'A story that opens like Aladdin's Cave and ends like a Greek myth of Nemesis cannot fail to capture the imagination of all men and women. . . .'

Lady Burghclere

The Complete
Tutankhamun

The King · The Tomb · The Royal Treasure

by Nicholas Reeves

Foreword by
the Seventh Earl of Carnarvon

519 illustrations, 65 in color

Thames & Hudson

For Claire, Kate, Elizabeth and Harriet

Half-title: *One of the four calcite stoppers (nos. 266c–f) from the king's canopic chest.* Frontispiece: *Face of the solid-gold, innermost coffin (no. 255) which held the body of Tutankhamun.*

A note on spellings

Because the hieroglyphs preserve no more than the consonantal skeleton of the Egyptian language, the ancient pronunciation cannot usually be established. For this reason, Egyptian names exhibit a variety of modern spellings, and often based upon the Greek form rather than the Egyptian. 'Tutankhamun' is here employed as the preferred spelling, but other versions of the king's name exist – including Tut.ankh.Amen, Tutankhamen, Tut 'ankh Amun, Tutankhamon, Tutenkhamon, Tutanchamun and Tutenchamun; these variants have been retained where appropriate in book titles and quotations.

© 1990 Thames & Hudson Ltd, London
Text © 1990 Nicholas Reeves

First published in hardcover in the United States of America in 1990 by Thames & Hudson Inc., 500 Fifth Avenue, New York, New York 10110

thamesandhudsonusa.com

First paperback edition 1995
Reprinted 2005

Library of Congress Catalog Card Number 90-70202

ISBN-13: 978-0-500-27810-9
ISBN-10: 0-500-27810-5

Printed in China

Contents

I
Tutankhamun and His Time

II
Search and Discovery

Foreword by the Seventh Earl of Carnarvon

I met Mr Howard Carter on his last visit to Highclere in April 1933 when I was nine years old. I remember him well with his bow tie, and being fascinated by some of the descriptions he was giving my mother of Egypt and the Valley of the Kings.

When my father died, the interest was rekindled: an inventory had to be taken of the contents of Highclere Castle, and it was during this period that the remains of my grandfather's Egyptian collection were found. I was lucky then to have the advice and help of Dr Nicholas Reeves in identifying and cataloguing this collection, and finally putting it on display. Dr Reeves's knowledge of the period of Tutankhamun is quite remarkable and he and his wife, Claire, have been immensely helpful to me and my family in presenting these wonderful artifacts to the public.

I have since started to collect a few pieces myself and hope that over the years, we shall be able to enhance the collection, which is so popular with the public when they visit the Castle.

Dr Reeves's fascinating book will surely become an important addition to the record of the history of Tutankhamun as well as encouraging more and more people from all over the world to visit the Valley of the Kings.

Carnarvon

(Opposite) Tutankhamun receives flowers from his wife, Ankhesenamun: the ivory-veneered lid of box no. 540 + 551.

Chronology and Family Relationships

The precise dates of the Egyptian dynasties and the pharaohs who ruled during them are still the subject of much scholarly debate. The dates employed here are based on the chronology developed by Prof John Baines and Dr Jaromír Málek and put forward in their *Atlas of Ancient Egypt*. Details of the rulers of the New Kingdom have been given in full; the names of Tutankhamun and those monarchs in his immediate family have been highlighted in italics.

Late Predynastic	*c.* 3000 BC

Early Dynastic Period	
1st–3rd dynasties	2920–2575

Old Kingdom	
4th–8th dynasties	2575–2134

First Intermediate Period	
9th–11th dynasties	2134–2040

Middle Kingdom	
11th–14th dynasties	2040–1640

Second Intermediate Period	
15th–17th dynasties	1640–1532

New Kingdom

18th dynasty	1550–1319
Ahmose	1550–1525
Amenophis I	1525–1504
Tuthmosis I	1504–1492
Tuthmosis II	1492–1479
Tuthmosis III	1479–1425
Hatshepsut	1473–1458
Amenophis II	1427–1401
Tuthmosis IV	1401–1391
Amenophis III	1391–1353
Amenophis IV/Akhenaten	1353–1335
Smenkhkare (Nefertiti?)	1335–1333
Tutankhamun	1333–1323
Ay	1323–1319
19th dynasty	1319–1196
Horemheb	1319–1307
Ramesses I	1307–1306
Sethos I	1306–1290
Ramesses II	1290–1224
Merenptah	1224–1214
Sethos II	1214–1204
Amenmesse (usurper during reign of Sethos II)	
Siptah	1204–1198
Twosre	1198–1196
20th dynasty	1196–1070
Sethnakht	1196–1194
Ramesses III	1194–1163
Ramesses IV	1163–1156
Ramesses V	1156–1151
Ramesses VI	1151–1143
Ramesses VII	1143–1136
Ramesses VIII	1136–1131
Ramesses IX	1131–1112
Ramesses X	1112–1100
Ramesses XI	1100–1070

Third Intermediate Period	
21st–25th dynasties	1070–712

Late Period	
25th dynasty–2nd Persian Period	712–332

Graeco-Roman Period	
Macedonian dynasty-Roman emperors	
	332 BC–AD 395

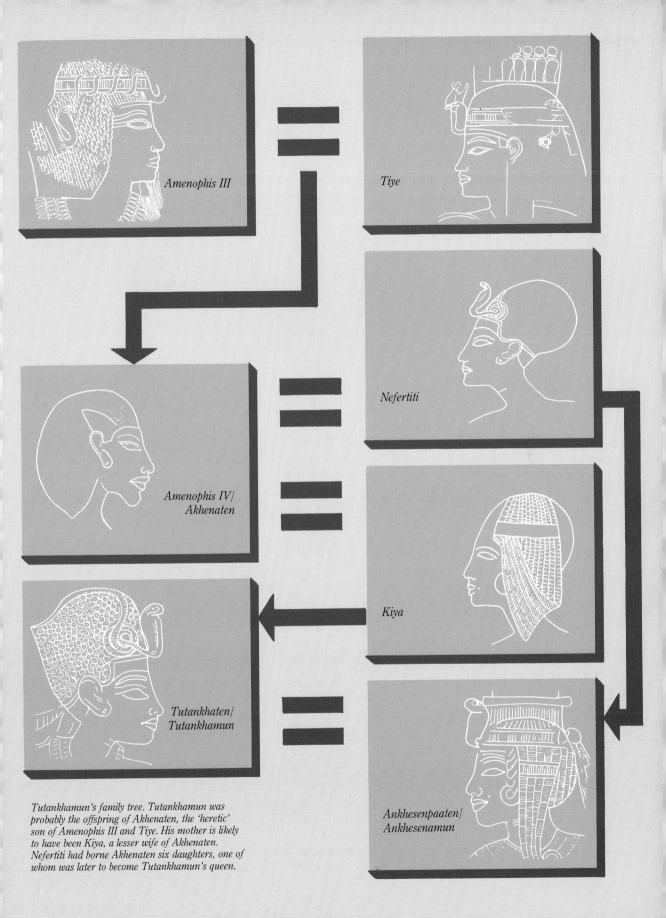

Amenophis III

Tiye

Amenophis IV/
Akhenaten

Nefertiti

Kiya

Tutankhaten/
Tutankhamun

Ankhesenpaaten/
Ankhesenamun

Tutankhamun's family tree. Tutankhamun was
probably the offspring of Akhenaten, the 'heretic'
son of Amenophis III and Tiye. His mother is likely
to have been Kiya, a lesser wife of Akhenaten.
Nefertiti had borne Akhenaten six daughters, one of
whom was later to become Tutankhamun's queen.

Introduction:
Discovering Tutankhamun

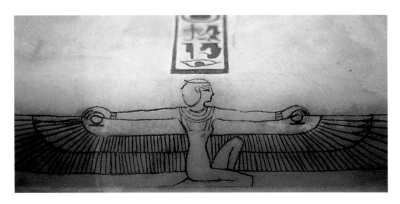

A goddess spreads her wings protectively around the royal viscera: a detail of the lid of Tutankhamun's canopic chest (no. 266b), carved from a single block of translucent calcite and delicately picked out in dark blue.

❛ When I started out for Egypt I had anticipated finding something, but I never dreamt that I should find such a tomb as this. ❜

George Herbert, fifth Earl of Carnarvon

The Earl of Carnarvon and Howard Carter could never have imagined the wonders that lay ahead as, late in the afternoon of 26 November 1922, they made a small peep-hole in the blocked inner doorway of the unimposing tomb recently brought to light in the Valley of the Kings.

'Mr Carter, holding a candle before him, put his head in', Lord Carnarvon was to recall shortly after the event. 'He did not say anything for two or three minutes, but kept me in rather painful suspense. I thought I had been disappointed again, and I said, "Can you see anything?" "Yes, yes," he replied, "it is wonderful."'

Here before them, crammed in from floor to ceiling, barely lit by the excavators' flickering light, lay a breathtaking array of funerary furniture and ritual figures, untouched for an eternity and seemingly in perfect condition; and everywhere the glint of gold. The enormity of the discovery did not take long to sink in; as Carnarvon excitedly scribbled to the Egyptologist Alan Gardiner the day after viewing the tomb for the first time: 'There is enough stuff to fill the whole upstairs Egyptian section of the B[ritish] M[useum]. I imagine it is the greatest find ever made.'

And so it was to prove. Tutankhamun, the obscure owner and occupant of this treasure-store, became overnight a household name. The discovery put Egyptology on the map, and 'Pharaoh's tomb' became the yardstick by which all archaeological discoveries would in future be measured. No archaeological find before or since has so captured the public imagination, thanks in great part to extensive coverage by the press. The newspapers were quick to appreciate that, as a story, Tutankhamun had it all: the thrill of the chase, the lure of buried treasure – and, with Lord Carnarvon's untimely death, a sting in the tail. Yet, for all the publicity the tomb of Tutankhamun generated at the time, and has continued steadily to generate since, it remains a tale but partly told.

Perhaps the real curse of the pharaohs is that Carter did not live to complete his publication of the tomb and its contents; he died, a disillusioned and exhausted man, in 1939. His three-volume *The Tomb of Tut.ankh.Amen*, which appeared between 1923 and 1933, had been intended merely as a taster for the definitive *Report upon the Tomb of Tut 'ankh Amun*, which would have been a very much larger work, an appropriate crown to Carter's extraordinary career. After a decade and a half devoted to the clearance of the tomb and the study of its contents, no one knew Tutankhamun and his treasures better than Carter himself.

Fortunately for posterity, Carter was a careful and meticulous worker, and made notes on every aspect of the discovery. These notes survive, together with Carter's fine drawings and reconstructions and the extensive series of superb photographs made by Harry Burton of New York's Metropolitan Museum of Art during the clearance of the tomb. Bequeathed to Carter's niece, Phyllis Walker, in 1939, this

(Right) Tutankhamun is welcomed into the realms of the dead by the goddess Nut: a detail from the north wall of the king's decorated Burial Chamber.

(Opposite) Tutankhamun as Horus harpooning Seth, a powerful allegory of order victorious over chaos: one of two closely similar images (nos. 275c, 275e) of brilliantly gilded wood recovered by Carter from the inner recesses of the Treasury.

archive was generously presented to the University of Oxford. It is now preserved in the Griffith Institute of the Ashmolean Museum as a resource of inestimable value, the basis of numerous specialist studies which have broadened our understanding not only of the tomb and the antiquities themselves but of the period in which Tutankhamun lived.

The gold mask, the jewels, the gilded figures, the richly inlaid furniture – these were merely the tip of a veritable iceberg of beads, boxes, stools, chariots, bows, arrows, shoes, gloves, underwear, food provisions, and much more besides. Tutankhamun's tomb contained everything, both ritual and personal, an Egyptian king might require for a happy and contented existence in the afterworld. It provides a unique insight into the nature of Tutan-

khamun's life on earth: through the objects from the tomb it is possible to see beyond the god-king to the boy-mortal. Who he was, why he died, what was buried with him – these are just some of the topics on which, with the help of Carter and his successors in the field, fresh light may now be shed.

Nicholas Reeves
January 1990

(Below) A photograph, taken shortly after the discovery, of (left to right) Lady Evelyn Herbert, her father Lord Carnarvon, Howard Carter, and 'Pecky' Callender, one of Carter's co-workers. They stand triumphant on the rock-cut staircase leading down into the tomb.

(Right) The calcite 'Wishing Cup' (no. 14), fashioned in the form of a white lotus. This delightful object, abandoned in the doorway of the Antechamber, was one of the first pieces revealed in the glimmer of the excavators' torches.

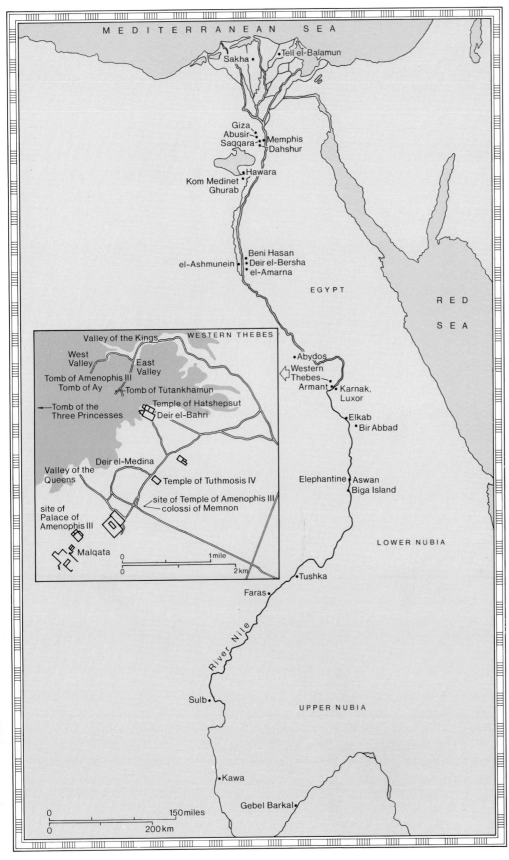

Egypt (left) and her northern
neighbours (above). The Nile
in ancient times, as today,
was bordered on either side
by inhospitable desert. By its
annual ebb and flow, the river
sustained life and gave a vital
rhythm to the existence of the
country's inhabitants. The
precious, silt-rich strip of
'black land' was reserved for
the living; the dead were
consigned to the lifeless
desert, in cemeteries generally
sited on the west bank, where
the sun-god Re was seen to
'die' at the end of each day.
During the New Kingdom,
Egypt's principal necropolis
was situated in Western
Thebes. Here, following a
brief reign and surrounded
by his treasures, the young
king Tutankhamun was laid
to rest in a rock-cut tomb
close to his forefathers. The
site was a dried-up river bed
known to the world as the
Valley of the Kings.

Tutankhamun lived and died against a backdrop of one of the richest and most sophisticated periods of Egyptian history, an age of international power-politics, religious turmoil, and unbounded artistic and literary creativity brought to fruition largely by the will of one man: his father, the heretic Pharaoh Akhenaten.

The king's only known son, Tutankhamun succeeded to the throne as a mere child following the brief intervening reign of the enigmatic Smenkhkare. Tutankhamun's legacy was a country physically and spiritually drained following his father's neglect of the traditional pantheon and imposition of the Aten cult, centred upon the new capital at el-Amarna. With the boy's accession, the Amarna experiment was brought to an end; the religious factions were reconciled and the country returned to relative normality.

But little of this was the young king's doing. Where Akhenaten had been strong, Tutankhamun was weak: behind the gold mask of the all-powerful god-ruler is the face of a vulnerable and manipulated little boy, a mere cipher for the deeds and aspirations of others.

Portrait of the child-king: detail of a gessoed and painted wooden head (no. 8) from the tomb.

I   Tutankhamun and His Time

The 18th Dynasty Before Amarna

The presentation of Asiatic tribute: the rulers of northern foreign lands fall to their knees before Pharaoh, in a painted scene from the tomb of Sobkhotep (No. 63) at Thebes.

❛ So let my brother send me gold in very great quantity. For in my brother's land gold is as plentiful as dust. ❜

King Tushratta of Mitanni to Pharaoh Amenophis III

From the very beginnings of her recorded history, Egypt was a land apart, isolated from her neighbours by the natural boundaries of Mediterranean in the north, cataract region in the south, and deserts to east and west. There had always been links of sort with the outside world, but a new awareness of foreign lands, and what they had to offer, was forced upon the Egyptians by the gradual infiltration of Asiatics who eventually came to rule Egypt as the 'Hyksos' kings of the seventeenth–sixteenth centuries BC. Characterized by later generations as a humiliating 'blast of God', Hyksos rule brought with it nonetheless great advances in bronze-working, pottery-making, weaving, agriculture and warfare which interested the Egyptians greatly. The benefits of foreign contact indeed provided a stimulus to the expansionist policy of the New Kingdom (1550–1070 BC). The first step in this policy would be the expulsion of the Hyksos by the Theban prince Ahmose, founder of the 18th dynasty, the first dynasty of the New Kingdom.

The reign of Pharaoh Tuthmosis I, Ahmose's successor but one, witnessed a phenomenal extension of Egyptian power northwards to the Euphrates, and was balanced by a progression south beyond the fourth cataract. With consolidation under Tuthmosis III and Amenophis II, an initial phase of plunder and pillage was followed, in the north, by the establishment of vassal rulers and the imposition of tribute. In the south, Nubia was exploited directly under the viceroy or 'King's son of Kush'. Wealth poured into the coffers of the Egyptian king and of his principal god, Amon-Re, in the form of raw materials and manpower, not only from Egypt's vassals but by diplomatic exchange with the Hittites (in Anatolia), Mitanni (Naharin, in present-day northern Syria), Assyria, Babylon and the rulers of the Greek isles.

The courtyard of Amenophis III at Luxor Temple, with its massive papyriform columns.

(Far left) Amenophis III, 'the Magnificent', clutching the kingly heqa-sceptre and wearing the blue crown with uraeus-serpent and streamers and shebyu-collar: a fragment of limestone relief from the Theban tomb of Khaemhat (No. 57).

(Left) Queen Tiye, shown with coarsely braided wig, double uraeus and diadem inscribed at the front with her name: a small head of green steatite found by Flinders Petrie at Serabit el-Khadim in Sinai.

When Amenophis III came to the throne in 1391 BC, Egypt was at the centre of the world stage. As the diplomatic correspondence found at el-Amarna reveals, during the 37 recorded years of his reign the king and his influential queen, Tiye, reaped in full the benefits of an empire stable and at peace. A god incarnate, Pharaoh was sufficiently powerful to short-change his neighbours in the diplomacy of gift-giving, and received their princesses into his harim with no thought of exchange. Great building works were undertaken, including a new palace complex with a vast, man-made lake at Malqata on the west bank of the Nile at Thebes, and temples, shrines and other structures at Luxor, Karnak, Sulb and elsewhere. The king's mortuary temple, its position today marked by the famed 'Colossi of Memnon', was perhaps the most sumptuous of all:

'. . . a monument of eternity and everlastingness, of fine sandstone worked with gold throughout . . . [its] pavements . . . made pure with silver, all its doors with fine gold'.

Egypt in the reign of Amenophis III, 'the Magnificent', was a nation at the height of her power and prestige; she was, at the same time, an Egypt effete, decadent and ripe for change. The change would come with a vengeance with the theological crisis of the succeeding reign.

Amenophis III was buried in a large, rock-cut sepulchre begun by his father, Tuthmosis IV, in the western annexe of the Valley of the Kings. This tomb, No. 22 in the Valley sequence, was first noted by two members of Napoleon's Egyptian expedition in 1799. Its L-shaped ground-plan, characteristic of 18th-dynasty royal tombs, was elaborated by the addition of two extra rooms off the enlarged, easternmost store-chambers of the decorated burial chamber. One of these 'suites' is thought to have been intended for the king's principal wife, Tiye – though, since she outlived her husband, it would seem never actually to have been employed. The great royal wife was probably buried at el-Amarna by her son, Akhenaten, though during the reign of Tutankhamun her mummy was transferred to Thebes for reburial in Tomb 55 in the Valley of the Kings (p. 20). The remains of both king and queen have been identified among a group of royal mummies found in the tomb of Amenophis II (No. 35) in 1898, where they had been hidden at the time the necropolis was dismantled at the end of the New Kingdom.

The burial of Amenophis III was perhaps the most magnificent of any Egyptian king, in a sepulchre scarcely less splendid than his mortuary temple. The broken fragments yielded by Carnarvon and Carter's clearance of the tomb in 1915 (p. 48) would offer many tantalizing hints of its former glory.

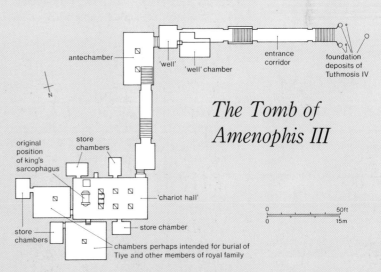

The Tomb of Amenophis III

antechamber

'well'

'well' chamber

entrance corridor

foundation deposits of Tuthmosis IV

N

original position of king's sarcophagus

store chambers

'chariot hall'

store chamber

store chambers

chambers perhaps intended for burial of Tiye and other members of royal family

0   50ft
0   15m

Akhenaten and the Amarna Age

(Right) Akhenaten, Nefertiti and Meritaten receive 'life' from the Aten in return for their offerings. Detail from a calcite relief excavated by Petrie (assisted by Howard Carter) at el-Amarna in 1891.

(Far right) The earlier (top) and later (below) forms of the Aten's names.

The elongated face of Amenophis IV from one of a series of striking colossal statues (perhaps the work of the sculptor Bek) erected in the king's temple complex at Karnak.

❛ The good god, sole one of Re,
 Whose goodness Aten fashioned,
 Useful, truthful, to his maker,
 Who contents him with that which pleases his *ka*.
 Who serves him who begot him,
 Who guides the land for him who enthroned him,
 Who provisions his house of eternity
 With millions, hundred-thousands of things.
 Who exalts Aten, magnifies his name,
 Who causes the land to belong to his maker . . . ❜

Boundary stela S at el-Amarna

With the premature death of the heir-apparent, Tuthmosis, the succession passed in 1353 BC to Prince Amenophis, a younger son of Amenophis III and his chief consort, Tiye. The new king, who had perhaps acted as co-regent with his father for a short while before the latter's death, was to waste little time in asserting himself.

Amenophis IV was to reign for 17 years, and to stamp his character upon every aspect of Egyptian life and culture. The main feature of his rule was an exclusive, even fanatical, personal devotion to the Aten. A relatively minor aspect of the sun-god, Re-Horakhty, the Aten had already achieved a certain prominence under Tuthmosis IV and Amenophis III. From Year 2 of Amenophis IV, the names of the Aten were written in oval cartouches, like those of the king. In addition, the Aten was shown as a god in its own right: a solar disc (or globe) emitting rays which end in hands presenting 'life' (the hieroglyph *ankh*) to the noses of both the king and his principal queen, Nefertiti.

The disc was to be the symbol of a new order imposed upon his subjects by Pharaoh. Its basic tenet is spelled out in the Great Hymn to the Aten, a version of which is inscribed upon the tomb-walls of the courtier Ay (destined to be Tutankhamun's successor) at el-Amarna: there is but one god, the Aten, the sole creator and gentle benefactor of mankind. In this hymn, a masterpiece of literature perhaps composed by the king himself, the true nature of the Amarna revolution nevertheless stands revealed:

'There is no other who knows you,
Only your son Neferkheprure-waenre [Amenophis IV] . . .'

Since access to the god would be through the intermediacy of Pharaoh alone, the Aten and his spokesman became in effect one and the same: Pharaoh worshipped the disc, and the populace worshipped him. Whether by intention or not, the traditional god-king had become divine-dictator.

The early years of the reign were taken up with extensive building works at Karnak, monuments later dismantled by Pharaoh's successors and the thousands of sandstone *talatat*-blocks re-employed as building rubble. By Year 6, Amenophis IV had changed his name (which may be translated 'Amun-is-content') to Akhenaten ('He-who-is-beneficial-to-the-Aten') – coincident, it seems, with the start of work on a new capital: Akhetaten ('Horizon-of-the-Aten'), dedicated to the worship of the disc at el-Amarna in Middle Egypt. This new city, its territory demarcated by a series of 'boundary stelae', was in all probability the birthplace of Tutankhamun. Here, maintained by a strong military presence, the Aten reigned supreme.

The Aten's official name exists in two principal forms. The earlier first occurs accompanying the falcon-headed form of the god, and, subsequently, within a pair of cartouches (stressing the ambiguity between god and king), as the earlier name-form of the rayed sun disc. In the Aten's later name form, adopted in about Year 9 of the reign, all mention of Horakhty and Shu has been dropped. This name change probably marked the pinnacle of Akhenaten's hostility towards the old order. It was accompanied by the erasure from all accessible monuments of any reference to Amun and the old polytheistic religion, including the Amen- element in his father's and his own original name.

This persecution was to mark the beginning of the end. With the closure of the traditional shrines, the economic stability of the Egyptian state was seriously undermined; while, with the day-to-day running of the country left unsupervised in the hands of lesser men, exploitation of the disorientated populace was rife. This neglect would earn Pharaoh the posthumous sobriquet 'criminal of Akhetaten'.

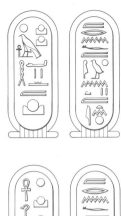

The Art of Amarna

The Amarna period has given its name to a unique and markedly stylized art, at its best highly sensual, at its worst wholly repellant, in which many of the age-old formalizations were abandoned. Gone are representations of the king-as-hero, to be replaced by grotesque images of the long-faced, pot-bellied reality which was Pharaoh, 'living according to *maat* ["right"]', in perfect harmony with his loving family and taking fullest pleasure in the beauties of nature. And here again, remarkably, the impetus seems to have come from above: as the royal sculptor Bek records, he was 'one whom his majesty himself instructed'.

Extract from the Great Hymn to the Aten, inscribed in the tomb of the god's father Ay (No. 25) at el-Amarna:

How many are your deeds,
Though hidden from sight,
O Sole God beside whom there is none!
You made the earth as you wished, you alone,
All peoples, herds, and flocks;
All upon earth that walk on legs,
All on high that fly on wings,
The lands of Khor [Syria] and Kush [Nubia],
The land of Egypt.

Psalm 104, 24

O lord, how manifold are thy works!
In wisdom hast thou made them all;
The earth is full of thy creatures.

The similarity between certain passages in this Hymn to the Aten and Psalm 104 has often been remarked upon. A recent view is that 'The resemblances are . . . likely to be the result of the generic similarity between Egyptian hymns and biblical psalms' rather than a 'specific literary interdependence'.

Akhenaten's Burial and the Enigma of Tomb 55

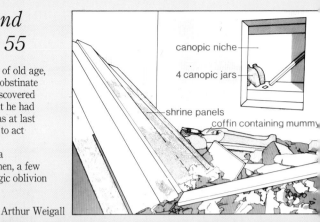

canopic niche

4 canopic jars

shrine panels

coffin containing mummy

*(Right above and below) The
devastated state of the Tomb
55 burial chamber as found.*

❛ . . . owing to some curious idiosyncracy of old age,
Mr. Davis entertained a most violent and obstinate
objection to the suggestion that he had discovered
the body of Akhenaten. He had hoped that he had
found Queen Taia [Tiye], and when he was at last
forced to abandon this fallacy, he seemed to act
almost as though desiring to obscure the
identification of the body. He was still in a
passionate state of mind in this regard when, a few
years later, his brain gave way, and a tragic oblivion
descended upon him. ❜

Arthur Weigall

*(Below) Seal impression
recovered by Ayrton from
Tomb 55. The type, depicting
a foreign captive between a
rampant lion and a crocodile,
would later turn up in the
tomb of Tutankhamun.*

*(Bottom) Tomb 55, shown
underlying the larger tomb of
Ramesses IX. A side-chamber
of the Ramessid tomb is
unfinished: when the walls
began to sound hollow, work
was stopped and the 'lost'
tomb investigated.*

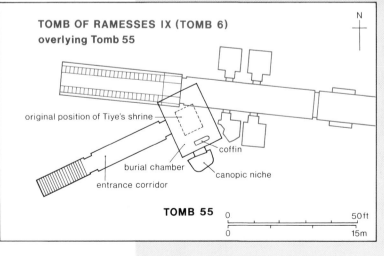

TOMB OF RAMESSES IX (TOMB 6) overlying Tomb 55

N

original position of Tiye's shrine

coffin

burial chamber

canopic niche

entrance corridor

TOMB 55

0   50 ft

0   15 m

In accordance with the vow proclaimed on boundary
stelae K and X, Akhenaten prepared a tomb for
himself in the cliffs at el-Amarna, abandoning the
tomb excavation already begun in the Valley of the
Kings (probably No. 25 in the West Valley) together
with what had already been produced in the way of
funerary furniture.

The Amarna tomb was discovered at the
beginning of the century by the Italian excavator
Alexandre Barsanti; it was found to contain little
more than a few broken *shabtis* (funerary figures),
remains of the king's sarcophagus, and fragments of
the canopic chest intended to hold his embalmed
internal organs. Whether Akhenaten was ever buried
at el-Amarna has been questioned. Since an *ad hoc*
burial chamber had been cut from an antechamber in
the unfinished tomb, there can be little doubt that he
was; though when the royal burial-ground was
evacuated following the abandonment of Akhetaten,

the king's body appears to have been transferred by his son Tutankhamun to the Valley of the Kings.

The remains of this Theban reburial seem to have been brought to light in Tomb 55 during work sponsored by Theodore M. Davis (pp. 37–9) in 1907. Tomb 55 is one of the most controversial discoveries ever made in Egypt. Excavated by the English archaeologist Edward R. Ayrton under trying circumstances and in due course poorly published by Davis himself, no consensus has yet been reached on its precise nature or on the identity of its occupant. A single-chambered corridor tomb, it contained an assortment of objects, including a coffined mummy, a gilded wooden shrine, four canopic jars, and a set of so-called 'magic bricks'. The material falls neatly into two groups. The principal element of the first group was the shrine, originally prepared for Akhenaten's mother and giving the title to Davis's published account of the find, *The Tomb of Queen Tiyi*. The second group included the coffined mummy, canopic jars and 'magic bricks', objects which the inscriptions on the bricks would seem to associate with Akhenaten himself.

In all likelihood, the shrine indicates Tiye's original presence within the tomb. Her mummy and most of her funerary equipment, however, were missing, perhaps removed when the tomb was stumbled upon during the course of quarrying the overlying tomb of Ramesses IX (No. 6); the dismantled shrine had been abandoned when the workers discovered that it could not be extracted without first clearing the rubble that filled the corridor. The mummy of Tiye has been recognized by American researchers among those bodies later cached in the tomb of Amenophis II (No. 35), though the identification is not universally accepted.

The Tomb 55 coffin and canopic jars had been prepared originally for Kiya, a secondary wife of

Akhenaten and perhaps Tutankhamun's mother (p. 9). The names of the subsequent owner had been excised from the coffin, presumably at the time the mummy of Queen Tiye was removed from the chamber. Physical and blood-group similarities between the unidentified occupant of the coffin and the mummy of Tutankhamun (p. 117) are remarkable; indeed archaeological considerations suggest that the anonymous body ought to be that of Akhenaten himself, Tutankhamun's father. However, the estimated age at death of the Tomb 55 corpse – reduced since the initial analysis from 25/26 + to 20 years – remains problematic; even by the most conservative reckoning, Akhenaten must have been at least 30 when he died.

(Above) Kiya: a calcite canopic-jar lid from Tomb 55, superimposed upon a photograph of the coffin.

(Below) One of the gilded side-panels from Queen Tiye's shrine, and a line-drawn detail by Harold Jones.

Nefertiti and the Succession

Akhenaten's principal wife was the beautiful Nefertiti, subject of the famous limestone portrait bust in West Berlin (21300). Research over the last decade and a half has indicated that the importance of the queen during the Amarna period was probably far greater than previously recognized.

(Left) Painted limestone bust of Nefertiti, from the studio of the sculptor Djehutymose at el-Amarna. The delicate balance of the piece has been achieved by the ruse of completing the crown in lighter-weight plaster. Perhaps because of the head's instructional role, only one eye-inlay is present.

(Right) Limestone stela dedicated by the soldier Pase, formerly believed to show Akhenaten and his co-regent, 'Smenkhkare'. The stela was never completed, and neither individual is named; the three empty cartouches on the right indicate, nonetheless, that the figures are those of Akhenaten and his queen, Nefertiti. The queen's exceptional status is shown by the fact that she wears the kingly double-crown of Upper and Lower Egypt.

Nefertiti's origins are still uncertain, but from quite early in the reign she was shown in the company of her husband almost as an equal, he and she receiving the 'blessing' of the Aten's rays as junior members of the Aten triad (family grouping of three gods). By Year 6 of the reign, the queen's devotion to the Aten was publicly signalled by a change in her name from plain 'Nefertiti' ('The-radiant-one-is-come') to 'Nefernefruaten-Nefertiti' ('The-Aten-is-radiant-of-radiance [because] the-beautiful-one-is-come'). Her status continued to increase until, on a private stela belonging to a soldier by the name of Pase (East Berlin 17813), Nefertiti is shown seated beside her husband wearing the kingly double crown. After Year 13 or thereabouts, at the height of her power and influence, she drops from view. This disappearance used to be attributed to a fall from grace, with which scholars associated what they supposed to be several appropriated images and inscriptions of Nefertiti at el-Amarna and elsewhere (monuments which are now known to have been usurped from Akhenaten's secondary wife, Kiya).

It is surely no coincidence that the disappearance of Nefernefruaten-Nefertiti should have coincided with the advent of a new co-regent, Ankhkheprure Nefernefruaten, formerly identified as an older brother or half-brother of Tutankhamun. And, indeed, the indications are that queen and co-regent were one and the same: the co-regent not only bears one of the queen's names, 'beloved of Akhenaten',

but 'his' nomen occurs on a number of faience ring bezels in the feminine form Ankh*et*kheprure.

Akhenaten died in his 17th regnal year, leaving Egypt and her empire in tatters after the years of introspection and neglect. Subsequent developments are difficult to follow. The appearance of a king Ankhkheprure Smenkhkare-djeserkhepru is documented towards the end of Akhenaten's reign, and it is tempting to see this ruler as the ultimate manifestation of the former great royal wife, Nefertiti. She it may well have been who, in a desperate attempt to retain power after Akhenaten's death, wrote to Suppiluliumas I, king of the Hittites, asking for a son to marry and consolidate her position. A copy of the letter was found in the Hittite archives at Hattusas in modern Turkey, and is an indication of the depths to which proud Egypt had sunk:

'My husband died. A son I have not. But to thee, they say, the sons are many. If thou wouldst give me one son of thine, he would become my husband. Never shall I pick out a servant of mine and make him my husband! . . . I am afraid!'

Suppiluliumas was astounded, and sceptical: 'such a thing has never happened before in my whole life'. There was an interchange of messengers, and a son, Zannanza, duly despatched, only to be murdered en route to Egypt. Smenkhkare disappears after a brief independent reign, and the spotlight shifts to a child no more than nine years of age: Tutankhaten, better known today by his later name of Tutankhamun.

Fragmentary limestone inscription from the North Palace at el-Amarna. The column of text on the left was erased in antiquity and reinscribed for the king's daughter Meritaten. The 'victim' of these usurpations was Kiya, as traces of the original text on this and other monuments reveal – not Nefertiti, as was once thought.

Nefertiti, wearing her characteristic, flat-topped crown, makes offerings to the Aten on a limestone temple block from el-Ashmunein.

Who Was Tutankhamun?

(Above) Inscription recording the king's royal filiation: 'King's bodily son, his beloved, Tutankhuaten'.

(Below left) Plaster mask from el-Amarna. The large ear-ornaments probably identify the subject as Kiya.

(Below right) Return to orthodoxy: the 'Restoration Stela'.

(Opposite page, top) The hand of Amun sets the blue crown on Tutankhamun's head.

(Opposite, below) The royal birth? A fragmentary scene from the tomb of Akhenaten at el-Amarna.

' The mystery of his life still eludes us – the shadows move but the dark is never quite dispersed. '

Howard Carter

Despite the richness of his burial, Tutankhamun remains an enigmatic figure. To judge from his mummy (p. 116), he died perhaps as young as 16 or 17 years of age, having been born, presumably at 'Akhetaten (modern el-Amarna), during the latter half of the reign of Akhenaten. Although his royal stock has sometimes been questioned, an inscription brought to light at el-Ashmunein across the river from el-Amarna confirms that Tutankhuaten (as he is there named) was indeed the son of a king. Official policy during the boy's reign seems to have been to stress his association with Amenophis III. Nevertheless, in the absence of a long co-regency between Amenophis III and Akhenaten, the probability must be that Tutankhamun was a son of the latter.

Firm evidence is lacking to establish with certainty the identity of Tutankhamun's mother, though a degree of informed speculation is possible. Nefertiti appears to have borne Akhenaten no sons; but she was not his only wife. Among the king's secondary wives and concubines, one in particular stands out: the lady Kiya, identified by some with the Mitannian princess Tadukhepa, daughter of Tushratta, sent to Egypt to cement treaty relations between the two countries at the start of the reign.

Kiya is peculiarly prominent in the sculptural record at el-Amarna and her special position in the king's favour is reflected in her unique title: Greatly Beloved Wife. In a number of Amarna reliefs, Kiya is shown in the company of a daughter. The question is: might she also have given the king a son?

Chronological considerations by no means rule out the possibility. The indications are that Kiya was in favour before Year 9 or 10 of Akhenaten's reign, but after Year 11 – at about the time of Tutankhamun's birth – she disappears from view to have her several monuments at el-Amarna appropriated by Nefertiti's daughter, Meritaten. One theory is that Kiya died in childbirth, as a fragmentary mourning scene in Akhenaten's tomb perhaps records. But it is equally possible that she fell from grace, victim of a court intrigue engineered by the jealous Nefertiti; indeed, it may be no coincidence that the meteoric rise in the status of Nefertiti seems to have begun in earnest only after Kiya's demise.

Whatever the identity and the eventual fate of his mother, Tutankhamun came to the throne in 1333 BC, as Tutankhaten, a young child. He was to rule Egypt for nine years or more, though there can be little doubt that for most of this time the reins of government were firmly in the hands of others – Ay, perhaps a relative of the King, and the general Horemheb, each of whom would succeed to the throne. Tutankhaten's queen was Ankhesenpaaten, the somewhat older third daughter of Akhenaten and Nefertiti; the match may have been made to unite opposing royal factions.

Hard facts relating to Tutankhamun's period of rule are few. References to at least one Asiatic and perhaps a Nubian military campaign have been discerned in relief fragments from Karnak and Luxor, as well as in the superb sculptured reliefs of Horemheb's Memphite tomb and in the painted scenes of Nubian and Asiatic tribute in the tomb of

the viceroy Huy at Thebes – though whether Pharaoh himself ever took the field has been doubted. But the principal event of the reign was in the domestic sphere. Early on the administrative capital of Egypt was moved back from el-Amarna to Memphis, with Thebes re-established as the country's religious centre. At the same time, by abandoning the -aten forms of their names in Year 2, the royal couple signalled the formal resurgence of Amun and the traditional pantheon following the years of proscription under Akhenaten. Promulgated by decree at Memphis and recorded in the retrospectively-dated 'Restoration Stela' (extant in two copies, later usurped by Horemheb), this one event marks the reign as pivotal to the subsequent course of Egyptian history.

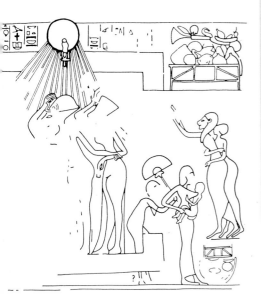

The Names of Tutankhamun

At his accession to the throne an Egyptian king adopted a formal 'titulary', a sequence of five titled names. The combination of names chosen was unique to each ruler.

1 the HORUS name: *Ka-nakht tut-mesut*, 'Strong bull, fitting-of-created-forms'

2 the NEBTY* or 'HE-OF-THE-TWO-LADIES' name: *Nefer-hepu segereh-tawy sehetep-netjeru nebu*, 'Dynamic-of-laws, who-calms-the-Two-Lands, who-propitiates-all-the-gods' (variants: (i) *Wer-ah-Amun*, 'Great-of-the-palace-of-Amun'; (ii) . . . *neb-er-djer*, '. . . -lord-of-all')

variants (i)

(ii)

3 the GOLDEN FALCON* name: *Wetjes-khau sehetep-netjeru*, 'Who-displays-the-regalia, who-propitiates-the-gods' (variants: (i) *Heqa-maat sehetep-netjeru*, 'The-one-who-brings-together-the-cosmic-order, who-propitiates-the-gods'; (ii) *Wetjes-khau-yotef-Re*, 'Who-displays-the-regalia-of-his-father-Re'; (iii) *Wetjes-khau tjes-tawy em* . . ., 'Who-displays-the-regalia, who-keeps-the-Two-Lands-together . . .')

variants (i)

(ii)

(iii)

4 the PRENOMEN, which commonly follows the group *nesu-bity*, 'dual king', traditionally rendered 'King of Upper and Lower Egypt': *Nebkheprure*, 'The-lordly-manifestation-of-Re'

5 the NOMEN, introduced by *sa-ra*, 'Son of Re': *Tutankhamun heqa-Iunu-shema*, 'Living-image-of-Amun, ruler-of-Upper-Egyptian-Heliopolis' (earlier variant: *Tutankhaten*, 'Living-image-of-the-Aten')'

earlier variant

Of these names, those most frequently encountered are the prenomen and the nomen, written within an oval rope border, or cartouche.

* Those names marked with an asterisk are not attested with the Tutankh*aten* ('Living-image-of-the-Aten') form of nomen.

The Archaeology of Tutankhamun's Reign

It comes as a surprise to many people to learn that not everything inscribed with the name of Tutankhamun originates from his tomb. The young king's short reign was a time of reconstruction following the devastation of Akhenaten's latter years, and the period following the return to Thebes was marked by a significant increase in artistic and architectural activity throughout Egypt – though since a good number of the monuments for which Tutankhamun was responsible were subsequently usurped by his successors, the extent of this activity is less obvious than it might be.

The following listing (which is, of necessity, selective) will give some indication of the range of monuments and artefacts of Tutankhamun that has come down to us – from splendid, long-dismantled temple precincts to the humblest of discarded seal impressions.

El-Amarna

An important block originating from el-Amarna (though recovered from el-Ashmunein on the opposite bank of the river) records the fact that Tutankhamun was the son of a king (p. 24). A fragmentary stela (Berlin 14197) from el-Amarna represents Tutankhamun (as Tutankhaten) offering to Amun and Mut. Many faience finger-rings inscribed with the king's prenomen (less commonly, his nomen) have been found at this site. Whether as Tutankhaten the king had begun to prepare a tomb for himself at el-Amarna is unknown, though one of the abandoned workings in the royal wadi there (perhaps No. 27?) might conceivably be attributed to him.

Thebes

Karnak
The work of reconstruction referred to in the 'Restoration Stelae' went on apace at the great temple complex of Karnak. A figure of Tutankhamun was added to the decoration of the third pylon. The dismantling of the Akhenaten temples appears to have begun during the young king's reign, as also

(Right) The moon-god Khons, son of Amun and Mut: a black granite statue with the facial features of Tutankhamun, found beneath the pavement of the god's sanctuary in the Great Temple of Amun at Karnak.

(Below) Plan of Karnak, showing the Great Temple of Amun and the precinct of his consort, the goddess Mut.

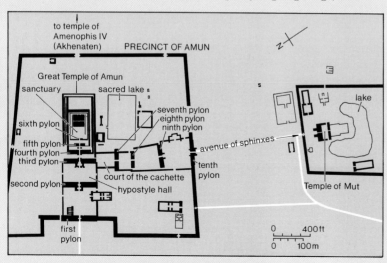

to temple of Amenophis IV (Akhenaten)

PRECINCT OF AMUN

Great Temple of Amun
sanctuary
sacred lake
sixth pylon
seventh pylon
eighth pylon
ninth pylon
fifth pylon
fourth pylon
third pylon
avenue of sphinxes
tenth pylon
second pylon
court of the cachette
hypostyle hall
first pylon
lake
Temple of Mut

0   400 ft
0   100 m

the restoration of Atenist damage to the east face of the sixth pylon and elsewhere. Other works attributed to Tutankhamun include the avenue of ram-headed sphinxes between the tenth pylon and the precinct of Amun's consort, the goddess Mut, and the decoration of the exterior enclosure wall of the court of the *cachette* (so-called because of the large collection of hidden statuary which was brought to light there in 1903). Two structures, now dismantled and represented by scattered blocks, were called the 'Mansion-of-Nebkheprure-in-Thebes' and the 'Mansion-of-Nebkheprure-beloved-of-Amun-who-sets-Thebes-in-order'.

Several stelae of Tutankhamun are known from Karnak, including the well-known restoration texts (Cairo CG 34183–4), one of which was perhaps erected in front of the third pylon. Another stela of the king before Amun and Mut stands before the north face of the seventh pylon.

A great deal of sculpture from the reign has been found at Karnak, either of the king himself or of deities represented with his facial features. A colossal seated figure of a king identified as Tutankhamun, and an inscribed statue-base, were excavated from the court of the Mut Temple, as was a once finely inlaid calcite sphinx (Luxor J 49). Two standing statues of the king (Cairo CG 42091-2) were recovered from the floor of court 1 in the Great Temple (the

court of the *cachette*). A fourth piece from the *cachette* (Cairo CG 42097) shows Tutankhamun seated between Amun and Mut. A statue in the Louvre depicts the young king protected by the seated Amun (Louvre E 11609); probably from Karnak is an indurated limestone head from a coronation group of the king, with the hand of Amun resting upon his blue crown, in New York (MMA 50.6). A black granite dyad, or pair-statue, representing Tutankhamun standing with Amun (who is shown in ithyphallic form) is in the British Museum (EA 21); it probably also comes from Karnak, as does a second black granite statue in the British Museum (EA 75) representing the king with attributes of the Nile god Hapy. A fine double statue of indurated limestone, now in Turin (768), from 'Thebes' and again probably Karnak, shows the king with Amun. A colossal figure of Amun with the features of Tutankhamun stands in the courtyard of the god's sanctuary; it has been suggested that its companion figure, representing the female aspect of the god, Amunet, was carved during the reign of Ay. A statue of Amun with the features of the king was recovered from the *cachette* (Cairo JE 38049), while detached heads of Amun are in Cairo (Cairo CG 38002), Copenhagen (Ny Carlsberg Glyptothek ÆIN 35), and elsewhere. A black granite statue of Khons (Cairo CG 38488) comes from the Great Temple.

Colossal statue of Amun at Karnak, carved in the image of Tutankhamun and originally inscribed with his name. The monument was subsequently usurped by Horemheb.

(See p. 37.)

Temple of Luxor

The unfinished Processional Colonnade of Amenophis III at Luxor was decorated during the reign of Tutankhamun, with portraits of the king on the door jambs of the north wall. The scenes of the Opet-festival on the east and west walls were subsequently usurped by Horemheb.

In 1989, a series of test-borings made in the colonnaded court of the Temple of Luxor unexpectedly brought to light a group of 22 statues, the so-called 'Luxor *cachette*', buried in about the fourth century BC. Among their number were several fragments of a blue-painted calcite sphinx inscribed upon its shoulder with the cartouche of Tutankhamun.

Western Thebes

Two faience ring bezels and a clay seal impression of Tutankhamun (perhaps also a limestone lintel usurped by Horemheb) were found among the ruins of the palace of Amenophis III at Malqata.

Tutankhamun's mortuary temple was probably erected in the vicinity of Ramesses III's later funerary monument at Medinet Habu. Two colossal quartzite statues from this temple, which was employed to celebrate the cult of the dead king, were found reused in the mortuary temple of Ay and Horemheb, inscribed by Ay (Cairo JE 59869 + 60134?; Chicago OrInst 14088). A high priest of Tutankhamun's funerary cult, Userhat, is attested on a stela fragment in the Metropolitan Museum of Art in New York (MMA 05.4.2); a *shabti* figure in the British Museum (EA 38721) carries the inscription of a *wab*-priest of the king called Pairy.

Tutankhamun's tomb is that now numbered 62 in the Valley of the Kings; other objects bearing the king's name have been recovered from Pit 54 (New York, MMA 09.184.1–170, 214–697, 788–805) and Tomb 58 (Cairo JE 57438). A blue faience cup of Tutankhamun has also been found in the Valley (Cairo JE 38330). (See p. 37.)

A wooden 'astronomical instrument' now in Chicago (OrInst 12144), with restoration text on behalf of Tutankhamun's 'great-grandfather' Tuthmosis IV, probably comes from the latter's destroyed mortuary temple at Thebes.

Memphis

A 'House of Nebkheprure', presumably a temple at Memphis, is mentioned on the monument of a treasury official, May, from the pyramid complex of Sahure at Abusir. A limestone lintel of Tutankhamun in East Berlin, and a second lintel (Cairo JE 88131 (part)), usurped by Horemheb and found reused within the Ptah Temple enclosure in the construction of the tomb of Shoshenq, the god's high priest, perhaps originate from one or more other structures of Tutankhamun at Memphis. An uninscribed 'bust' of the king(?) (Cairo JE 55032) was found at Kom el-Fakhry.

An inscribed limestone lintel of Tutankhamun (Cairo JE 57195) was discovered built into the mud-brick 'Resthouse of Tutankhamun' situated to the west of Chephren's valley temple at Giza. Among other objects of the reign from Giza is a broken stela, found in the vicinity of the Sphinx, in which a courtier(?) is shown adoring the royal couple.

The third of the sacred Apis-bull burials brought to light in the Serapeum enclosure at Saqqara by the French Egyptologist Auguste Mariette had been made during the reign of Tutankhamun. Four canopic jars (S 1151–4) and three inscribed glass pendants (456) from the burial are in the Louvre.

Other sites

A fragmentary box of gilded wood was found by the French Egyptologist Émile Amélineau at Abydos in the 1890s (part, Amiens, Musée de Picardie); while Flinders Petrie, digging at Kom Medinet Ghurab, brought to light several faience rings and a wooden cubit rod of Tutankhamun, now in University College London (Petrie Museum, UC 16050). A calcite jar of the king (UC 16021) also originates from here. A block with the cartouches of Tutankhamun was noted by J. Gardner Wilkinson at Bir Abbad in the Wadi Abbad, en route to the Red Sea.

In Nubia, Tutankhamun built temples at Kawa (ancient Gem(pa)aten) and Faras. A fragmentary granite group of the king between Amun and Mut(?) and a steatite head of the king(?), both from the latter site, are in Khartoum Museum (3766 and 5829). Two granite lions in the British Museum (EA 1–2) were found at Gebel Barkal, where they had been carried by the ruler of Meroë, Amanislo. Initiated by Amenophis III, one (EA 2) was inscribed with a dedication text of Tutankhamun and originally set up at Sulb by Ay.

In Palestine, a gold ring inscribed with the king's prenomen (Jerusalem, Arch. Museum 33.1708) was found at Tell el-Ajjul, in the family tomb of an 'Egyptian governor'. Also from Palestine may be noted a faience ring, found at Tell el-Safi/Tell Zakariya.

Among the unprovenanced objects from the reign might be mentioned three fragmentary stelae, one of Year 4 (West Berlin 345/67, with an endowment text) and two of Year 8 (Liverpool, Institute of Archaeology E 90 and E 583 – the latter with a royal decree for Maya). A kneeling bronze figure of Tutankhamun is in Philadelphia (University Museum, E 14295). Other miscellaneous objects of Tutankhamun include an inscribed box-knob (Baltimore, WAG 48.405), fragmentary faience throwsticks (British Museum EA 54822; Petrie Museum, UC 12496), an inscribed copper dish in the British Museum (EA 43040), and a fragmentary faience collar terminal (Eton College, Myers Museum, ECM 1887) with a representation of the king drinking from a lotus chalice.

(Above) Red-granite lion from Gebel Barkal, inscribed with a dedication text of Tutankhamun.

(Opposite) Part of the processional colonnade of Amenophis III at Luxor Temple: the portrait is that of Tutankhamun, the altered cartouches those of his successor-but-one, Horemheb.

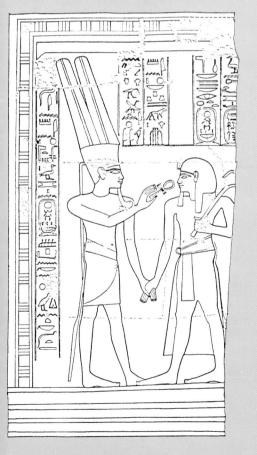

(Left) Amon-Re presents the hieroglyph for 'life' to the nose of his son, Tutankhamun: a wall detail from Temple A at Kawa.

(Right) Tutankhamun drinking from a white lotus chalice: a scene in relief on a fragmentary faience collar terminal.

All the King's Men

The god's father Ay: detail from a fragment of gold foil found by Davis in Tomb 58 in the Valley of the Kings.

Pharaoh Tutankhamun was a semi-divine being standing at the top of the hierarchical pyramid of Egyptian society. The intercessor between gods and men, ruling an essentially agricultural populace whose principal concern was the annual ebb and flow of the life-giving river Nile, the king's contact with his people was in practice limited. Surrounded at court by an inner circle of advisers and friends, the day to day running of the realm – the collection of taxes, regulation of agriculture, and administration of justice – was delegated to an army of officials whose tentacles radiated out from Memphis, Egypt's administrative capital, through the length and breadth of the country.

So far as the names of these officials is concerned, Egypt during the reign of Tutankhamun is a jigsaw for which most of the pieces are missing. For the vast majority of Tutankhamun's contemporaries, high-ranking or low, administrators, priests, military men, or peasants, nothing whatsoever is known. Even for the exceptions, archaeology has provided little more than disembodied names, gleaned from those few closely datable monuments the king's favour had enabled his men to bequeath to posterity. The following are a selection.

The inner circle

Ay

The principal member of the king's inner circle was the god's father Ay, perhaps to be recognized as the father of Nefertiti and thus step-grandfather to Tutankhamun. By virtue of his position as principal adviser to Tutankhamun, controlling access to and influencing his ward, a great deal of power was concentrated in Ay's hands. Following the king's untimely death, Ay, presumably by virtue of his links to the royal line, would rule as Pharaoh in his own right. He was buried after a brief reign in Tomb 23 in the western annexe of the Valley of the Kings. A number of fragments of gold foil discovered by Theodore M. Davis in Tomb 58 in the main Valley (p. 38) had evidently formed part of Ay's burial furniture.

Horemheb

The *de facto* influence at court of the god's father Ay was balanced by the *de jure* power of the military officer Horemheb, whose titles included those of commander-in-chief of the army and deputy of the king. By force of arms, Horemheb was able to reassert Egyptian suzerainty abroad and ensure the

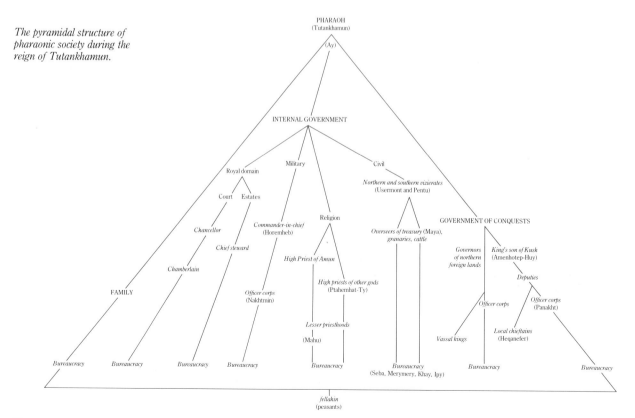

The pyramidal structure of pharaonic society during the reign of Tutankhamun.

continuation of tribute from Egypt's northern and southern neighbours. Horemheb's successes are depicted in his finely decorated private tomb, which was brought to light in the New Kingdom necropolis at Saqqara a few years ago; following his accession, a second tomb was prepared in the Valley of the Kings (No. 57). An uninscribed limestone dyad in the British Museum (EA 36) may well come from his Saqqara tomb chapel. A fine granite statue of Horemheb as a scribe is in the Metropolitan Museum of Art in New York (MMA 23.10.1); a similar, though headless, statue of the man, from Karnak, is in Cairo (CG 42129).

Nakhtmin

A second military officer of note was Nakhtmin (or Minnakht), evidently a close relative of Ay who is best known today for the five large wooden *shabti* figures he presented to the burial of Tutankhamun (p. 139). On a statue of the man probably carved during the reign of Ay, Nakhtmin is designated 'king's son'. If Ay had intended that Nakhtmin should succeed him, it was an ambition which Horemheb was destined to foil.

Maya

Among the titles recorded on the wooden *shabti* and bier figure presented by Maya to the burial of Tutankhamun (p. 137) are those of overseer of works in the Place of Eternity (i.e. the royal cemetery) and overseer of the treasury (meaning in this instance, perhaps, the funerary storerooms). Maya's gifts, like those of Nakhtmin, suggest a close personal attachment to the king. He seems to have taken responsibility not only for the preparation of Tutankhamun's burial but also for its restoration; he was to undertake a similar restoration, with his assistant Djehutymose (p. 97), in the tomb of Tuthmosis IV (No. 43, where he left a graffito) in Year 8 of Horemheb. The finely decorated tomb of Maya was recently discovered close to that of Horemheb at Saqqara; statues of the man and his wife, Meryet, from the tomb chapel, are now in Leiden (AST 1–3).

Officials and administrators

Usermont and Pentu

The vizierate, or 'prime-ministership', of Egypt at this period was divided into a northern and a southern office. Usermont, one vizier from the reign of Tutankhamun, is known from two statue fragments (one, from Armant, Cairo Temp. 22/6/37/1) and a stone sarcophagus from the Theban area. A second vizier, Pentu, perhaps the owner of Tomb 5 at el-Amarna, is recorded on a wine-jar docket (no. 490) from Tutankhamun's tomb (p. 203). Usermont and

(Above left) Horemheb, commander-in-chief of the army and deputy of the king.

(Above right) The military officer Nakhtmin.

(Below) The necropolis official Maya.

Seba, mayor of Thinis, as represented on one of two surviving stelae.

Pentu are perhaps the two viziers depicted among the funerary procession which decorates one wall of the Burial Chamber in Tutankhamun's tomb (p. 72).

Huy and the Nubian contingent

The viceroy of Kush under Tutankhamun, whose job was to oversee Egyptian exploitation of the gold-rich country and ensure the free-flow of tribute, was one Amenhotep-Huy; the man's decorated tomb (No. 40) is at Thebes. Statues of Huy have been found at Elkab and Abusir (East Berlin 19900), with inscriptions at Faras and a graffito at Biga. Stelae of Huy are in Cairo (JE 37463, with a hymn to the *ka* or 'spirit' of the king) and Berlin (17332). Taemwadjsi, the probable wife of Huy and 'chief of the harim of Tutankhamun' – an institution of which, regretta-

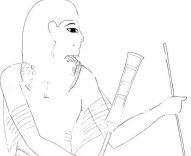

Amenhotep-Huy, viceroy of Kush during the reign of Tutankhamun.

bly, we know next to nothing – is attested at Faras (Khartoum 3745 and 4449), Kawa (Khartoum 2690) and also at Thebes (in the tomb of Yuya and Tjuyu: Cairo CG 51083). Mentioned in the tomb of Huy is one Heqanefer, a local chieftain whose own tomb has come to light at Tushka in lower Nubia.

Other named officials

Among the less-exalted contemporaries of Tutankhamun is the mayor of Thinis, Seba, who is known from two stelae: one in the Louvre (C 87), the other, a fragment, in the Fitzwilliam Museum, Cambridge (E SS 54). The stela of one Panakht, governor of Kawa during the reign, is in Khartoum (2680). Memphis stelae are attested for the royal scribe Merymery (Cairo CG 34186) and an unnamed treasury official (Petrie Museum, University College London, UC 14470). A 'servant of Amun' named Mahu is known from a stela found at Deir el-Medina.

Other probable contemporaries include the scribe Khay, whose statue is in Berlin (2294), the chief steward and fan-bearer Ipy, whose stela is in Leningrad (Hermitage 1072), and two canopic jars in Leiden (AAL 4c, d), and Ptahemhat-Ty, high priest of Ptah (stela, British Museum EA 972, and other monuments). A wooden scribal palette belonging to an unnamed official of the king, from 'Thebes', is in the Louvre (N 2241).

See further pp. 28–9.

> ❛ Woe to him that assaileth thee [O Amun]! Thy City endures, whereas he that assaileth thee is cast down ❜

Prayer to Amun on an ostracon from Thebes

For most of his reign Tutankhamun was the pawn of others; but inevitably, as he grew older, the boy's pliability will have lessened. With his wife's apparent inability to carry children to full-term, the inheritance would pass to Ay, an elderly man with little time left. X-rays of Tutankhamun's skull reveal damage consistent with the king's having received a blow to the head: Ay's gnawing ambition for power may well have driven him to murder.

Tutankhamun was interred by King Ay in a hastily adapted private sepulchre (No. 62) in the Valley of the Kings in around 1323 BC – to judge from the flowers and fruits buried with him, during the first half of March. Doubtless this small tomb had been pressed into service only because work on Tutankhamun's intended place of burial, Tomb 23 in the West Valley, had scarcely begun; the excavation would be employed by his successor.

Ay's brief reign of only four years appears to have continued the policies begun under his young predecessor. Ay died in 1319 BC, and the period immediately following may have been marked by a struggle for the throne between Nakhtmin, the 'king's son' whom some have seen as Ay's appointed successor, and the general Horemheb. It was perhaps during this troubled time that Tutankhamun's tomb was entered by thieves (p. 95).

With the accession of Horemheb, who dated his reign retrospectively from the death of Amenophis III, the reaction to the Amarna pharaohs began in earnest with the continued dismantling of Akhenaten's monuments, the usurpation of those of Tutankhamun, and the general work of reconstruction.

Ay's perhaps tenuous claim to the throne may have been strengthened by forging close links with Tutankhamun's widow, Ankhesenamun. An alliance is suggested by a glass ring-bezel in which the names of the two are found combined. The ring was first spotted by Percy Newberry, who conveyed news of it to Carter in this letter preserved among the Carter papers in Oxford.

Destruction of the Amarna legacy continued in the 19th dynasty, of which Horemheb may be seen as spiritual founder: within 50 years of Akhenaten's death, the heretic king, Nefernefruaten, Smenkhkare, Tutankhamun and Ay had been struck from the records. It was as if they had never existed.

(Far left) Horemheb as Pharaoh: a broken calcite canopic stopper found by Theodore Davis in the king's tomb in the Valley of the Kings.

(Left) King Ay represented as a Nile-god: fragment from a throne base of indurated limestone.

By a curious irony, it was the very oblivion to which Tutankhamun had been consigned that would ensure the survival of his burial. Consistently omitted by his Ramessid successors from the lists of Egypt's former kings, he was soon forgotten. With time, the site of his tomb began to blend in perfectly with its surroundings – to be missed not only by Ramesses VI who quarried a tomb for himself within a few metres of it, but more importantly when the royal tombs were dismantled following the abandonment of the Valley of the Kings by Ramesses XI (1100–1070 BC).

Egyptologists scrutinizing the fragmentary remains of the period were somewhat better informed. A few objects had been found inscribed with Tutankhamun's name, and the likelihood was, they reasoned, that the king had been interred in the royal burial-ground at Thebes. Indications that this might indeed be the case were in due course uncovered by Theodore Davis's team, and in 1909 a small undecorated chamber was brought to light which Davis imagined to be the tomb itself.

Howard Carter, for one, thought differently. He believed that Tutankhamun's burial still awaited discovery, and that it might even be intact. For five years he and Lord Carnarvon systematically cleared the Valley of the Kings down to bedrock in search of this archaeological Holy Grail. Their perseverance was rewarded when, at 10 am on Saturday, 4 November 1922, workmen reported the discovery of a step cut into the rock of the Valley floor beneath the foundations of a group of huts erected during the quarrying of the tomb of Ramesses VI. It was the beginning of a stairway leading down to a walled-up doorway. Tutankhamun had been found.

The Valley of the Kings and the tomb of Tutankhamun.

'The Valley of the Tombs is Now Exhausted'

‘ . . . if Mr. Theodore Davis, of Boston, for whom I was excavating in 1914, had not stopped his last 'dig' too soon I am convinced he would have discovered the present tomb of King Tutankhamen. We came within six feet of it. Just then Mr. Davis feared that further digging would undermine the adjacent roadway and ordered me to cease work. ’

Harry Burton

The Valley of the Kings is situated about 5km (3mi) to the west of modern Luxor on the opposite bank of the Nile. It in fact comprises two valleys: an eastern wadi, the Valley of the Kings proper; and a western

annexe, Wadyein or the West Valley. The first king to be buried here was Tuthmosis I and, with but few exceptions, every king of the New Kingdom was to prepare for burial within its confines; Tutankhamun was perhaps the seventh monarch to do so. To date, excavation has brought to light some 80 or more tombs and pits.

The last king to be interred in the Valley was perhaps Ramesses X. Under his successor, Ramesses XI, a start was made on dismantling the royal burial-ground, the immense riches of which were proving an irresistible temptation to thieves. The tomb furniture was broken-up for the reuse of its materials, and the occupants, denuded of their jewels, were reinterred in a handful of easily guarded hiding-places or caches. Had modern explorers fully appreciated the thoroughness of this dismantling, their search for intact tombs might never have begun.

But the lure of buried treasure was the motivation of almost all who have dug in the Valley of the Kings, from the son of Sheikh Mamam in the mid-eighteenth century down to Carnarvon and Carter in this. More often than not the participants in the

The main wadi of the Valley of the Kings, highlighting the principal excavations (sponsor/excavator and date of discovery) carried out between 1900 and the discovery of the tomb of Tutankhamun in 1922.

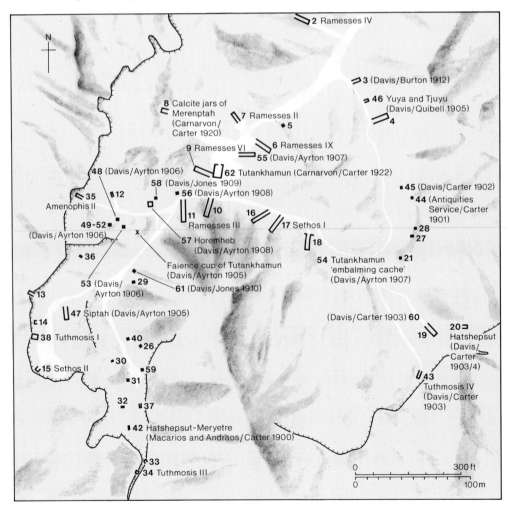

chase were blinded to the interest and importance of what burial furniture the ancients had left behind; recording was skimped and the finds lost for good. For all its colourful characters and abundance of incident, the story of excavation in the Valley of the Kings is a sorry one.

Theodore Davis: Patron and Excavator

Had Theodore Davis stumbled upon Tutankhamun, the story of the Valley's archaeological destruction might have been sorrier still. Davis, a retired American lawyer, began excavating in the Valley in 1902, at first under the supervision of Howard Carter (in his capacity as Inspector-General of Monuments of Upper Egypt), later employing his own archaeologists: Edward R. Ayrton, Harold and Cyril Jones and, finally, Harry Burton. Davis had prodigious good luck, between 1902 and 1914 uncovering no fewer than 30 tombs of varying significance. His interest in careful clearance work was minimal, however, and his employment of photography and the most basic conservation methods almost non-existent; while his splendid series of publications manages to record everything but the facts.

Davis came close to finding Tutankhamun on several occasions – horrifyingly close, if Burton is to be believed. His first brush with the king came in 1905/6, when Ayrton brought to light a small faience cup bearing the king's prenomen, discovered 'under a rock' not far from private tomb No. 48. The second came with the discovery of Pit 54 in 1907, containing embalming and other debris associated with the king's burial. On 10 January 1909 a third

The first clue to Tutankhamun's presence in the Valley: an inscribed faience cup found by Ayrton during the 1905/6 season. It is identical to others later recovered from the king's tomb, and had perhaps been removed from the burial by robbers under the mistaken impression that it was made of glass – a valuable commodity during the late 18th dynasty.

Theodore M. Davis, striking an appropriately 'archaeological' pose in jodhpurs and puttees. The rakish young man to his left is the archaeologist Edward R. Ayrton; on Davis's right stand Arthur Weigall, Inspector-General of Antiquities for Upper Egypt, and his wife Hortense. From a photograph taken by Benjamin Stone in 1907.

*Fragment of gold foil,
recovered by Harold Jones
from Tomb 58 though
originating in the tomb of
King Ay (No. 23). Ay is
shown in his chariot, firing
arrows at a copper target.
Two foreign captives are
bound to the target-stand; a
further two make obeisance
before the king.*

find was made: a small, undecorated chamber
(No. 58) containing a fine calcite *shabti* figure and
several fragments of gold foil and other fittings
stripped from one or more chariots and from harness
originally buried in Tomb 23 (that of Ay). The gold
bore the names both of Tutankhamun and of Ay, the
latter as commoner and pharaoh, and at once
became confused in Davis's mind with the blue
faience cup and the contents of Pit 54. A man with a
penchant for tying up loose ends, Davis concluded
that he had found the tomb of Tutankhamun
himself; and that being so, he opined, 'I fear that the
Valley of the Tombs is now exhausted'.

Pit 54

Pit 54, 1.9 by 1.25m (6ft by 4ft) and perhaps a metre
and half (about 5ft) deep, was opened by Ayrton on
21 December 1907. In it, he found a collection of large
storage jars – perhaps a dozen in all – which Davis
ordered to be carried up to his excavation house in
the West Valley. Following a disastrous official
opening of the jars in the presence of the British
Consul-General, Sir Eldon Gorst (who, Herbert
Winlock records, merely complimented Davis on his
cook and left), the debris the jars contained was
consigned to a storeroom. The material included
small clay seal impressions bearing the name of
Tutankhamun, fragments of linen bearing hieratic
dockets dating to Years 6 and 8 of the king, linen
bundles of natron (sodium carbonate, a naturally
occurring salt used in embalming), a few bones,
masses of broken pottery, faded floral collars and a
miniature mask of gilded cartonnage (p. 123). Davis's
only use for the find was to demonstrate to guests,
by tearing the papyrus collars to shreds before their

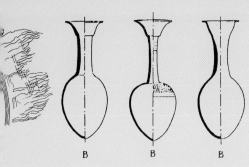

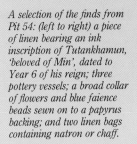

A selection of the finds from Pit 54: (left to right) a piece of linen bearing an ink inscription of Tutankhamun, 'beloved of Min', dated to Year 6 of his reign; three pottery vessels; a broad collar of flowers and blue faience beads sewn on to a papyrus backing; and two linen bags containing natron or chaff.

eyes, how strong the material could be after 3,000 years in the ground.

What Ayrton had brought to light in Pit 54 was in fact of immense interest. Winlock, of New York's Metropolitan Museum of Art, believed that these jars contained the remains of a funerary meal and ritually unclean mummification debris which had had to be buried away from the tomb with which it was associated; to judge from the inscribed linen and the seals employed, the owner of this material was Tutankhamun himself. Winlock was very close to the truth. The assemblage was indeed associated with the burial of Tutankhamun; but its find-spot had nothing to do with ritual impurity. As fragments recovered from Tutankhamun's tomb were to show, the Davis jars had originally been placed in the empty entrance corridor. They were removed to Pit 54 after the first robbery (p. 95), when the decision was taken to fill the entrance corridor with rubble as a deterrent to further theft.

Pit 54 (left), an abandoned 'commencement' for a tomb pressed into service in antiquity for objects orginally stored in the corridor of the tomb of Tutankhamun. The photograph (far left) shows the location of the pit in the Valley. (Below) Two mud seal impressions from Pit 54, that on the left inscribed with the king's prenomen, 'beloved of Khnum, manifold of praises'.

Howard Carter: Early Days

Howard Carter as a young man (right): an oil-painting recently discovered in the Tower – the attic – of Highclere Castle, Lord Carnarvon's stately home. It was perhaps the work of Samuel Carter, Howard's father, an animal painter of repute but, as the rather bovine jaw suggests, less skilled at reproducing the human form.

Cat in the marshes (below): a delightful detail from the 12th-dynasty tomb of Khnumhotep (No. 3) at Beni Hasan, reproduced in watercolour by Howard Carter in 1893 for the Egypt Exploration Fund.

Akhenaten: the fragmentary face (below right) from a statue of indurated limestone, discovered during the course of Carter's work with Flinders Petrie at el-Amarna. The fragment passed into the collection of Lord Amherst, Carter's sponsor on the Petrie dig, and was later acquired by Lord Carnarvon when the Amherst collection was dispersed in 1921.

❝ Mr. Carter is a good-natured lad whose interest is entirely in painting and natural history; . . . it is of no use to me to work him up as an excavator. ❞

W.M. Flinders Petrie

Howard Carter first opened his eyes to the world in London, at 10 Rich Terrace, Kensington, on 9 May 1874, the youngest of 11 children born to Samuel John Carter, an animal painter and illustrator for the *Illustrated London News*, and his wife Martha Joyce Sands. Much of his youth was spent in Norfolk, at the Carter family home in the quiet village of Swaffham. His formal education was minimal, a fact of which Carter was always painfully aware – 'It is said that nature thrusts some of us into the world miserably incomplete' – and which may at least partially explain the abrupt and defensive manner which accompanied him throughout his life. But his inherited artistic skills were considerable, and in the summer of 1891 were brought by the future Lady Amherst of nearby Didlington to the notice of the young Percy Newberry, an Egyptologist working at that time for the Egypt Exploration Fund (EEF). Impressed by his talent, Newberry employed Carter to help ink-in tracings of tomb scenes at Beni Hasan, and in October that same year the 17-year-old artist visited Egypt to work at Beni Hasan and later at Deir el-Bersha. While in Egypt, he undertook to excavate at el-Amarna on behalf of William Amhurst Tyssen-Amherst (later first Baron Amherst of Hackney), under Flinders Petrie. Petrie, unimpressed, dismissed the would-be archaeologist in a single paragraph, damning him with faint praise.

Whatever the dour Petrie may have thought, Carter's enthusiasm for archaeology was real and intense, and he agreed with alacrity to return to Egypt the following year as draughtsman with the EEF. It was as a member of the EEF Archaeological Survey team that he first encountered Thebes, spending the better part of the next six years copying the scenes and inscriptions of the magnificent mortuary temple of Hatshepsut, the 18th-dynasty woman-pharaoh, at Deir el-Bahri.

The potential which Petrie failed to see was left to the French Egyptologist Gaston Maspero to recognize. Maspero had recently been re-appointed head of the Egyptian Antiquities Service, the government department he had already served with distinction between 1881 and 1886. One of his first acts, in 1899, was to appoint Carter to the newly established post of Inspector-General of Monuments of Upper Egypt.

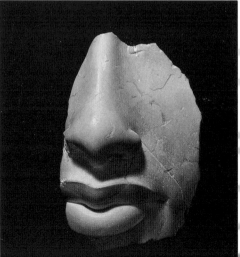

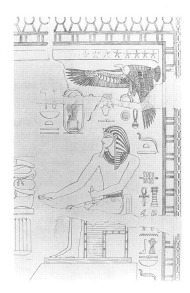

Carter took up his new position in January, 1900, and from this time on began to take an active and increasing interest in the vast Theban necropolis. His introduction to the Valley of the Kings came almost at once, with the rearrangement and partial removal to the Giza Museum of the royal mummies found in the tomb of Amenophis II (No. 35) in 1898; the tomb was about to be opened to the public. Over the following years, Carter undertook the clearance of several new but plundered tombs, not only for the Antiquities Service, but on behalf of Theodore Davis (p. 37) whose triumphs over the years Carter was in office would include the discovery of two new private sepulchres (Nos. 45 and 60) and one royal – that of Tuthmosis IV (No. 43).

Carter did his job well, and was a valued member of the Antiquities Service, repaid by transfer to the more prestigious post at Saqqara in the north in 1904. His sudden and unnecessary resignation within months came as a shock to everyone.

Howard Carter's drawing of the right exterior surface of the chariot body discovered by Davis in the tomb of Tuthmosis IV (No. 43) in 1903. The original is of wood, overlaid with canvas and with gesso carved in fine low relief; until the discovery of the tomb of Tutankhamun in 1922, it was the most substantial portion of an Egyptian royal chariot known.

The magnificent setting of Hatshepsut's mortuary temple (above), looking down from the path leading over the cliff to the Valley of the Kings.

(Above left) Queen Hatshepsut seated before a table of offerings: a detail from the wall decoration of her mortuary temple at Deir el-Bahri, where Carter was employed as principal copyist by the Egypt Exploration Fund for much of the 1890s.

41

Howard Carter: the Lean Years

> ❛ I have a hot temper, and that amount of tenacity of purpose which unfriendly observers sometimes call obstinacy, and which nowadays . . . it pleases my enemies to term . . . *un mauvaise caractère*. Well, that I can't help! ❜
>
> Howard Carter

Carter's telegram informing Lord Cromer of the fracas in the tomb of the sacred bulls at Saqqara. When Carter refused to apologize for his over-zealous ejection from the tomb of an unruly party of French tourists, he was obliged to resign.

Carter as a down-and-out: a pencil sketch made c. 1909 by Arthur Weigall, Carter's eventual successor as Inspector of Antiquities in Luxor.

Carter's *mauvaise caractère* was to dog him throughout his life. One particular incident shortly after his move to Saqqara cost him his government career.

The affair was trivial enough, and not a little comic. A group of 14 French tourists visiting Saqqara on 8 January 1905, when informed that they would require a ticket to see the Serapeum, burial place of the sacred Apis bulls, began to abuse both the local inspectors and the *ghafirs* (tomb guards). Eventually, all but three members of the party, several of whom were 'very much the worse for liquor', agreed to pay, and both paying and non-paying members of the party forced their way *en masse* past the ticket collector into the darkness of the tomb. Discovering that there were no candles available to them, the tourists promptly rushed out again, and demanded their money back. Carter was sent for. Playing it by the book, he refused to make any refund and, in no uncertain terms, told the French to leave. The ensuing affray left both sides 'cut and knocked about', and it is hardly surprising that the French should have lodged a formal complaint. Carter, hauled before Lord Cromer, then British Consul-General, was asked to explain himself. Much sympathy was expressed for Carter's predicament, but it was considered diplomatic that he should offer an apology. Carter, with righteous indignation, refused: so far as he was concerned, he had only done his duty, and if the demand for an apology were to be pressed, he would resign – and resign he did.

Maspero was very much distressed by the affair, 'and wrote to several of Carter's friends saying that he did not know what the Antiquities Department

COFFER BEARING THE NAMES OF AMENOTHES III.

Limestone relief with the head of King Tuthmosis III (far left), from Deir el-Bahri: from the portfolio of colour reproductions of his work, Six Portraits of the Thothmes Family, *published privately by Carter (perhaps with Lord Carnarvon's help) sometime before 1910.*

Gilded wooden casket (left centre) of Amenophis III with blue faience inlay, and detail of the gilded and inlaid outer wooden coffin of Tjuyu (left): two of the watercolours produced by Carter for Theodore Davis's publication The Tomb of Iouiya and Touiyou, which appeared in 1907.

would do without him, and begged us to persuade him to return.' But Carter, being Carter, went his own way.

For some months he eked out a meagre living as a 'gentleman-dealer' and artist, supplementing the few Egyptological commissions which came his way – notably the recording of the objects discovered by Theodore Davis in the tomb of Yuya and Tjuyu (No. 46) – by painting the sights and scenes of both ancient and modern Egypt in rather charming watercolours which he sold to visiting tourists. Business was anything but brisk. Had Carter been less of a perfectionist, matters might have been different; but, both at this period and later, he seems to have discarded as many paintings as he produced – and no doubt as many were given away as gifts as were sold. An introduction to the Earl of Carnarvon offered the chance of a new start.

The Gentleman Dealer

'There is no one more familiar with the Egyptian market or more closely in touch with all its best possibilities . . . I need only point to our own "Carnarvon Collection", which [Carter] formed for Carnarvon over a long period of years, to illustrate his excellence of judgement and sense of the beautiful.'

Albert M. Lythgoe

Egypt in the first decade of this century was a very different place from the Egypt of today. If not actually encouraged, it was at least tolerated that an archaeologist might, on occasion, indulge in the purchase and resale of antiquities. Carter's activities as a 'gentleman dealer' seem to date from this 'low' period in his career, and to have continued throughout his life, profiting him well. His purchases for Lord Carnarvon (p. 47) and 'intermediary' activities on behalf of the Metropolitan Museum of Art, most notably in the acquisition of the £53,000 'Treasure of Three Princesses', are well known. But Carter also put his eye to good use buying, on 15 per cent commission, for private collectors, including the Englishman J.J. Acworth (many of whose pieces are now in the British Museum). Carter seems also to have sold through various Cairo dealers, including E. A. Abemayor and the well-patronized Nicolas Tano, whose shop was across from Shepheard's, the favoured haunt of many English tourists.

A herding and fishing scene: two limestone relief fragments from a 5th dynasty tomb, acquired by Carter for the Detroit Institute of Arts in 1930.

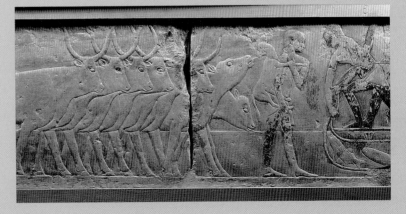

Lord Carnarvon

The debonair George Edward Stanhope Molyneux Herbert (right), fifth Earl of Carnarvon: a painting by Howard Carter's brother, William.

A wooden cat-coffin, the sole find of Lord Carnarvon's first season, which the excavator proudly presented to the Cairo Museum.

The Winter Palace Hotel in Luxor, Carnarvon's bolt-hole during the digging seasons at Thebes.

‘ We once had the pleasure of entertaining Rudyard Kipling at the headquarters of our Expedition in Thebes. He described the life of the field archaeologist very happily by saying: "It furnishes a scholarly pursuit with all the excitement of a gold prospector's life". That goes far toward explaining why a sporting gentleman like the late Earl of Carnarvon was willing to spend so much money and so many discouraging years looking for an unplundered tomb in the Valley of the Kings. ’

Ambrose Lansing

Lord Carnarvon's introduction to Egyptology was a somewhat circuitous one. The infant sport of motoring had been a particular passion, and although he considered himself to be a careful 'automobilist', Carnarvon was never able to resist the temptation to speed which the new mode of transport offered. He was brought before the magistrates on several occasions, one report in *The Autocar* describing how, 'like "a flash"', he had whizzed past pedestrians and cyclists at terrifying speeds of up to 20 miles an hour.

The inevitable accident came in 1901, in Germany. Though saved from death by the quick thinking of his chauffeur, Edward Trotman, the fifth Earl was left appallingly weak, his spare frame ('I only weigh 8st 12lbs and cannot go up') increasingly vulnerable to the cold and damp of the English climate. He began to winter abroad, and in 1903 visited Egypt for the first time.

Though the climate suited him well, Carnarvon soon found life in Cairo rather dull. He took to Egyptology simply as a congenial way of passing the interminable winter days, little realizing the extent to which this new hobby would come to dominate his life. At Lord Cromer's request, he was granted a concession to dig in a much turned-over area of Sheikh Abd el-Qurna, an unpromising site (but convenient for the Winter Palace Hotel) which had been assigned to Carnarvon in an attempt to cool his archaeological ardour. Each day Lord Carnarvon sat himself in his large screened cage, protected from the flies and the dust, to watch his men work; sometimes he was joined by his wife, 'dressed for a garden party rather than the desert, with charming patent-leather, high-heeled shoes and a good deal of jewellery flashing in the sunlight'. Finds were predictably few: after six weeks of frantic digging Lord Carnarvon had little to show for his efforts except a mummified cat, still contained in its cat-shaped wooden coffin.

But Carnarvon was flushed with pride at his discovery, and found his enthusiasm heightened rather than dampened. He was, nonetheless, well aware of his limitations as an archaeologist, and determined to secure a more promising concession by presenting a less amateur face to the authorities. He again consulted Lord Cromer, who made enquiries of Maspero and suggested he meet Howard Carter.

Excavations 1907–1914

'The finds extend from the XIIIth Dynasty to the Ptolemaic period, and are particularly rich for Dynasties XVII and XVIII. They include coffins, furniture, musical instruments, toys, an inlaid board for a game . . . and hieratic and demotic texts of great historical interest.'

Francis Llewellyn Griffith

The fiasco of the first season would have put off most would-be excavators. Not so Carnarvon, who determined to press on, extending his Theban concession and applying for permission to work at Aswan. 'I thought I would have two strings as I am not sure I will get my wife to stay another whole 2 months at Luxor.' And later he wrote, 'If I get what I want I shall bring out a learned man as I have not time to learn up all the requisite data.'

Under the watchful supervision of his 'learned man' – Howard Carter – Lord Carnarvon's second season began. Despite his interest in Aswan, the work was confined to the Theban west bank. The results of this 'small excavation at Gurneh' were immensely successful, Carter turning up not only the decorated tomb of Tetiky, an early 18th-dynasty mayor of Thebes, but a further tomb (No. 9 in the excavators' sequence) containing two wooden tablets. The more important of these was inscribed on the one face with extracts from the precepts of Ptahhotep, a series of instructions for moral guidance, and, on the other, part of a text recording the first steps in the expulsion of the Hyksos by the 17th dynasty King Kamose.

The following years produced equally successful results, Carter bringing to light a whole series of important private tombs dating from the end of the Middle Kingdom to the start of the New, and two

(Left) Howard Carter and an unidentified woman stand behind Gaston Maspero, the French director of the Antiquities Service, and his wife during a visit to Carnarvon's work at Thebes in 1913. The photographer was Lord Carnarvon himself.

Pay-day (below left): Howard Carter settles accounts with his workmen at the end of the month. Another photograph from Lord Carnarvon's personal album.

Excavating at Thebes (below): winding queues of workmen carry spoil from the excavations, many with baskets balanced precariously upon their heads.

(Above) Unlike many archaeologists of the day, Carter was not afraid of dirtying his hands. Here he is seen pulling on his cardigan after exploring a swelteringly hot underground tomb-chamber brought to light by his workmen. A photograph by Lord Carnarvon, 1913.

(Above right) Lord Carnarvon and his dog on site during the clearance of Tomb 47 at Thebes. The spoil from the interior of the tomb is being passed back by the line of basket-boys for dumping away from the area of work.

(Below left) A pair of base-silver bracelets, part of the hoard of jewellery found in a pottery jar at Tell el-Balamun. Carter dated the pieces to the 'late Ptolemaic' period – that is, c. 100 BC; more recent opinion is that the jewellery dates from Roman times, more than two centuries later.

(Far right) Detail from a funerary papyrus of the 12th century BC: a coloured vignette showing the lady owner, hands raised in adoration of the god Osiris. From Carnarvon and Carter's 1907/8 season at Thebes.

'lost' temples of Queen Hatshepsut and Ramesses IV. In 1912 the report of the first seasons' work was published in appropriately lavish style as *Five Years' Explorations at Thebes, a record of work done 1907–1911*. The volume received wide acclaim; the Carnarvon–Carter team had made its mark.

In 1912, while continuing the digging at Thebes, Carnarvon and Carter decided to try their luck at Sakha (ancient Xoïs) in the Delta. But Fortune, who had smiled so sweetly on their Theban endeavours, seemed less interested in the excavators' northern efforts. The team – envisaged as comprising Lord and Lady Carnarvon, Carter, Percy Newberry, Lord Carnarvon's servant, Lady Carnarvon's maid, Carnarvon's ever-present physician, Dr Johnson, a cook and some 50 workers – had to abandon the place after no more than a fortnight 'on account of the number of cobras and cerastes [horned vipers] that infested the whole area'.

The following year, having been foiled in their attempts to dig at Dahshur, Carnarvon and Carter turned their attention to another Delta site, Tell el-

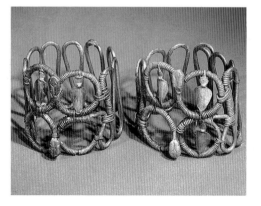

Balamun. There were no snakes, but, as at Sakha, the yield was uninspiring. Despite a brief revival of interest caused by the discovery of a hoard of Graeco-Roman silver jewellery, work was abandoned after a few trial soundings. Somewhat disheartened, Lord Carnarvon returned home.

Carnarvon the Collector

> 'To amass such a collection it was not merely a question of riches, nor even of expert assistance. It was a case of inspiration, of taste, of *flair* which cannot be acquired from any amount of study.'
>
> Jean Capart

In Howard Carter, Lord Carnarvon evidently recognized not only a talented archaeologist but a kindred spirit. Carnarvon was keen to continue digging, but the not-inconsiderable expense of such work had been brought home to him by the experiences of his first, independent season. Carter came up with a business-like suggestion which appealed to Carnarvon's pocket and added a little spice to their venture. According to the fifth Earl's son and successor, 'Carter suggested . . . that some of the expenses of the work might well be defrayed by buying antiques in the bazaar in Cairo or elsewhere to sell them to collectors at a handsome profit. Carter proved very adept at this business and I . . . heard them talk of many good deals brought off in this fashion.'

Both the Metropolitan Museum of Art and the British Museum benefited from this arrangement, though whether the scheme ever realized much profit after Carter's salary had been paid (£400 a year in 1907; £200 a month in 1911) is perhaps doubtful. Much of their 'stock' seems to have passed directly in to Lord Carnarvon's own collection. Carnarvon's taste for Egyptian art was developing rapidly, and by the time of his death in 1923 what had started off as a somewhat random assortment of purchased and excavated pieces ranked as one of the finest private collections of Egyptian art in the world.

The prices paid by the cognoscenti for Egyptian antiquities at this time were high. 'You have heard, of course,' Carnarvon wrote to Wallis Budge of the British Museum in 1912, 'that Morgan had bought the coptic MSS you refused for 80,000£' (a figure which even Carnarvon was forced to admit 'I personally can scarcely credit'). While to Budge again, in March 1913, he wrote, 'I saw a head just like your little red head in the Museum but a trifle bigger in green basalt, price asked 1500. . . .' The prices paid by Carter, if more reasonable, were anything but low, as his diaries and surviving letters record. A green stone head of Tuthmosis III, said to come from the tomb of Amenophis I at Thebes (p. 48), cost £151; three carnelian bracelet plaques of Amenophis III and Tiye (p. 48) Carter acquired for £350, with a multiple *kohl*-tube of Hatshepsut thrown in for good measure. It was a rich man's market, and in this market Lord Carnarvon could easily hold his own.

The Carnarvon collection, when it came to be listed by Carter in November 1924, numbered some 1,218 objects or groups of objects. These antiquities, according to the terms of his will of 29 October 1919, Carnarvon left to his wife Almina, advising that 'Should she find it necessary to sell . . . I suggest that the nation – *i.e.* the British Museum – be given the first refusal at £20,000, far below its value . . .' And if the British Museum didn't want them, 'I would suggest that the collection be offered to the Metropolitan, New York, Mr. Carter to have charge of the negotiations and to fix the price.'

For obvious reasons, Lady Carnarvon was unenthusiastic about offering the collection to the nation at a knock-down price rather than at its true value, which stood then at over £35,000. The difficulty, however, advised by Carter, she determined to meet head on.

The Director of the British Museum was asked whether his institution would like to acquire the collection for the sum specified in Lord Carnarvon's will; if so, payment should be made in full by 4 pm that same day. The Museum could not meet the deadline, and Lady Carnarvon, her conscience cleared, offered the collection to the Metropolitan in New York for $145,000. They snapped it up.

Small basalt head (above) of a Tuthmosid pharaoh wearing the nemes-*headdress, purchased by Carter in 1912 from the Cairo dealer Blanchard for £151. Carter later claimed to have found a fragment from this same head during the course of his work at the tomb of Amenophis I which, if correct, will have been the original find-spot of the piece.*

The spectacular centrepiece of the Carnarvon collection (left): a solid gold statuette of Amon-Re, king of the gods, said to have been found north of the Temple of Amun at Karnak in 1916. Although originally assigned by Carter to the middle years of the 18th dynasty, a Third Intermediate Period date now seems more likely.

Royal Tombs 1914–1922

' I believe I really have found the tomb of Amenhotep [Amenophis] I . . . '

Carnarvon to Wallis Budge

From the very beginnings of their association, Lord Carnarvon and Howard Carter had had as their ultimate aim work in the New Kingdom royal necropolis. The concession for the Valley of the Kings, however, was still held by Theodore Davis (whom Carnarvon, like many people, actively disliked: 'I told [Maspero] I should not speak to the man again'). News of Carter's latest discovery offered a way forward.

The discovery was a tomb which the Theban locals had been plundering secretly for some time. Eventually, after much detective work, Carter had tracked it down. It proved to be that of Amenophis I, a joint burial prepared for the king and his mother Ahmose-Nofretiri, who shared a funerary temple on the edge of the nearby cultivation. The burial had been dismantled in antiquity, and the mummies of the royal pair had been removed, ultimately finding their way to the Deir el-Bahri cache. But those who had carried out the salvage operation some 3,000 years before – and the modern robbers who had stumbled upon the tomb – had left much behind. Carter's clearance brought to light a mass of inscribed vessel fragments, a large heart-scarab of blue frit and a collection of fragments from the Third Intermediate Period burials which had been introduced into the tomb after Amenophis I and his mother had gone. It was Carnarvon's first royal tomb, and it spurred him on to greater things.

Some months before his death on 23 February 1915, Theodore Davis had abandoned the Valley concession, opening the way at last for Carnarvon and Carter. Plans for work at Hawara, at the pyramid complex of Ammenemes III, were abandoned, and by 8 February 1915 Carter had commenced work at the tomb of Amenophis III (No. 22) in the western annexe of the Valley of the Kings. Carnarvon had been influenced in his choice by Carter's acquisition on the Luxor antiquities market in 1912 of three fine bracelet plaques of carnelian, which appeared to have once adorned the mummy of the king. If the tomb had produced objects of this quality, it might well contain other pieces of artistic interest.

The excavators' efforts were not to be in vain. Though the tomb of Amenophis III, like that of Amenophis I and Ahmose-Nofretiri, had apparently been dismantled by the necropolis administration during the tenth century BC, Carter was able to salvage a great deal from the smashed debris left behind. Four of an original five foundation deposits inscribed for Tuthmosis IV (the father of Amenophis III) were found undisturbed at the entrance to the tomb, indicating that work on quarrying the sepulchre had begun during that king's reign. Within the tomb, clearance of the well and well-chamber produced a whole range of funerary objects, including fragments of serpentine, calcite, faience and wooden *shabtis*, broken vessels, pieces of a superb pectoral ornament of blue faience, quantities of beads, sequins and amulets, and one corner of a bracelet plaque in blue faience from the same series that had started Carnarvon and Carter on their search.

The European war, however, was making its effects felt even in Egypt. Carnarvon was stranded in England, and Carter's energies were taken up more and more with essential war work as a diplomatic courier. In 1916, he did find the time to clear on Lord Carnarvon's behalf a newly discovered cliff-tomb in the Wadi Sikket Taqa el-Zeide, which

Carter's sketch of three superb bracelet plaques of carnelian purchased for Lord Carnarvon in October 1912 from the Luxor dealer Jusef Hasan.

A selection of objects from the foundation deposits uncovered by Carter at the entrance to the tomb of Amenophis III; these included miniature tools of wood and copper-alloy, model vessels of pottery and limestone, and several blue faience cartouche-plaques inscribed with the prenomen or nomen of Amenophis III's father, Tuthmosis IV.

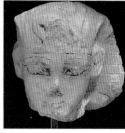

Calcite head with black eye detail, from a large shabti-*figure of Amenophis III. The head is inscribed in pencil with the excavator's number, 99, identifying it as a piece recovered from the well-chamber of the king's tomb on 2 March 1915.*

(Left) Excavating the Valley of the Kings down to bedrock in search of Tutankhamun: a photograph taken by Carter on 24 January 1920. The work of shifting the thousands of tons of limestone chip was facilitated by the use of a hand-propelled Decauville railway, seen here running diagonally from the centre of the photograph.

(Below left) The cache of calcite jars found at the entrance to the tomb of Merenptah in the Valley of the Kings on 26 February 1920. Lady Carnarvon, in a rare foray into her husband's work, is said to have dug out the jars herself. (Below) One of the six vessels presented to Lord Carnarvon, inscribed with the cartouches of Ramesses II.

ad been prepared for Hatshepsut while still Tuth-
nosis II's queen. But the tomb had never been used,
nd, apart from the abandoned sarcophagus, there
vere no finds.

By 1917, Carter was able to start work in the
Valley of the Kings proper, and over the following
ears, with brief interruptions, he proceeded to clear
ne Valley down to bedrock in the search for a single
omb: that of Tutankhamun. Countless boys and
en laboured to move thousands upon thousands of
ons of limestone rubble by basket and hand-
ropelled Decauville railway. But finds were few.

Apart from ostraca (flakes of limestone employed by
the ancient quarrying teams to jot down their lists
and accounts), the only discovery of note was a
group of calcite jars buried at the entrance to the
tomb of Merenptah. To judge from the hieratic
dockets they bore, these tired and worn-out vessels
had been employed to contain oils used in the final
preparations for burial of Merenptah's body. Of
these 13 jars, six were presented to the excavators. It
was a generous share of a miserable tally, but a poor
return on Lord Carnarvon's considerable
investment.

The Discovery

‹ At last have made wonderful discovery in Valley; a
magnificent tomb with seals intact; re-covered same for
your arrival; congratulations. ›

Howard Carter to Lord Carnarvo[n]

The disappointments, like the costs of excavating
this remote part of the world, were beginning [to]
mount up. Lord Carnarvon's enthusiasm was on th[e]
wane, and by the end of the bleak 1921/2 season h[e]
had decided to call it a day. Much as Carnarv[on]
hated to admit it, Davis's view that the Valley of th[e]
Kings was worked out seemed to have been corre[ct].
He and his excavator were obviously chasing [a]
chimera.

Carter was summoned to Highclere to receive th[e]
bad news. Carnarvon was clearly as disappointed a[s]
his associate when, after reviewing their work of th[e]
past few years, he stated that, with such littl[e]
prospect of success, he could no longer continue t[o]
finance the search. Carter had been expecting a[s]
much, and countered with a proposition he hope[d]
would appeal to Carnarvon's sporting instinct[s]:
Carter would finance from his own pocket on[e]
further season, clearing the last triangle of groun[d]
which he felt might yet yield results – and if a fin[d]
were made, it would belong to Carnarvon as holde[r]
of the concession. Impressed by Carter's commit[-]
ment, the fifth Earl relented: he agreed to a fina[l]
season, but he, not Carter, would foot the bill.

AN EGYPTIAN
TREASURE.

THE WONDERFUL
DISCOVERIES IN EGYPT

LORD CARNARVON'S OWN
COMPLETE ACCOUNT.

NEW CAVE OF ALADDIN

MATCHLESS WORKS OF ART

We are able to print to-day a complete accoun[t]
the Earl of Carnarvon of the wonder[ful]
ancient royal trea[sures]

Perseverance is rewarded

The race, then, was still on, though it is difficult to believe that Carter harboured much optimism when, on 1 November 1922, a Wednesday morning, work began. Three days later the outlook had brightened considerably. For, 'some thirteen feet [3.9m] below the entrance to the tomb of Ramesses VI, and a similar depth from the present bed level of The Valley', the top of a sunken staircase had come to light. By late afternoon on the following day 12 steps

had been cleared, and the upper part of a plastered blocking stood revealed, stamped over its entire surface with large though blurred oval seals. It was a discovery as puzzling as it was exciting:

'The design was certainly of the Eighteenth Dynasty. Could it be the tomb of a noble buried here by royal consent? Was it a royal cache, a hiding-place to which a mummy and its equipment had been removed for safety? Or was it actually the tomb of the king for whom I had spent so many years in search?'

In 1921 the Committee of the Egypt Exploration Society in London reported that 'it seems to be becoming more and more difficult, in fact almost impossible, to excite in the general public that interest in archaeology generally, and in Egyptian archaeology in particular, which we feel our country should take.' When, a few months later, news of Carnarvon and Carter's discovery of the tomb of Tutankhamun in the Valley of the Kings (left and opposite below) hit the headlines (opposite above), all that changed for good.

After several hours of digging, the rock-cut outline of the mysterious tomb entrance (left) could be clearly discerned.

Carter re-examined the seal impressions for a name – but to no avail. For the moment, the question of ownership would have to remain unanswered. Mustering all his will-power, he ordered his men to refill the staircase, and next day dashed off the now-famous telegram to Carnarvon, who was still in England.

Two-and-a-half weeks later, on 23 November, Lord Carnarvon and his daughter, Lady Evelyn Herbert, stepped off the train at Luxor; and the following day work began in earnest.

The mouth of the tomb fully cleared (right), showing the entrance stairway and modern retaining wall. A marker-stone visible in the top left-hand corner of the photograph carries the 'interlinked Cs' Carnarvon crest – its resemblance to a skull and crossbones earning the excavators the nickname 'The Buccaneers' – and a grid reference to Carter's map of the area.

Lord Carnarvon and Lady Evelyn Herbert, arriving at Luxor station on 23 November 1922, are met by Howard Carter and the governor of Qena province.

With the stairwell entirely freed, the full expanse of the plastered doorway could be seen. 'On the lower part the seal impressions were much clearer, and we were able without any difficulty to make out on several of them the name of Tut.ankh.Amen.' The diggers' elation was tempered by the observation that here, at the top left-hand corner of the blocking, were signs of reclosing: the deposit, whatever its true nature, had evidently been tampered with in antiquity – a reluctant conclusion the debris already encountered on the steps of the tomb only served to reinforce.

Piece by piece, the blocking was removed, and little by little a descending corridor was revealed, filled to the ceiling with packed limestone chip, through which a tunnel had been dug and anciently refilled. By 4 o'clock on the afternoon of 26 November the corridor was empty, and before the

171

The plastered door blockings had been stamped all over with a range of large oval seals, including the famous motif of the jackal triumphant over nine bound captives; the detail shown here is from the blocking to the Annexe. A drawing by Carter of the jackal and nine captives device, to the right in the photograph, is shown above.

53

(Right) As the rubble fill of the entrance corridor was removed, a second blocking came into view. Beyond lay the Antechamber and its shimmering contents.

(Right centre) The Burial Chamber blocking, photographed before Carnarvon and Carter broke through the anciently replastered robbers' hole, visible at the bottom of the picture, on 28 November 1922. Their clumsy concealment of this hole with a basket lid and a handful of rushes (far right, above) was probably undertaken for tactical reasons: Carnarvon, wishing to strike the best deal he could with the press, was anxious to maintain the suspense for as long as possible.

(Far right, below) The entrance to the tomb of Ramesses VI was quarried directly above that of Tutankhamun, contributing significantly to the survival of the boy-king's burial.

excavators loomed a second door, again faced with plaster, stamped over its entire surface with oval seals and reclosed at the top left-hand corner.

The first glimpse

Not knowing what to expect – perhaps a second staircase – Carter made a small hole in the sealed doorway and inserted a candle to test for foul gases. He then peered into the void beyond:

'At first I could see nothing, the hot air escaping from the chamber causing the candle flame to flicker, but presently, as my eyes grew accustomed to the light, details of the room within emerged slowly from the mist, strange animals, statues, and gold – everywhere the glint of gold.'

This was it, so much sooner than expected – 'the day of days,' Carter wrote, 'the most wonderful that I have ever lived through, and certainly one whose like I can never hope to see again.'

Enlarging the hole, and accompanied by Lady Evelyn and Callender, Carter and Carnarvon clambered down into the Antechamber where they stood, dumbstruck. Slowly, carefully, they moved between the heaps of treasure, their minds in a whirl, unable to believe what their eyes were seeing. After what must have seemed like an eternity, the party stumbled back to Carter's house for a fitful rest before resuming exploration the next day.

With Callender's electric lighting now installed the scene was less real than ever, the sparkle of the gold more dazzling than before. But the layout of the

deposit was now clear. Beneath the couch, on the west wall, was the entrance to a second chamber (the Annexe), while an area of stamped plaster between two 'guardian statues' standing against the north wall of the antechamber marked the entrance to a third chamber, the blocking of which showed signs of having been resealed in the middle at the bottom. As is now common knowledge, and as was undoubtedly their prerogative, Carnarvon and Carter entered this third chamber within a short time of the discovery – to judge from a letter written by Carnarvon to Alan Gardiner, on the evening of 28 November; this was the day before the official opening of the tomb, by which time record photographs of the ancient sealed reclosure had been taken. Dismantling the resealed section, Carter wriggled through first, followed by Carnarvon and Lady Evelyn; Callender proved too large for the hole. The chamber was filled with a huge gilded shrine, while beyond lay a fourth chamber, with open doorway through which could be glimpsed ever more beautiful things watched over by a reclining figure of the Anubis dog, divine guardian of the royal cemetery. But it was the shrine which attracted everyone's attention. The nature of the deposit was now clear: 'I have got Tutankhamen (that is certain) and I believe . . . intact.'

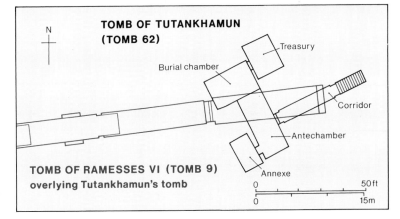

TOMB OF TUTANKHAMUN (TOMB 62)

N

Treasury

Burial chamber

Corridor

Antechamber

Annexe

TOMB OF RAMESSES VI (TOMB 9) overlying Tutankhamun's tomb

0   50 ft
0   15 m

The Excavation Team

‹ While in Cairo I had time to take stock of the position, and it became more and more clear to me that assistance – and that on a big scale – was necessary if the work in the tomb was to be carried out in a satisfactory manner. The question was, where to turn for this assistance. ›

Howard Carter

It did not take Carnarvon and Carter long to appreciate the enormity of the discovery and its implications. 'Carter has weeks of work ahead of him', Carnarvon optimistically forecast soon after entering the tomb for the first time. Arthur Callender, a close friend of Carter, had been on hand since 9 November, but his assistance was clearly not enough. Fortunately, Albert Lythgoe, Curator of the Metropolitan Museum's Egyptian Department, had cabled to offer congratulations and any help he could. Carter took Lythgoe at his word, and at the beginning of December telegraphed the following request.

'Thanks message [of congratulations]. Discovery colossal and need every assistance. Could you consider loan of Burton in recording in time being? Costs to us. Immediate reply would oblige. Every regards, Carter, Continental, Cairo'.

Lythgoe was quick to reply. On 7 December he cabled the following message:

'Only too delighted to assist in every possible way. Please call upon Burton and any other members of our staff. Am cabling Burton to that effect. Lythgoe.'

The close ties that already existed between Carter, Carnarvon and the Metropolitan Museum were strengthened. It was a generosity which would in due course be rewarded by Carter engineering the Met's acquisition of the Carnarvon collection.

Within a matter of days, Carter received further offers of help, on 9 December from Alfred Lucas, a chemist with the Egyptian Government, and on 12 December from Arthur Mace, an Egyptologist with the Metropolitan Expedition. Six days later, James Henry Breasted, Director of the Oriental Institute in Chicago, arrived to begin work on the seal impressions which covered the plastered blockings. Hauser and Hall, two architects with the Metropolitan team, began work on drawing a plan of the objects in position. And on 3 January, the British philologist Alan Gardiner arrived to start work on the inscriptions.

After three and a half thousand years of silence, the tomb was a-hum with activity. The numbers would increase with the arrival of Carter's old friend Percy Newberry as work got under way. It was a showpiece of academic co-operation that was in due course to draw in Douglas Derry of the Cairo Anatomy School and Saleh Bey Hamdi of Alexandria to conduct the postmortem examination of the mummy; Battiscombe Gunn, to work on the ostraca for the final publication; the botanist L.A. Boodle from Kew Gardens; James R. Ogden, the Harrogate jeweller, to report on aspects of the goldwork; Alexander Scott and H.J. Plenderleith of the British Museum, for analytical assistance; G.F. Hulme of the Geological Survey of Egypt; and others.

Members of the Team

Lord Carnarvon (1866–1923)
Carnarvon first visited Egypt in 1903 in search of the warmer climes which his frail health required. His interest in archaeology turned into a consuming passion following his introduction to Howard Carter in 1907. Carnarvon's untimely death on 5 April 1923 would rob Egyptology – and Carter – of an influential friend and ally.

Howard Carter (1874–1939)
Carter was Lord Carnarvon's field-director. Following the death of his employer, Carter directed the clearance of the tomb on behalf of Almina, Lady Carnarvon. He also supervised the conservation of the tomb furniture, its transportation to Cairo and, in the early stages, its installation in the Cairo Museum. Despite his enormous talent and resource, Carter was a stubborn man, 'by nature nervous and high-strung', who alienated many with whom he came into contact: the first few years of the clearance were to be very difficult.

Arthur Cruttenden Mace (1874–1928)
Arthur Mace was a former student and distant cousin of Flinders Petrie, for whom he dug at Dendera, Hiw and Abydos. After a spell with George A. Reisner, working at Giza and Naga el-Der, Mace had joined the Metropolitan Museum in 1901 as Assistant Curator of Egyptian Art. Mace's sound common sense and practical skills were invaluable to Carter, and he co-authored the first volume of *The Tomb of Tut.ankh.Amen*. In 1924 Mace's health failed, and to Carter's regret he left Egypt for good.

Alfred Lucas (1867–1945)
Alfred Lucas, Manchester born, was from 1923–32 Chemist to the Antiquities Service. For nine seasons he would work closely with Carter in the consolidation of Tutankhamun's burial equipment, and in analyzing the various materials brought to light in the tomb. Carter estimated that without conservation barely 10 per cent of the tomb's contents would have reached Cairo in a state fit for exhibition. Thanks to Lucas's skills, barely 0.25 per cent of the objects was lost. As well as drawing upon his skills at preservation, Carter was to rely heavily on Lucas's forensic talents in his reconstruction of the robberies to which the tomb had been subjected after Tutankhamun's burial.

Henry (Harry) Burton (1879–1940)
The services of Harry Burton, Lincolnshire-born though a resident of Florence, were loaned by the Metropolitan Museum's Egyptian Expedition, which he had joined in 1914. Burton had previously dug for Theodore Davis in the Valley of the Kings, but was attached to the Metropolitan and Carter teams as photographer. The hundreds of glass negatives he took during the course of the Tutankhamun clearance provide an unparalleled body of reference and are among the finest archaeological photographs ever made.

Arthur R. ('Pecky') Callender (d. 1936)
Arthur Callender, by profession an architect and engineer, was a long-standing friend of Carter's. He had retired as manager of the Egyptian branch railways in 1920, and was invited to join the excavating team at the beginning of November, 1922. A careful and dependable worker, well-used to Carter's moods, Callender's skills would be put to good use during the dismantling and removal of the large gilded shrines from Tutankhamun's tomb.

Percy Edward Newberry (1869–1949)
Percy Newberry, sometime Professor of Egyptology at the University of Liverpool and Carter's erstwhile mentor, worked closely with the Tutankhamun team for several seasons. Newberry's special interest was the botanical specimens from the tomb, upon a selection of which he would briefly report in the second volume of *The Tomb of Tut.ankh.Amen*. Mrs Newberry gave invaluable help in the mending of a number of the textiles from the tomb, including the ill-fated pall (p. 101).

Alan Henderson Gardiner (1879–1963)
Gardiner, independently wealthy, was the foremost philologist of his generation, and a useful political ally. A friend to the sponsor rather than to the excavator, Gardiner's co-operation was vital for a successful completion of the enterprise, which Carter was sufficiently professional to appreciate. But beneath a veneer of cordiality there was little love lost between the two. As Carter had written of Gardiner some years earlier: 'the more I see of him the less I like him, and I am . . . sure that as far as any real friendship goes he is not to be trusted . . .'

James Henry Breasted (1865–1935)
Breasted was founder and first director of the Oriental Institute of the University of Chicago. His reputation as an historian of ancient Egypt was second to none, and he was invited by Carnarvon 'to do all the historical work involved in the discovery and its eventual publication'; although 'this was a staggering assignment', as events transpired the actual historical yield of the tomb would turn out to be extremely meagre. In the end, most of Breasted's efforts would be expended upon the great number of seal impressions stamped upon the door-blockings of the various chambers of the tomb.

Walter Hauser (1893–1959)
Hauser, an American, had been trained as an architect, and joined the Metropolitan's Egyptian Expedition in 1919 following a brief period of teaching at the Massachusetts Institute of Technology (MIT). Herbert Winlock's right-hand man, Hauser, with Lindsley Foote Hall, would be responsible for producing invaluable scale drawings of the Antechamber *in situ*. Personal difficulties with Carter soon brought the association to an end.

Lindsley Foote Hall (1883–1969)
Hall was another product of MIT, where he too had trained as a draughtsman. He joined the Metropolitan Museum's Egyptian Expedition in 1913. He would work closely with Hauser in producing accurate scale drawings of Tutankhamun's tomb furniture *in situ* before clearance of the Antechamber began. Like Hauser, Hall found Carter a difficult man to work for, and his association with the project likewise came to an abrupt halt.

Richard Adamson
Acting Sergeant Richard Adamson, because of his lowly rank, was mentioned in none of the contemporary accounts of the discovery. He was to serve as a guard to the Carnarvon expedition for seven seasons, from October 1922. Adamson claimed that most nights he would sleep in the Antechamber, playing opera records on a gramophone provided by Carter; as one recent interviewer was told, 'The scratchy strains of music coming from the tomb were enough to scare off any robbers.'

Clearing the Tomb

'Excitement had gripped us hitherto, and given us no pause for thought, but now for the first time we began to realize what a prodigious task we had in front of us, and what a responsibility it entailed. This was no ordinary find, to be disposed of in a normal season's work; nor was there any precedent to show us how to handle it. The thing was outside all experience, bewildering, and for the moment it seemed as though there were more to be done than any human agency could accomplish.'

Howard Carter

Howard Carter's clearance of the tomb of Tutankhamun, and his preservation of the treasures to make them fit for removal to Cairo, took almost a decade; had the tomb been found by anyone else, it would have been cleared and any surviving contents put on display within a month. The difference underlines the caution with which Carter approached his task, and the immense burden of responsibility he felt.

Through all the distractions and difficulties of the first two seasons (p. 64), Carter and his team pressed on with the clearance in a thorough and methodical way, maintaining the fullest records ('no matter how trivial a discovery appears at the moment . . . notes may afterwards afford most valuable information')

(Below) Emptying the inner recesses of the tomb.

and lavishing time and money on the preservation of the antiquities as they were brought out. The expedition had from the start been employing the tomb of Ramesses XI (No. 4) as a storeroom for supplies and for minor finds from the stairwell and corridor (a number of which would be re-excavated half a century later by The Brooklyn Museum). This was now supplemented by the tomb of Sethos II, which would be used as a secure field conservation laboratory and photographic studio. Tomb 55, conveniently situated across the path from Tutankh-

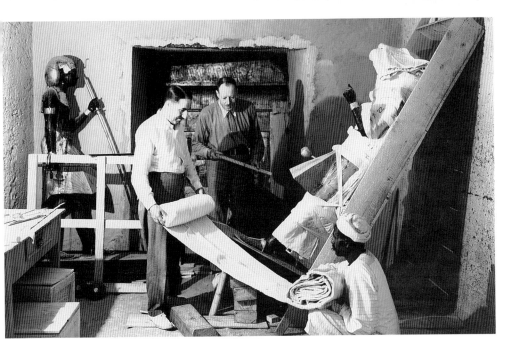

amun, was pressed into service as a darkroom for Harry Burton.

A routine was rapidly established for processing the seemingly endless flow of treasures and conservation challenges issuing forth from the tomb. Each object or group of objects was given a reference number; *in situ* photographs were then taken, with and without reference number cards in position, the camera carefully positioned so that every object showed in at least one of the shots. A brief description, with sketch where appropriate, was made of each object by Carter or Mace on a numbered record card; the object was located on a ground-plan of the tomb being prepared by Hall and Hauser (for the Antechamber only); and the piece was removed to the laboratory for treatment by Lucas and Mace, with further photography and recording. A final photograph was taken as conserved. All this for many thousands of objects, over several seasons, in sweltering heat (24–29°C (75.2 84.2°F)), with continued harassment from the press (who were soon complaining about the excessive

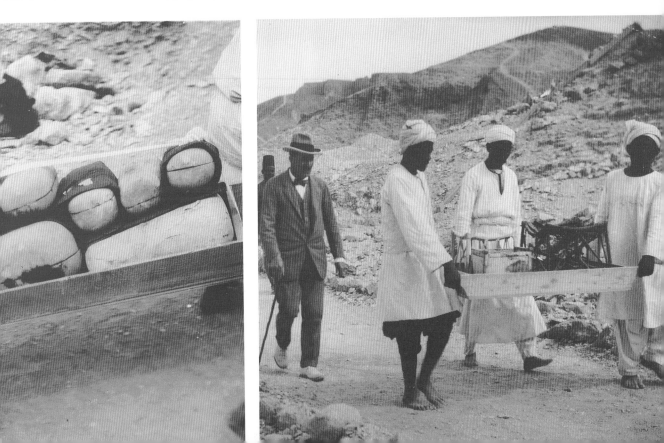

(Above) Safely conserved and packed in specially built crates for transport to Cairo, the antiquities are transferred to the river, along the same 'road by which they had passed, under such different circumstances, 3,000 years before.'

(Right) The clearance of Tutankhamun's tomb seems to have been the first ever archaeological expedition to have its own resident chemist. Lucas's experiments in the field (shown here is a page from one of his notebooks, recording attempts at treating the sadly decayed leather products from the tomb) were crucial in stabilizing the condition of the more fragile objects for the long and difficult journey to Cairo.

amount of time the clearance was taking), from visitors (more than 12,000 at the height of the hysteria, between 1 January and 15 March 1926), and from the Egyptian Government itself.

Clearance of the Antechamber began on 27 December 1922, took seven weeks, and used up more than a mile of cotton wadding and 32 bales of calico. At the end of this, as of each future season, the antiquities were crated up with care, using hundreds of feet of timber, and transported to the river en route to Cairo by hand-propelled Decauville railway. Though a relatively short distance, the journey to the boat took more than 15 hours, without shade, during the height of the summer, with constant leap-frogging of the meagre number of rail-lengths provided by the Antiquities Service. Only the gold coffin and mask, and one or two other lots, would not be transported by river: 'These were conveyed by train in a special "Service Car" with an armed guard from the Egyptian army in the adjoining carriage, both car and carriage being shunted from the Cairo railway station directly into the yard of the Museum.'

Carter's numbering system

The tomb of Tutankhamun, now designated Valley Tomb 62, was No. 433 in Carter's sequence of discoveries since 1915. Every fragment, object or

group of objects from 'Tomb 433' was assigned an object number ranging from 1 to 620; subdivisions for objects within a numbered group were noted by the use of single or multiple letters – a, b, c, etc., where appropriate aa, bb, cc, aaa, bbb, ccc, or even 4a, 4b (for aaaa, bbbb), etc. Additional subdivisions were noted by bracketed Arabic numerals. Group no. 620 is anomalous in that it was given 123 numbered subdivisions: 620:1 to 620:123.

The distribution of object numbers throughout the tomb was as follows:

1a–3	entrance staircase
4	first sealed doorway
5a–12t	Corridor
13	second sealed doorway
14–170	Antechamber
28	sealed doorway into the Burial Chamber
172–260	Burial Chamber
261–336	Treasury
171	partially dismantled Annexe blocking
337–620:123	Annexe

'It had been our privilege to find the most important collection of Egyptian antiquities that had ever seen the light, and it was for us to show that we were worthy of the trust.'

Howard Carter

(Above left) Arthur Callender, Carter's long-standing friend, engaged in recording work outside the tomb of Sethos II. In the background, engaged in conversation, can be seen Alfred Lucas and Alexander Scott of the British Museum.

(Above right) Carter's skills as an artist were to prove immensely useful as the clearance got under way, the clarity and accuracy of his 'sketches' providing instant identification for many of the thousands of objects the clearance was to reveal.

(Left) At the end of each season, for security against theft and flood, the tomb entrance was covered over. Beneath the rubble fill, closing off the entrance to the corridor, was a watertight wooden blocking erected over a wooden portcullis (shown here guarded by a local policeman). At the far end of the corridor was a second screening sheet and a padlocked steel gate.

The Death of Lord Carnarvon

(Opposite) Carnarvon's death certificate. On it rests the ivory-handled razor with which the fifth Earl infected the fateful mosquito bite, resulting in his death.

(Below) Ever since his motoring accident in Germany in 1901, Carnarvon's constitution had been anything but strong. He is seen here resting on the shaded veranda of Carter's house at Elwat el-Dibun.

' Our great sorrow during the last few days has been Carnarvon's serious illness. He . . . is not yet out of danger. It is difficult to think that only last Friday he and I dined and spent the evening together. It would be terrible if – but I just won't think of it. '

Alan Gardiner to his wife Heddie

The unexpected death of Lord Carnarvon was a watershed in the history of the tomb clearance. Overnight Carter was thrust fully into the limelight, adding to his own immensely stressful duties as excavator the full burden of public relations, which had hitherto been handled with great style by his late employer.

But all of this was in the future as Lord Carnarvon departed for Aswan on 28 February for a few days rest following the excitement of the official opening of the Burial Chamber (p. 82). Whether before or after his arrival at Aswan, Carnarvon was bitten on the cheek by a mosquito. Shaving with his cut-throat razor, he inadvertently opened the bite, which reddened angrily. Despite treating the wound with iodine from his well-stocked medicine chest, a fever set in and Lord Carnarvon, worn out by events and running a temperature of 38.3°C (101°F), allowed his daughter Evelyn to confine him to bed to rest and recover. This seemed to do the trick, and two days later he was up and about, eager to visit the tomb. When her father suffered a relapse almost immediately, Lady Evelyn made arrangements for him to be moved to the Continental-Savoy in Cairo, on 14 March. But it was too late. Ever since his car accident, the 57-year-old Earl had been a weak man; further weakened, as he was, by the present

The Curse

'. . . all sane people should dismiss such inventions with contempt.'

Howard Cart[er]

Lord Carnarvon's death focused popular attention on a warning made just two weeks before by the novelist Marie Corelli that 'the most dire punishmen[t] follows any rash intruder into a sealed tomb'. The public chose to ignore the fact that Lord Carnarvon's constitution had never been strong, and indeed that his annual pilgrimage to Egypt had been undertaken primarily on health grounds: it preferred to regard his sudden passing as the inevitable consequence of having disturbed Pharaoh's rest.

"THE CURS[E]
Superstitious Legend Roun[d]
MARIE CORELLI'S
Conan Doyle Puts Suspici[on]
When Lord Carnarvon
morning of April 5, fr[om]
ng a mosquito-bi[te]

infection, in the days before penicillin, he fell an easy prey to pneumonia. His wife was summoned from England, arriving by air in a Puss Moth with her husband's physician, Dr Johnson. Before long their son, Lord Porchester, had joined them, just in time to spend a few hours with his delirious father. By the morning of 5 April it was all over: as Carter records in his diary, 'Poor Ld. C. died during the early hours of the morning.'

The show of emotion from family, friends and colleagues was matched by the black frame sported by the Cairo newspapers. For, despite the uproar caused by his exclusivity agreement with *The Times* (p. 64), Carnarvon had been much loved and respected in Egypt.

Arrangements were made for the body of the fifth Earl to be embalmed without delay for transport to England and burial on Beacon Hill overlooking his beloved Highclere. Meanwhile, in Egypt, Howard Carter was left at the helm of what was now Lady Carnarvon's 'ship'. Sadly, he was to prove a poor sailor.

Death by association

Rumour was rife. On the day the tomb was opened, Carter's pet canary was swallowed by a cobra – the cobra being the very serpent on Pharaoh's brow which spits fire at his enemies; at the precise moment of Carnarvon's death, it was said, the lights of Cairo inexplicably went out; while at the same time, in England, Carnarvon's three-legged terrier bitch, Susie, howled and dropped dead.

The demise of anyone who had been even remotely connected with Carnarvon, Carter or the discovery was immediately seized upon as further evidence for the efficacy of Tutankhamun's vengeance: Carnarvon's younger brother, Aubrey Herbert, died suddenly in September 1923; an X-ray specialist passed away unexpectedly while en route to Egypt to examine the king's mummy; the American railroad magnate Jay Gould died of pneumonia, the result of a cold contracted during a visit to the tomb; the Egyptian Ali Kemel Fahmy Bey was shot by his wife in the London Savoy some time after viewing the discovery; Arthur Mace, Carter's right-hand man, suffered a breakdown of health and died before the tomb had been fully cleared; the

Arthur Conan Doyle attributed responsibility for Carnarvon's death to 'elementals – not souls, not spirits – created by Tutankhamen's priests to guard the tomb'. Modern explanations of 'the curse' tend to be framed in more 'scientific' terms: infection by long-dormant micro-organisms (histoplasmosis) is a current favourite.

French Egyptologist Georges Bénédite died as the result of a fall after seeing the tomb. Carter's secretary Richard Bethell died in unusual circumstances at the Bath Club in 1929; Bethell's father, Lord Westbury, who had never seen the tomb but possessed a small collection of Egyptian antiquities, committed suicide a short time later; while an 8-year-old child was accidentally killed by Lord Westbury's hearse. These were just a few of the claimed victims. Such a catalogue of tragedy, public opinion maintained, could hardly be fortuitous.

Statistics drawn up for his own amusement by the American Egyptologist Herbert E. Winlock in 1934 paint a rather different picture. Of the 26 people who had been present at the opening of the tomb, six had died within a decade. Of the 22 who had witnessed the opening of the sarcophagus, only two had died. While of the 10 who had been present at the mummy's unwrapping, none had yet succumbed to 'the curse'. Indeed, Carter himself did not die until 1939, at the age of 64; Harry Burton, the expedition photographer, died in 1940, aged 60. Lord Carnarvon's daughter, Lady Evelyn Herbert (later Lady Evelyn Beauchamp), born in 1901 and one of the first to enter the tomb, lived until 1980. Others involved closely with the discovery included Professor Percy E. Newberry, Carter's friend and mentor, who died in 1949, aged 80; Dr (later Sir) Alan H. Gardiner, who studied the tomb's inscriptions, died in 1963, aged 84; while Dr D.E. Derry, who performed the autopsy on the king's mummy, died at the age of 87 in 1969.

As an imaginary inscription was purported to proclaim, 'Death shall come on swift wings to him that toucheth the tomb of Pharaoh.' It cannot be denied, however, that Death was peculiarly selective in his choice of victims, and surprisingly long in coming for those who were perhaps closest to the work.

Arthur Weigall (above), the former Antiquities Service Inspector, who for a time was employed as a special correspondent for the Daily Mail. Observing Carnarvon's good humour at the opening of the Burial Chamber doorway, Weigall is reputed to have commented: 'If he goes down in that spirit, I give him six weeks to live.' Just over six weeks later, the fifth Earl was dead.

Politics

Howard Carter, a glamorous visitor, Pierre Lacau and members of the Egyptian government pose for the camera in front of the tomb of Sethos II. But behind the smiles trouble was brewing.

' . . . the atmosphere of Luxor is rather nerve-wracking at present. The Winter Palace is a scream. No one talks of anything but the tomb, newspaper men swarm, and you daren't say a word without looking round everywhere to see if anyone is listening. Some of them are trying to make mischief between Carnarvon and the Department of Antiquities, and all Luxor takes sides one way or the other. Archaeology plus journalism is bad enough, but when you add Politics it becomes a little too much. . . . '

Arthur Mace to his wife Winifred

' The whole is a disagreeable business and Carter is such an autocrat that to be thwarted at every turn takes all reason from him. '

Winifred Mace to her mother

If there was ever a wrong time to die, Lord Carnarvon chose it. Not only was he robbed of the satisfaction of seeing Tutankhamun unveiled, but the man he left behind to deal with what was developing into a very tricky political situation was to prove totally lacking in diplomacy and finesse. Carter was a superb excavator, but the public-relations role he now found himself playing was one for which he could not have been less well suited.

The seeds of disaster had been sown by Carnarvon himself when, on 9 January 1923, he signed a contract with *The Times* of London, in which he agreed that all details of the discovery would henceforth be channelled through that newspaper. At the time, both financially and practically, it seemed a sensible move; but politically it was to be a disaster. The *Times* agreement was felt to be an affront, not only to the local Egyptian press, but to the rest of the world's newspapers, and the excavators had to suffer on-going guerilla warfare and mischief-making from the *Times*'s competitors – one of whom, the *Daily Mail*, had employed Carter's old rival, Arthur Weigall, as their special correspondent. For the Egyptian nationalists, the *Times* agreement provided a God-given stick with which to beat not only the British 'colonialists', but foreigners in general. It would eventually prove the expedition's undoing.

Tension in the tomb

With the official 'discovery', on 16 February 1923, that the king still lay undisturbed within his tomb, pressure to see the find became worse. There was also the nagging question of a division of the objects: was the tomb to be classified as intact or otherwise? If 'intact', the Egyptian Government would, under the terms of the concession, be entitled to deny the excavators' claims to any share of the objects recovered.

Carter and Carnarvon began to argue between themselves as to the best way of dealing with the difficulties which the discovery was continuing to present; in due course they fell out altogether – Carter, on 23 February 1923, going so far as to demand that Carnarvon never enter his house again. It was an indication of how fraught the situation had become. The cloud of gloom which descended on the Tutankhamun camp following Lord Carnarvon's death, on 5 April 1923, was intensified by the realization of how much more vulnerable without their influential sponsor the expedition now was.

The second season began in October 1923. Carter had spent the summer in England, where he visited Highclere to persuade Lady Carnarvon to renew the concession under her own name. To this she had readily agreed, as she did also to renewing the *Times* contract which had been the cause of so much grief the previous season. This year the fuss was to be even worse, thanks largely to Carter's poor handling of the situation. As a first step in the downward

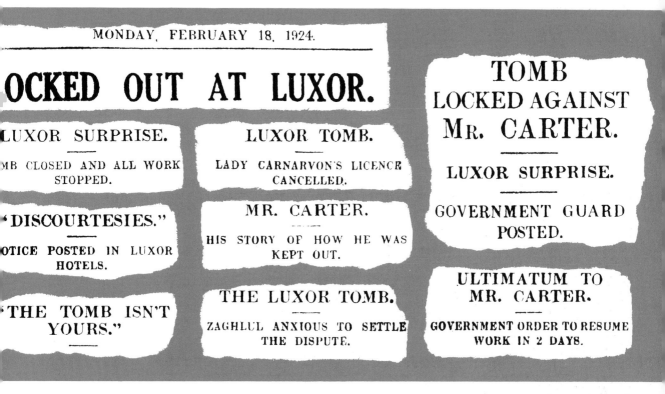

MONDAY, FEBRUARY 18, 1924.

OCKED OUT AT LUXOR.

TOMB
LOCKED AGAINST
MR. CARTER.

LUXOR SURPRISE.

MB CLOSED AND ALL WORK
STOPPED.

LUXOR TOMB.

LADY CARNARVON'S LICENCE
CANCELLED.

LUXOR SURPRISE.

"DISCOURTESIES."

OTICE POSTED IN LUXOR
HOTELS.

MR. CARTER.

HIS STORY OF HOW HE WAS
KEPT OUT.

GOVERNMENT GUARD
POSTED.

"THE TOMB ISN'T
YOURS."

THE LUXOR TOMB.

ZAGHLUL ANXIOUS TO SETTLE
THE DISPUTE.

ULTIMATUM TO
MR. CARTER.

GOVERNMENT ORDER TO RESUME
WORK IN 2 DAYS.

piral, with the clear aim of circumventing a call om journalists that all or none be present when an nnouncement on the find was to be made, Carter ecided that Merton, the *Times*'s correspondent, ould no longer be regarded as a pressman but as a member of the excavating team. *The Times* would still be first with the news.

The Egyptian Government – and in particular Pierre Lacau, Maspero's successor as Director-General of the Antiquities Service – had been under increasing pressure to take action over the *Times* embargo, not least by the Nationalists who much resented the lack of Egyptian involvement in the enterprise. Admittance and an immediate briefing of the Egyptian press would have been a sensible first step towards soothing ruffled feelings – but stubbornly Carter refused to budge. He saw it as a matter of principle. A sniping war broke out, and the awkwardness between Lacau and Carter escalated rapidly into unpleasantness. As early as 23 December 1923, the wife of Carter's co-worker, Mace, was articulating the ultimate threat: '. . . there are so many troubles Mr Carter might even close the work down, then who knows what will happen . . . .'

Matters came to a head following the official lifting of the sarcophagus lid on 12 February 1924. Carter's intention that wives of the expedition members should visit the tomb on the following day was thwarted by the newly appointed Nationalist Minister of Public Works, Morcos Bey Hanna – no friend to the English since their attempt to have him hanged for his political activities some years before. Carter could see nothing in the Minister's action except a personal insult to himself, to his colleagues and to England; Mace saw it more as petty jealousy, 'spoiling the dream of every Egyptologist'. Carter, 'looking desperately ill and in a fury', carried out his

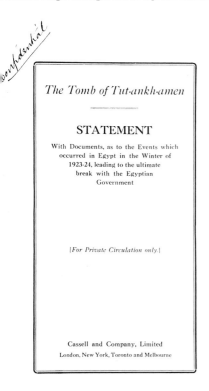

The Tomb of Tut·ankh·amen

STATEMENT

With Documents, as to the Events which occurred in Egypt in the Winter of 1923-24, leading to the ultimate break with the Egyptian Government

[For Private Circulation only.]

Cassell and Company, Limited
London, New York, Toronto and Melbourne

(Above) Lord Carnarvon's agreement with The Times *generated much ill-feeling in the rival press, both European and Egyptian. The sniping continued after Carnarvon's death, and would culminate in Carter's lock-out from the tomb.*

(Left) The cover of Carter's privately printed pamphlet, containing 'a full statement of the facts which have led us to the present position with the Egyptian government'. This rare volume recounts in minute detail, letter by letter, conversation by conversation, the events leading up to Carter's suspension of work at the tomb in February 1924. One of the appendices, removed by Carter from many copies of the booklet, contained embarrassing transcripts of Herbert Winlock's coded telegrams and letters warning Carter of the discovery in the Ramesses XI storeroom. The printing of this ill-judged pamphlet would cost Carter the support of many friends and allies.

Tutankhamun as the sun-god Re bursting forth from the primeval lotus (no. 8). Carter, seeking to explain its presence in a crate in Ramesses XI's tomb, stated that it had been found in the Corridor, objects from which were 'not yet fully registered.'

threat: he closed the tomb, leaving the sarcophagus lid hanging precariously by its ropes, and posted a notice in the lobby of the Winter Palace in Luxor, explaining the reason for his team's action:

'Owing to the impossible restrictions and discourtesies of the Egyptian Public Works Department and its antiquity service, all my collaborators, as a protest, have refused to work any further upon their scientific investigations in the tomb.'

It was archaeology's first strike, and Carter's biggest mistake. For, by abandoning the clearance, Carter had played into Lacau's hands: he had infringed the terms of his concession, and it was duly cancelled. The Egyptian Government declared that it would itself complete the work. Legal action to re-establish his claim to the tomb came to nothing, and Carter left for England and his American lecture tour, fuming with indignation and frustration at having been so completely outmanoeuvred.

Resolution and recovery

In Carter's absence, matters went from bad to worse with the discovery of a gessoed wooden head of the king packed as if ready to be shipped out of the country. But for the terrorist murder of the British Sirdar, Sir Lee Stack, on 19 November, and a subsequent drastic tightening of British control over Egypt, Carter might never have returned. As luck would have it, the departure of the Nationalist Government meant that he did – but on the Egyptians' terms. Carter received the new concession, still in Lady Carnarvon's name, on 13 January 1925; *The Times* lost its monopoly of news on the discovery, and the Carnarvon estate, despite vague promises of one or two duplicates when the tomb had been fully cleared, was obliged to abandon any formal claim to the king's treasures. As compensation for expenses incurred in the work however, the Carnarvon estate in 1930 received the sum of £36,000. It marked the end of their commitment; the final seasons would be financed by the Egyptians and by Carter himself.

There were sighs of relief all round, even from Lacau, when Carter was at last able to continue with the monumental task of clearing and recording the tomb: 'there is no better person to whom this delicate stuff could have been entrusted', was Winlock's view. In truth, it was a job no one else wanted. Work on clearing the tomb and conserving the objects would continue for more than seven years, and the study of its contents and preparations for publication would hang as a burden around Carter's neck for the rest of his life.

Lectures

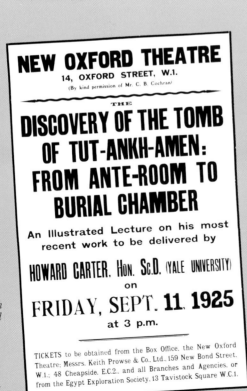

Poster announcing Carter's lecture at the New Oxford Theatre, London. Press reports could not have been more favourable: 'Little imagination was needed to penetrate the simple and unassuming manner in which Mr. Carter told his story, and to experience the thrills of excitement as he revealed the romance surrounding every stage in the great adventure which was destined to be crowned with such surprising results.'

'The question of lectures is going to be a rather serious one. I don't think Carter has ever given one in his life, and he doesn't in the least know how to set about it. . . .'

Arthur Mace to his wife Winifred

The unprecedented public interest aroused by the discovery had to be satisfied, and Carter's first lectures were at the New Oxford Theatre in London on 21 and 25 September 1923. On Saturday, 12 April 1924, Carter embarked upon an extended lecture tour of the United States and Canada. From the end of April until the middle of June, Carter enthralled audience after audience with one of his two prepared texts, the first a general lecture on the tomb, the second describing his most recent work of clearance. It was something of a whistle-stop tour, taking in New York, Philadelphia, New Haven, Baltimore, Washington (where he gave a private talk at the White House to President Calvin Coolidge), Worcester, Boston, Hartford, Pittsburgh, Chicago, Cincinnati, Detroit (with Henry Ford among the audience), Cleveland, Columbus, Buffalo, Toronto, Montreal and Ottawa. Mace need not have worried: Carter turned out to be a convincing and witty speaker. The tour was a sparkling success, crowned by the presentation of an honorary doctorate from Yale University on 18 June.

These triumphs were only the first of many, to be followed by lectures in Madrid in November 1924 and by an English tour. Lecture halls proved too small to receive the numbers applying for tickets; theatres were filled to capacity. Carter had well and truly arrived.

> ❝ What a curious and unhappy fatality seems to surround the tomb of Tutankhamun.... ❞

Edward Robinson

Howard Carter finally completed his work of conservation on the Tutankhamun objects in the spring of 1932, four years after the last chamber had been cleared and almost a decade after the initial discovery. The third and final part of 'the preliminary narrative', *The Tomb of Tut.ankh.Amen*, appeared in 1933, and the next years were occupied with the preparation of the definitive, six-volume work on the discovery, which was to be entitled *A Report upon the Tomb of Tut 'ankh Amun*. But progress was slow, and reading through his notes one gains the impression that the task to which Carter had given his life at the end proved too much for him.

Carter died in London, at 48 Albert Court, his Kensington home, on 2 March 1939, having been blessed with fame and fortune, though denied any public honour. By the will he had made in 1931, Carter's papers and personal possessions passed to his niece, Phyllis Walker. His furniture was auctioned at Sotheby's in December 1939, his books two months later, on 22 February. A portion of Carter's small but choice collection of antiquities passed via King Farouk to the Cairo Museum; other pieces were sold, through the London dealers Spink, and objects from it now grace half a dozen collections around the world.'Castle Carter', the house at Elwat el-Diban on the Theban west bank, scene of so much excitement during the digging years, passed to the Metropolitan Museum of Art. It was, in so many ways, the end of an era.

Howard Carter: the Final Curtain

Carter the gentleman: after an oil painting by his brother, William. Carter's sophisticated air owed not a little to the influence of Lord Carnarvon and his circle.

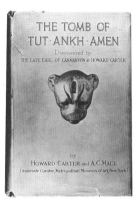

THE TOMB OF TUT·ANKH·AMEN
Discovered by
THE LATE EARL OF CARNARVON & HOWARD CARTER

by
HOWARD CARTER and A.C. MACE
(Associate Curator, Metropolitan Museum of Art, New York)

Volume 1 of The Tomb of Tut.ankh.Amen. *Much of the text of this splendid, three-part work was ghost-written by Carter's close friend, Percy White.*

Carter's last will and testament, dated 14 July 1931, by which the bulk of his estate was left to his niece, Phyllis Walker. Carter's executors were Harry Burton, who advised the niece on the disposal of Carter's antiquities, and Captain Bruce Ingram, editor of the Illustrated London News.

The tomb, when found, proved something of an enigma. The narrow corridor and the minimal area of its ground plan indicated clearly that it had never been intended for the burial of a king. The excavators' first impressions were that they had found merely a cache of objects – albeit wonderful objects – salvaged from the Amarna royal cemetery, a cache perhaps related in some way to the Tomb 55 deposit across the Valley path. But, with the increasing prominence of Tutankhamun's name, and with the entry by Carnarvon and Carter into the Burial Chamber, all doubts were dispelled.

If the small and sparsely decorated tomb itself was a disappointment, its contents were not. The funerary furniture was magnificent, and it was difficult to comprehend either the quantity or the quality. But the tomb had clearly been robbed: How much had gone? When did the thefts take place? What had the robbers been looking for?

Carter's skill as a digger was unmatched, his thoroughness as a recorder unrivalled. Much that might, in less capable hands, have been lost forever was observed, noted, photographed, and preserved for posterity. Tutankhamun's is the richest burial ever to have been found in the Valley of the Kings; thanks to Carter, it is also the best documented. More than half a century after the discovery, it is possible not only to reconstruct the state in which the tomb was found, but also to check Carter's answers to the questions the discovery posed, and to re-examine the evidence upon which his answers were based.

The tomb of Tutankhamun at the time of the clearance.

III The Archaeology of the Tomb

Architecture

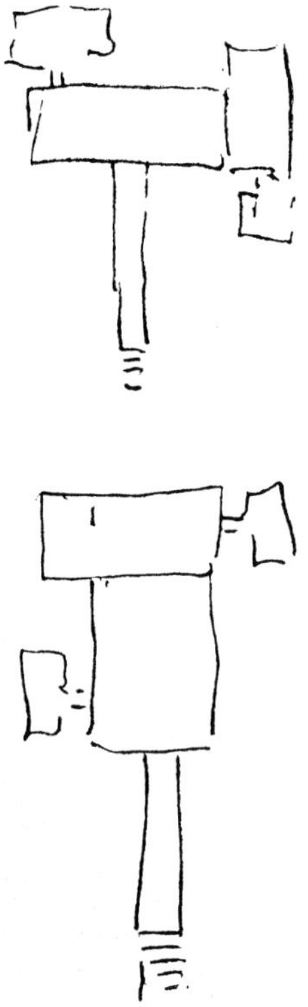

Carter's analysis of the Tutankhamun ground-plan. By swinging the chambers around 90 degrees, the Antechamber may be seen to correspond to the pillared hall of a more typical 18th dynasty royal tomb, the Burial Chamber to the sunken 'crypt'; the Annexe and Treasury represent two of the four side rooms which, in the traditional design, lead off the burial-chamber complex.

Tutankhamun's tomb is cut down into the bedrock of the Valley – a white, amorphous limestone with flinty masses and occasional veins of calcite – with a foothill of some 21m (69ft) rising directly above it. The entrance stairway comprises 16 steps, 1.68m (5ft 6⅛in) wide, roofed in by the living rock at its westernmost end. The last six steps of the staircase, together with the lintel and jambs, had been cut away in antiquity to enable the larger pieces of funerary furniture (such as the sarcophagus and shrines) to be introduced, the steps and jambs of the entrance doorway being subsequently reconstructed in stone and plaster and the lintel replaced with a heavy, limewashed wooden beam. They would be cut away again when the shrine panels were removed by Carter's team. Within the entrance doorway, still in position at the time of the discovery, was a blocking of dry limestone construction faced with a hard, light grey gypsum plaster and stamped over its entire surface with large oval seals. Beyond was a descending corridor, filled with rubble at the time of the discovery. It measured 8.08 by 1.68m (26ft 6in by 5ft 6⅛in) and 2m (6ft 6¾in) high. The corridor terminated in a rock-cut doorway, blocked in a similar manner to the outer doorway, which gave access to the Antechamber through the middle of the eastern wall.

The Antechamber and Annexe

The Antechamber is orientated north–south; 7.85 by 3.55m (25ft 9in by 13ft 3¾in), it measures 2.68m (8ft 9½in) in height and lies some 7.1m (23ft 3½in) below the floor of the Valley. The surfaces of the walls here and indeed throughout the tomb, with the exception of the Burial Chamber, are unsmoothed and exhibit a pinky 'glow'. A third doorway in the west wall of the Antechamber, 0.95m (3ft 1⅜in) wide and 1.3m (4ft 3⅛in) high, and again closed with a masonry blocking, is positioned to take advantage of a natural fissure in the rock. This blocking leads through into a second and smaller chamber, the Annexe, 4.35 by 2.6m (14ft 3¼in by 8ft 6⅜in) and 2.55m (8ft 4½in) high, again orientated north–south. The floor level of this chamber drops 0.9m (2ft 11⅜in) below that of the Antechamber. Carter records that 'The masons' guide and measuring marks in red are still visible upon the unfinished surfaces of the walls', and here as elsewhere in the tomb 'a few flakes of limestone from their chisels were left lying upon the floors'.

At the northern end of the Antechamber a dry partition wall of rough limestone splinters and dust had been constructed, 'bonded with pieces of timber' and plastered over. This partition wall was pierced by a doorway with a rough wooden lintel, 1.65m (5ft 5in) wide and 1.78m (5ft 10in) high. Like the doorways at either end of the corridor, and like that leading into the Annexe, this doorway had been closed off with rough stones and its plastered surface stamped with a series of large oval seals. 'When this partition wall was removed . . . it was discovered that the dynastic workmen had had to cut away a large portion of the rock of the northwest corner of the Antechamber, to allow sufficient room for the larger and longer panels of [the] shrines to pass into the burial chamber.' Also noted was a 'putt-hole' to take the beam employed in manoeuvring the sarcophagus, cut low in the west wall of the Antechamber.

The Burial Chamber and Treasury

Beyond the partition wall lay the Burial Chamber, 6.37 by 4.02m (20ft 10¾in by 13ft 2¼in), and some 3.63m (11ft 11in) high. The floor was 0.94m (3ft 1in) below that of the Antechamber and 8.05m (26ft 5in) below the Valley surface. Cut into the north, south, east and west walls of the Burial Chamber before it was painted were four niches for the tomb's 'magic bricks' (p. 135), found concealed with rough pieces of limestone plastered in place and painted over. Unlike the Annexe and the Antechamber, the Burial Chamber is orientated east-west, its walls (though not the ceiling) plastered with gypsum and decorated with painted scenes (p. 72). The plaster seems not to have been fully dry when the tomb was closed, a fact which accounts at least in part for the humidity damage suffered by a number of objects. Still visible at the northeast end of the Burial Chamber ceiling are 'traces of smoke, as from an oil lamp or torch' employed by the ancient artists.

A low doorway, 1.12m (3ft 8¼in) wide, in the east wall of the Burial chamber gives access to the Treasury. This room, 4.75 by 3.8m (15ft 7in by 12ft 5⅝in) and 2.33m (7ft 7¾in) high, is orientated north–south like the Annexe and the Antechamber.

On the whole, Carter considered the cutting of the tomb to be good, if showing a certain asymmetry in places where the mason's chisel ('minute particles' of which 'still adhered to the limestone surface') had taken advantage of the natural fissures in the rock. These same fissures may well have been responsible for the seepage of water into the tomb: 'With the exception of the sunken stairway and the descending passage, throughout the interior of the tomb, the walls, ceilings, and floors have been much discoloured by damp arising from infrequent saturations that took place in the past. And in many places, particularly on the painted surfaces in the burial chamber, the walls are disfigured by a fungoid growth [in part] nourished by that mois-

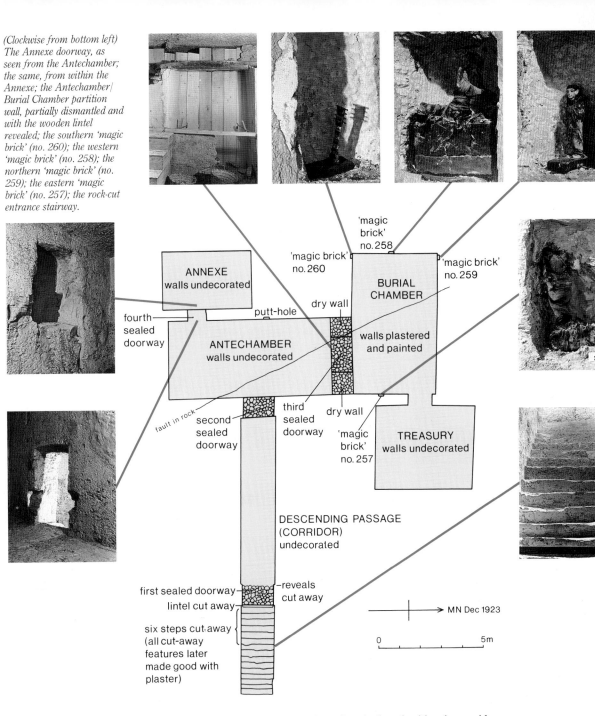

(Clockwise from bottom left) The Annexe doorway, as seen from the Antechamber; the same, from within the Annexe; the Antechamber/Burial Chamber partition wall, partially dismantled and with the wooden lintel revealed; the southern 'magic brick' (no. 260); the western 'magic brick' (no. 258); the northern 'magic brick' (no. 259); the eastern 'magic brick' (no. 257); the rock-cut entrance stairway.

ANNEXE
walls undecorated

'magic brick' no. 258

'magic brick' no. 260

'magic brick' no. 259

BURIAL CHAMBER

fourth sealed doorway

putt-hole

dry wall

ANTECHAMBER
walls undecorated

walls plastered and painted

fault in rock

second sealed doorway

third sealed doorway

dry wall

'magic brick' no. 257

TREASURY
walls undecorated

DESCENDING PASSAGE (CORRIDOR) undecorated

first sealed doorway
lintel cut away

reveals cut away

six steps cut away (all cut-away features later made good with plaster)

MN Dec 1923

0   5m

ture.' One particularly large fault runs from the southeast corner of the Antechamber through to the northwest corner of the Burial Chamber.

The tomb of Tutankhamun was clearly non-royal in form, showing a basic similarity to the tomb of Yuya and Tjuyu (No. 46) and to the enigmatic Tomb 55. But it was a private tomb (it has been suggested that of Ay himself) which had equally clearly been adapted – albeit in a very much restricted form – to the royal type: the Burial Chamber of Tutankhamun corresponds to the sunken sarcophagus 'crypt' of a

more normal royal tomb, though with only one side-room (the Treasury) instead of two; and the Antechamber, swung round, corresponds to the anterior, pillared section of the sarcophagus chamber, here again with one side-chamber (the Annexe) rather than two. Carter identified the tomb's architect as Maya, who presented two wooden figures to the burial (p. 139). This high official lived through several reigns and included among his titles those of Overseer of Works in the Place of Eternity and Overseer of Works in the West.

Wall Decoration

The only room with decoration of any sort is the Burial Chamber, whose paintings – 'rough, conventional and severely simple' – executed on a yellow-painted gypsum ground with white dado reflect its ancient ritual name: 'the House of Gold'.

The decoration, which is not dissimilar to that in the West Valley tomb of Ay (No. 23), occupies all four walls, with the scenes orientated towards the west wall. The scenes are marred by the presence of 'small brown fungus growths, the germs of which were possibly introduced either with the plaster or the sizing of the paint, and were nourished [in part] by the enclosed humidity that exuded from the plaster after the chamber had been sealed up.'

East wall

The decorated upper part of the east wall depicts the mummified king, his name written above in hieroglyphs, lying supine within a tall, garland-bedecked shrine, being dragged by five groups of men (12 in

total), dressed in white and wearing white mourning bands upon their brows. The last pair, with shaven heads and distinguishing dress, are the two viziers, or chief ministers, of Upper and Lower Egypt – perhaps Pentu and Usermont (p. 31). The remainder, as the inscription above their heads proclaims, are high officials of the palace. According to the text, they speak 'in one voice', saying 'Nebkheprure: come in peace, O god, protector of the land!'

North wall

The large painting on the north wall of the Burial Chamber subdivides into three separate scenes, ordered right to left.

The first scene depicts Tutankhamun's heir, the aged Ay, wearing the blue crown and dressed in the leopard skin of a *setem*-priest, the 'son' performing the necessary revivification ritual ('the opening of the mouth') for his 'father'; the dead boy here appears as Osiris, lord of the underworld. The names of both Tutankhamun and Ay are written above their heads in hieroglyphs.

In the second scene Tutankhamun, whose name again appears above his figure, has reverted to the costume of the living king although he has now entered the realm of the gods where he is greeted by the goddess Nut.

In the ultimate scene on the north wall, Tutankhamun, wearing the *nemes*-headcloth and followed closely by his *ka* or spiritual double, is welcomed

with an embrace into the underworld by Osiris, king of the dead, with whom he now becomes one.

South wall

The decoration of the south wall parallels that of the north wall. Here the king, wearing the bag-shaped *khat*-headdress, is welcomed into the realms of the underworld by Hathor, principal goddess of the west. Behind the king stands the embalmer god, the dog-headed Anubis; behind him, again identified by the hieroglyphs before her head, originally stood the goddess Isis. She was shown greeting the king in a

(Right) Figure of
Tutankhamun from the
south wall of the Burial
Chamber, with hypothetical
grid of 18 squares
superimposed to show
proportions.

(Far right) Amarna 20-
square grid superimposed
upon a figure of the king
from the north wall of the
Burial Chamber.

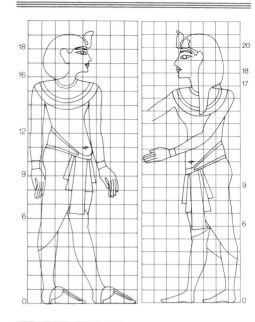

The west wall: focus and
culmination of the Burial
Chamber decoration.

similar fashion to Nut on the north wall; behind her
sat three minor deities of the underworld. The
figures were lost when the plastered partition wall
was dismantled by Carter's workmen to allow
removal of the shrines.

The proportions of the figures on this partition
wall, which was evidently decorated last and in
some haste after the shrines had been erected within
the Burial Chamber, differ from those employed
elsewhere in the tomb decoration. Clearly laid-out by
a different draughtsman, the proportions of the
figures are based not upon the Amarna canon of 20
squares but upon the more traditional 18-square
compositional grid.

West wall

The west wall, the focus and culmination of the
Burial Chamber's decorative scheme, is taken up by
an extract from the Book of *Amduat*, or 'What Is in
the Underworld'. The upper register is occupied by
the solar barque, preceded by five deities. Below
squat 12 baboon-deities of the first of the 12 hours of
the night through which the sun – and king – must
travel before achieving rebirth at dawn.

The Tomb Entrance

The ground immediately above the entrance to the tomb of Tutankhamun had been covered in antiquity by a collection of rough workmen's huts, built 0.9m (2ft 11⅜in) above bedrock and spreading over the entire area in front of the tomb of Ramesses VI (No. 9); they joined up with others on the opposite side of the path which had been uncovered by Ayrton in January 1907. Some of these huts Carter had already cleared in 1917, like Davis (p. 37) stopping work within a few feet of the tomb. Dismantling these structures five years later, 1–4 November 1922, in preparation for planning, a broken ostracon of Ramessid date was brought to light 'bearing [a] polytheistic sketch in bl[ack] and red of Horus and animals', together with an enclosure in stone which the excavator tentatively identified as an ancient '(?)Mortar trough' associated with work on Tomb 9.

The first step of Tutankhamun's tomb was uncovered on 4 November, immediately beneath the huts which had yielded these finds; a further 11 steps and the upper part of the plastered blocking were dug out the following day. No foundation deposits were found. The tomb entrance was immediately refilled, to be uncovered fully on 23–24 November after the arrival of Lord Carnarvon. Clearance of the lower staircase-fill revealed a number of antiquities (object nos. 1–3), including a green-glazed steatite scarab of Tuthmosis III, several clay seals from linen packages sporting the jackal and nine captives motif, a fragment of ivory, pieces of resin, turquoise-blue and chevron-patterned glass, stone and pottery, wine-jar dockets, jar seals, animal bones, wood and rush fragments, and the parts of two boxes. The first (no. 1k), inscribed with the names and titles of the co-regents Akhenaten and Nefernefruaten, and of the great royal wife Meritaten, carried a hieratic docket recording its original linen contents (p. 190); the second box (no. 1 l), the fastening knob of which carried the prenomen of Tutankhamun, was inscribed with a docket recording the silver vessels it had once contained (p. 190). Carter also claims to have turned up 'In the lower strata of rubbish that filled the staircase . . . a fragment with the name of Amen.hetep [Amenophis III]', though no further details of this object can now be traced.

Carter was puzzled:

'Why this mixture of names? The balance of evidence so far would seem to indicate a cache rather than a tomb, and at this stage in the proceedings we inclined more and more to the opinion that we were about to find a miscellaneous collection of objects of the Eighteenth Dynasty kings, brought from Tell el Amarna by Tut.ankh.Amen and deposited here for safety.'

(Top) Foundations of the Ramessid workmen's huts constructed above the entrance to Tutankhamun's tomb.

Carter's drawing of a green-glazed scarab (above) of Tuthmosis III (no. 1a), found in the rubble fill of the entrance stairway.

The descent into the tomb (left): the fully cleared stairway leading down to the first, outermost corridor blocking.

The Corridor

The corridor beyond the first blocking was opened on 25 November 1922, and found to be filled up to the ceiling with limestone rubble, 'probably the chip from its own excavation'. This fill, 'like the doorway, showed distinct signs of more than one opening and re-closing of the tomb, the untouched part consisting of clean white chip, mingled with dust, whereas the disturbed part was composed mainly of dark flint and chert. As sketched by Carter, the disturbed part of the fill occupied the entire upper left-hand corner of the corridor, and linked the refilled breach in the outer blocking with the refilled break in the blocking of the Antechamber doorway. It was clearly a robbers' tunnel (see p. 95).

By 26 November 9m (29ft 6in) of the corridor had been cleared, and the dimensions, so reminiscent of Tomb 55 (p. 20), 'seemed to substantiate our first conjecture that we had found a cache'. Penetration of the blocking would reveal all.

'Darkness and the iron testing rod told us that there was empty space. Perhaps another descending staircase, in accordance to [sic] the ordinary royal Theban tomb plan? Or may be a chamber? Candles were procured – the all important tell-tale for foul gases when opening an ancient subterranean excavation – I widened the breach and by means of the candle looked in, while Lord C., Lady E., and Callender with the *reises* [overseers] waited in anxious expectation. . . .'

(Above) The outer sealed doorway as first revealed, with the restored robbers' hole in its top-left corner.

(Right) Sections drawn by Carter on 26 November 1922, recording details of the corridor fill.

(Far right) A blue-painted nemset-vessel (no. 9) found in the corridor fill.

Distribution of Finds in Corridor

First part of passage

a fragments and lids of stone vessels
b red pottery 'foundation deposit' cups
c fragments of plaster jar seals
d fragments of mud (?)boxes
e splinters of gessoed and gilded wood
f splinters of wood
g fragments of faience
h pieces of felspar

'Lying upon floor near wall, far [south] side of passage', under fill

water skins
head of king rising from a lotus(?)

'Lying under the filling . . . upon the floor . . . [north] side and far end'

calcite vessels

In fill of passage

9   blue-painted *nemset*-vessel (near Antechamber blocking)
10 clay seals
11 wine-jar docket
12a faience pendants, some inlaid
12b portions of gold foil work
12c inlaid gold plaques from jewellery
12d faience rings (whole and broken)
12e fragments of faience, including gaming piece
12f faience floral pendants
12g bronze razors
12h fragments of resin (one showing inlay)
12i clay seal
12j fragments of ivory and ebony inlay
12k shells from (?)necklace
12l dried fruits
12m pieces of worked semi-precious stone
12n fragments of metalwork: gilded bronze; *shabti* yoke and basket; bronze arrowhead; gilded bronze staple
12o wooden labels
12p fragments of (?)felspar
12q fragments of glass
12r *dom*-palm nuts
12s pottery cup (like 5b)
12t fragments of stone vessel-lids

The fill of the corridor as it appeared following removal of the outer blocking, the refilled robber's tunnel clearly visible in the top left-hand corner.

The Antechamber

' Gradually the scene grew clearer, and we could pick out individual objects. First, right opposite to us – we had been conscious of them all the while, but refused to believe in them – were three great gilt couches, their sides carved in the form of monstrous animals, curiously attenuated in body, as they had to be to serve their purpose, but with heads of startling realism. Uncanny beasts enough to look upon at any time: seen as we saw them, their brilliant gilded surfaces picked out of the darkness by our electric torch, as though by limelight, their heads throwing grotesque distorted shadows on wall behind them, they were almost terrifying. Next, c the right, two statues caught and held our attention; t' life-sized figures of a king in black, facing each other like sentinels, gold kilted, gold sandalled, armed with mace and staff, the protective sacred cobra upon their foreheads.

' These were the dominant objects that caught the ey at first. Between them, around them, piled on top of them, there were countless others – exquisitely painte and inlaid caskets; alabaster vases, some beautifully carved in openwork designs; strange black shrines, fro the open door of one a great gilt snake peeping out; bouquets of flowers or leaves; beds; chairs beautifully carved; a golden inlaid throne; a heap of curious white oviform boxes; staves of all shapes and designs; benea our eyes, on the very threshold of the chamber, a beautiful lotiform cup of translucent alabaster; on the left a confused pile of overturned chariots, glistening with gold and inlay; and peeping from behind them another portrait of a king.

' Such were some of the objects that lay before us. . . .

Howard Car'

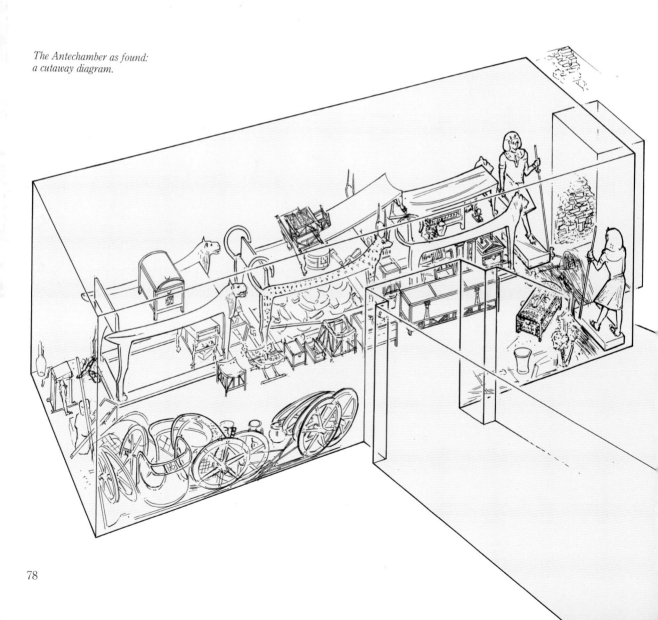

The Antechamber as found:
a cutaway diagram.

‘ The impression is overwhelming. It is a sight I have never dreamed of seeing; the ante-chamber of a Pharaoh's tomb still filled with magnificent equipment . . . still standing as it was placed there when the tomb was last closed in antiquity. ’

James Henry Breasted

The Antechamber presented a picture of organized chaos, its contents having been disturbed at least twice following the original closure of the tomb and only roughly put back in order before the final resealing. It contained 157 numbered groups of 600 to 700 objects (nos. 14–171) of a type which, in a normal New Kingdom royal burial, would have been placed in the pillared section of the burial chamber and in the anteroom preceding it. For the Czech Egyptologist Jaroslav Černý, this, the Antechamber, was the 'Hall of Waiting' mentioned in documents of the Ramessid period.

Between the objects a path had been cleared, perhaps in part by Carnarvon and Carter during their preliminary investigation of the tomb (p. 54). As an early photograph by Carter shows, the large Painted Box (no. 21) had certainly been moved between the time of the discovery and the start of photographing the Antechamber by Harry Burton on 18 December.

The clearance began in counter-clockwise fashion, starting with the funerary bouquets in the

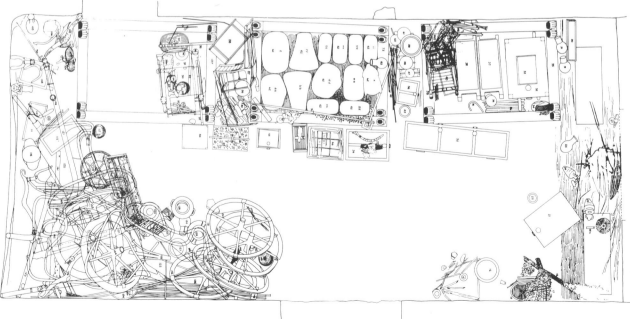

northeast corner (nos. 18 and 19a) and leaving the tangle of the chariots (nos. 120 *et seq*) to the end. The first object to be removed, on 27 December 1922, was the Painted Box (no. 21). 'Clearing the objects from the Antechamber was like playing a gigantic game of spillikins', Carter and Mace record. 'So crowded were they that it was a matter of extreme difficulty to move one without running serious risk of damaging others, and in some cases they were so inextricably tangled that an elaborate system of props and supports had to be devised to hold one object or group of objects in place while another was being removed. At such times life was a nightmare.' This nightmare finally came to an end on 16 February 1923: the Antechamber stood empty save for the pair of guardian statues (nos. 22 and 29), which would be removed at the start of the following season's work on the tomb.

(Opposite above) 'Wonderful things': the west wall of the Antechamber as first seen.

(Opposite below) Hall and Hauser's finished plan showing the Antechamber contents in situ. The path cleared to the Annexe doorway (probably at the time of Carnarvon and Carter's first entry) is clearly visible.

(Left) The northeast corner of the Antechamber, with Carnarvon and Carter's access-hole to the Burial Chamber concealed behind a basket-lid and handful of reeds: the Painted Box (no. 21) has been repositioned with its fastening knobs facing south rather than north as found.

The Burial Chamber

The official dismantling of the Burial Chamber blocking took place on 17 February 1923. Lord Carnarvon's brother, Mervyn Herbert, who was present at the opening, describes the scene:

'Rows of chairs had been arranged in the first chamber of the tomb, which had been entirely cleared except for the 2 statues of the King at one end. Between them was the sealed entrance and at the bottom of this sealed door was a little wooden platform which concealed the hole made in the wall where they had got in before. Porch [Carnarvon], poor old fellow, was nervous like a naughty schoolboy, fearing that they would discover that a hole had already been made. He was also, and most naturally, very excited; altho' he knew a good deal about what was there he cannot have helped feeling that this was one of the very great moments that happen to few people. He began by making a very nice speech to all of us – short and to the point – one of the main things being thanks to all the workers but principally to the Americans who had very generously given their services free. Then Carter made a speech – not very good – he was nervous, almost inarticulate and talked about science and the insecurity of the discovery.'

Then work began in earnest. Carter takes up the thread:

'. . . when, after about ten minutes' work, I had made a hole large enough to enable me to do so, I inserted an electric torch. An astonishing sight its light revealed, for there, within a yard of the doorway, stretching as far as one could see and blocking the entrance to the chamber, stood what to all appearances was a solid wall of gold. . . .

It was, beyond any question, the sepulchral chamber in which we stood, for there, towering above us, was one of the great gilt shrines beneath which kings were laid. So enormous was this structure . . . that it filled within a little the entire area of the chamber, a space of some two feet only separating it from the walls on all four sides, while its roof, with cornice top and torus moulding, reached almost to the ceiling. . . .'

The Burial Chamber, showing the coffined mummy enclosed in the quartzite sarcophagus and surrounded by its shrines: a cutaway diagram.

The first objects Carter removed were elements from two broad collars (no. 172) which had been dropped in the threshold by the tomb robbers. The work of clearance proceeded in an anti-clockwise fashion. Around the room, between the panels of the outermost shrine (no. 207) and the decorated walls were various objects: against the east wall stood a calcite lamp (no. 173), a resin-varnished wooden goose (no. 176), two reed and papyrus boxes (no. 178), a second calcite lamp (no. 174), and a wine jar (no. 180). Against the north wall was the ritual object no. 181 and eleven magical oars (nos. 182–92); in the northwest corner, the double shrine (no. 193) and an Anubis fetish (no. 194) in the form of an inflated animal skin 'full of solutions for preserving or washing the body' suspended on a pole. Against the west wall lay a second wine jar (no. 195); while in the southwest corner stood a second Anubis fetish (no. 202), as well as gilded wooden symbols which took the form of the hieroglyph *res*, 'to awake' (nos. 196, 199–201), and the clay supports on which they were intended to stand (no. 198a). A large funerary bouquet consisting of persea and olive (no. 205) also stood poignantly in the southwest corner of the Burial Chamber.

The opening: Carter takes a rest while Carnarvon peers over the partially dismantled Burial Chamber blocking.

(Below) The entrance to the Burial Chamber, with three-quarters of the sealed and plastered blocking removed to reveal the brilliant blue and gold of the outermost shrine.

Untouched for more than 3,000 years: Carter, Callender and one of the Egyptian foremen peer through the doors of the four gilded shrines to the sarcophagus within.

(Opposite left) Carter's unpublished plan of the Burial Chamber, showing the outermost coffin, the sarcophagus, the shrines, and the many objects scattered within and around.

(Opposite right) The narrow gap between the north wall and shrine, with magical wooden paddles and other ritual objects in position.

The doors of the shrine were located at the eastern end of the Burial Chamber. The outermost shrine had no seal – perhaps it had already been broken by the ancient robbers of the tomb (p. 96). Drawing back the bolts, the doors swung open to reveal a linen pall (no. 209), precisely as shown in the plan of the tomb of Ramesses IV, 'brown with age . . . rent by the weight of the gilt bronze marguerites sewn to its fabric'. Beneath this pall was a further shrine (no. 237), again bolted but this time with its seal – of

jackal and nine captives type – intact. Before its doors stood an elaborate calcite perfume vessel and stand (no. 210), a masterpiece of intricate carving flanked on either side by two Hapy-figures who secure the heraldic plants of Upper and Lower Egypt around the neck of the flask (see p. 198). To its right a second and somewhat smaller perfume jar (no. 211), again of calcite but cylindrical in form, carried on its lid a couchant lion with tongue of stained ivory (p. 198). At either side of the second shrine, in the

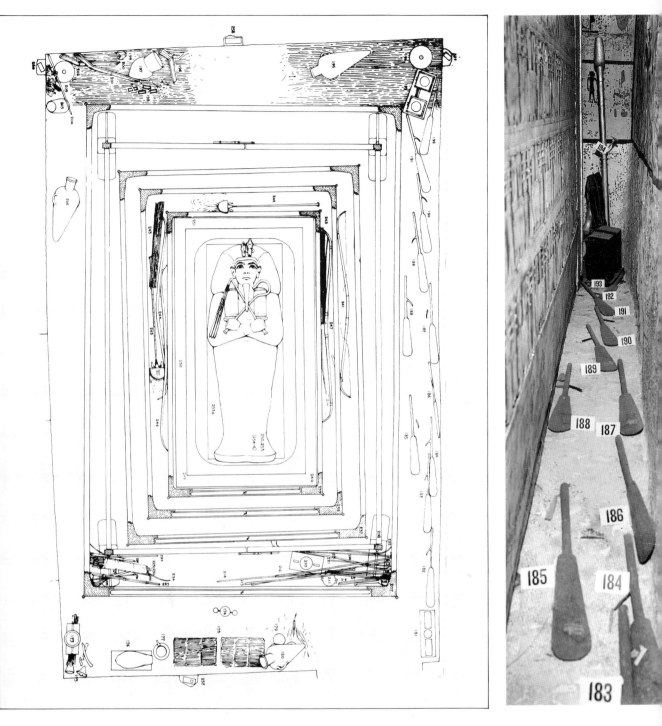

north- and southeast corners, stood a bundle of sticks, staves, bows and other objects (nos. 212–19, 221–36) (p. 174). The spaces between the second and third (no. 238) shrines was bare but for a single self bow (no. 241). Between the third and fourth (no. 239) were several items, most notably four bows and two groups of arrows (p. 174), and two fans (nos. 242–8) (p. 179). Within the fourth shrine lay a large *djed*-pillar of painted wood (no. 250), a bundle of reeds (no. 249), and the quartzite sarcophagus (no. 240).

Four concealed niches cut into the decorated walls of the Burial Chamber (p. 71) contained the 'magic bricks' (nos. 257–60) (p. 135).

Dismantling the shrines and opening the sarcophagus and coffins – comprising the bulk of the 88 object-groups the Burial Chamber contained (well over 300 individual pieces) – would take almost eight months, from November to May 1925.

The Treasury

'. . . a low door, eastwards from the sepulchral chamber, gave entrance to yet another chamber, smaller than the outer ones and not so lofty. This doorway, unlike the others, had not been closed and sealed . . . a single glance sufficed to tell us that here, within this little chamber, lay the greatest treasures of the tomb. Facing the doorway, on the farther side, stood the most beautiful monument that I have ever seen [the canopic shrine] – so lovely that it made one gasp with wonder and admiration . . .

' Immediately in front of the entrance lay the figure of the jackal god Anubis, upon his shrine, swathed in linen cloth, and resting upon a portable sled, and behind this the head of a bull upon a stand – emblems, these, of the underworld. In the south side of the chamber lay an endless number of black shrines and chests, all closed and sealed save one, whose open doors revealed statues of Tut.ankh.Amen standing upon black leopards. On the farther wall were more shrine-shaped boxes and miniature coffins of gilded wood . . . In the centre of the room, left of the Anubis and the bull, there was a row of magnificent caskets of ivory and wood, decorated and inlaid with gold and blue faience, one, whose lid we raised, containing a gorgeous ostrich-feather fan with ivory handle, fresh and strong to all appearance as when it left the maker's hand. There were also, distributed in different quarters of the chamber, a number of model boats with sails and rigging all complete, and, at the north side, yet another chariot.

' Such, from a hurried survey, were the contents of the innermost chamber. '

Howard Carter

Carter's description of the 'Innermost Treasury' was written in 1923; it was to be four more busy years before he was able to begin its clearance. During those years the entrance doorway would be blocked off with wooden boards, 'in order that, whilst dealing with the vast material in the Burial Chamber, we might not be distracted or tempted to disturb any of the objects. . . .'

The Treasury as found: a cutaway diagram.

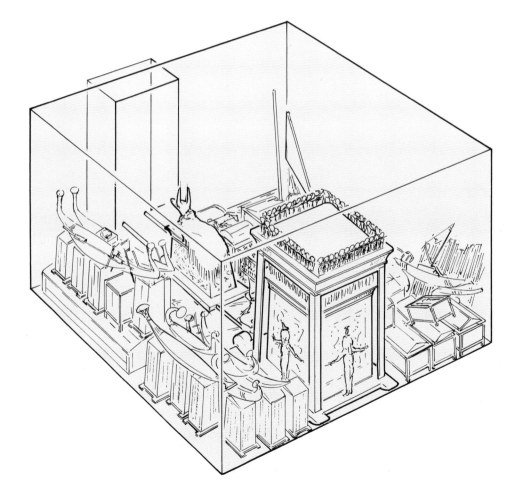

The entrance to the Treasury was dominated by a majestic image of Anubis, lord of the west, mounted upon a shrine equipped with carrying poles (no. 261).

(Below) To Anubis's right lay a row of jewel caskets (nos. 267–271), their sealed lids broken open and their contents rifled in antiquity; in front of the canopic shrine, carefully wrapped in linen, stood a gilded head of the Hathor cow (no. 264).

Clearance of the Treasury, which yielded 75 groups of objects (well in excess of 500 major pieces) principally of a 'purely funerary nature and of an intense religious character', began at the end of October 1926 with the removal of the Anubis jackal (no. 261) (p. 133) and the wooden cow head (no. 264) (p. 134). This was followed by the removal of the boxes, caskets, bow-case, model boats and chariot clutter which lay along the north wall, and the shrines, two mummified foetuses, further model boats and the Osiris bed which had been placed in the southern half of the room (nos. 265–336).

The robbers had been in here too, but had clearly operated with far more discernment, for, 'with rare exception, only those boxes which held objects of intrinsic value had been disturbed.' The thieves evidently knew their tomb.

(Above right) The southeast corner of the Treasury, with model boats piled upon a series of black varnished chests containing the king's gilded funerary statuettes.

(Right) The clutter of the south wall, with further shrine-shaped boxes and an intricately rigged boat (no. 276) resting upon the king's model granary (no. 277).

‘ Peering beneath the southernmost of the three great
couches, we noticed a small irregular hole in the wall.
Here was yet another sealed doorway, and a plunderers’
hole, which, unlike the others, had never been repaired.
Cautiously we crept under the couch, inserted our
portable light, and there before us lay another chamber,
rather smaller than the first, but even more crowded
with objects.
‘ The state of this inner room (afterwards called the
Annexe) simply defies description. In the Antechamber
there had been some sort of an attempt to tidy up after
the plunderers’ visit, but here everything was in
confusion, just as they had left it. ’

Howard Carter

The Annexe

The Annexe was for Carter equivalent to one of the
two side-rooms off the ‘crypt’ in a full-sized royal
tomb of the 18th dynasty; for Černý it was the
‘House-of-repelling-the-bowmen’ specified in the
docket of box 1k (p. 190). It was the last chamber to
be cleared, work beginning at the end of October,
1927, and ending in the spring of 1928. Though the
smallest of the chambers, its clearance would yield
some 283 groups of objects – half the numbered
groups from the entire tomb and well over 2,000
individual pieces. The material recovered was very
varied, thanks largely to the activities of the
restoration party, who appear to have compounded
the inconsistency of the original stocking and the
robbers’ destruction by throwing into the room
anything for which a satisfactory home could not be
found in the Antechamber.

Clearance of the Annexe was to be difficult indeed.
Because of the clutter, 1.8m (5ft 10⅞in) high in places,
the excavators had to be suspended on ropes above
the chamber floor (which lay more than a metre
below that of the Antechamber) until sufficient
space had been cleared for them to stand. Work
proceeded slowly and carefully, south to north,
again employing props and supports to prevent the
mountain of furniture collapsing into a broken heap
on the stone floor. To Carter’s surprise, the original
layout of the chamber could in due course be
salvaged. The distribution of the objects had been
rather more ordered than that which Carter first
encountered, but the range of material had been just
as disparate:

‘ . . . firstly, nearly forty pottery wine-jars were placed on
the floor at the northern end of this Annexe; next to
these were added at least thirty-five heavy alabaster
vessels containing oils and unguents; stacked beside
them, some even on top, were one hundred and sixteen
baskets of fruits; the remaining space was then used for
other furniture – boxes, stools, chairs and bedsteads, etc.
– that were piled on top of them.’

*A cutaway diagram of the
Annexe as found.*

The Annexe had been intended, then, as a storage chamber for the oils, unguents, foods and wines buried with Tutankhamun, though the reduced amount of space available and the disorganized manner in which the tomb seems to have been stocked had resulted in some overflow (notably the king's boxed meats) into the Antechamber. In its turn, the Annexe had served as a convenient storage area for items such as the beds, chairs, *shabti* figures and other items which might, with space, have been more appropriately placed in the Antechamber or the Treasury.

The chamber appears to have been the last one sealed by the necropolis officials before the final stocking of the Antechamber and the erection of the blocking at the end of the corridor; a number of fragments of gypsum plaster (no. 106d), one of which 'showed [a] cast of the flattened dish which had contained it', are probably to be associated with this ancient closure.

Photographs taken by Harry Burton during clearance of the Annexe. (Opposite) The south end, its hopeless tangle of funerary equipment surmounted by the wooden day-bed no. 377. (Above) The west wall, showing one of Carter's wooden props in place supporting the bed no. 466. (Left) The northeast corner, with the stool no. 467 precariously balanced beside bed nos. 466 and 497.

The Seal Impressions

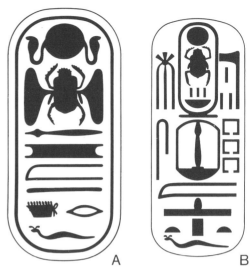

A

B

The door sealings

❝ The seals are in content testimonials certifying to the king's pious services on behalf of the gods during his life on earth . . . identical in function to the great Papyrus Harris, which is a vast testimonial of the same kind. Their further function was to enlist the protection of the gods for the king's tomb, just as is done in the Pyramid Texts. . . . *❞*

James Henry Breasted

Eight distinct types of large seal impression, presumably produced from matrices cut in wood, or perhaps steatite, were employed by members of the burial and restoration parties to stamp the plastered outer surfaces of the blockings erected at either end of the corridor and at the entrances into the Burial Chamber and the Annexe. To these eight blurred types Carter assigned the reference letters A–H. Types A–G date from the original closure of the tomb, type H (similar to E but without cartouche) to the reclosures following the robberies; for details of the distribution and Carter's count of the seals, refer to the table. The average size of the large sealings was 14.5cm by 6.6cm ($5\frac{7}{10}$ by $2\frac{3}{5}$in).

'The grouping of these seals was as haphazard as the perfunctory manner in which they were done. Each seal, or each official with his seal dabbed a number of impressions about the wet surface of the plaster, the blank spaces being filled up with impressions of the last employed.'

The distribution of the various types would indicate that not all seal-holders were present at or involved in the various stages in the closing of the tomb.

(Right) Alan H. Gardiner and James Henry Breasted, seen here standing outside the entrance to the tomb. Gardiner and Breasted were the first to decipher the blurred and imperfect impressions stamped upon the various door blockings, producing 'roughs' which Carter was then able to work up in preparation for the never-to-appear final publication of the tomb.

Seal type	Corridor (no. 4)	Antechamber (no. 13)	Burial Chamber (no. 28)	Annexe (no. 171)
A	13	x	55	
B	17	x	7	
C	8	x	1?	8
D	9	x		6
E	10	x	63	5
F			21	
G			4	14
H	7,28	x	x	x??

Key: 28 = 28 occurrences of the type, etc.
    x = number of occurrences uncertain

C

E

G

F

The large door-seal impressions (drawings after Carter):

A '[Neb]kheprure, great of love in the entire land'

B 'Nebkheprure, who creates [images of] the gods, who makes festive the temples with his offerings'

C 'Nebkheprure, King of Upper and Lower Egypt, who spends his life creating [images of] the gods, that they may give to him (?) the breath of life, incense, libations and offerings every day'

D 'Nebkheprure, who creates [the image of] Osiris and builds his temple as it was on the first occasion'

E 'Nebkheprure'

F 'Nebkheprure, beloved of Imentet, Osiris and Anubis'

G 'Anubis their [i.e. the four subject people's] overlord'

The seal at lower right is Carter's drawing of type D.

The object sealings

In addition to the large door-seals, several smaller types of seal impression were found attached (sometimes with a counter seal as corroboration) to lengths of cord or linen employed to close boxes and other objects within the tomb. Carter noted 11 types, to which he attached the reference letters I–S, a number of these displaying in their design certain correlations with the larger door sealings. These smaller sealings had been produced by pushing a signet into a pat of mud to produce a clear, relief impression. Signets of this sort appear to have been presented by the king to officials acting in his name, and in their details to have been unique to that individual. One of the seal impressions, type N, occurs also in Tomb 55; whoever the owner of the ring may have been, he not only took part in the stocking of Tutankhamun's tomb, but played a crucial role also in the Amarna reburial (p. 20).

There is little doubt that the majority, and probably all, of the smaller sealings are contemporary with the original tomb closing. It has been suggested that one of the smaller sealings from the tomb – type R – contains a version of the prenomen Neferkheprure (i.e. Akhenaten); but the break might just as easily conceal a reading of the prenomen of Tutankhamun. Two other seal-types – Q and S – have been considered later in date than the inter-

(Left) A photograph of the blocked and plastered entrance to the Burial Chamber, stamped over its entire surface with impressions of seal types A, B, C(?), E, F, and G. The resealed robbers' hole at the bottom of the doorway, breached by Carnarvon and Carter and concealed behind basketwork lid no. 26, carried impressions of seal type H.

(Below) The viceroy of Kush receives his seal of office: a detail from the Theban tomb of Amenhotep-Huy (No. 40).

(Right) One of the small jackal and nine captives seals (type J) from the tomb.

(Below) Drawings (after Carter) of the 11 types of small seal impression (I – S) from the tomb. The original Carter drawing to the left is of seal type P.

ment. Type Q, the first example of which had been found broken, was restored by Carter as 'Hor[em-heb]', giving rise to the notion that the latest robberies in the tomb took place before or during this reign when the tomb will have been finally reclosed and the disturbed objects resealed. Unfortunately, Carter's reading of the lower part of this impression can no longer be accepted as correct. As other examples show, the complete seal depicted the common motif of the royal falcon standing upon the sign for 'gold' (*nub*). So far as seal type S is concerned, it without doubt incorporated the cartouched prenomen of Tutankhamun's successor, Ay; but since Ay was already king when the funeral ceremony took place, its presence is of equivocal significance in dating the robberies in the tomb.

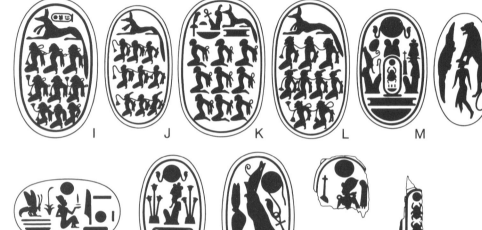

(Above) The controversial seal type Q from the shrine-shaped chest no. 304. Though incomplete and double-struck, the design of the complete seal evidently incorporated the non-specific royal epithet 'Golden falcon', and not the name 'Horemheb' as first restored by Carter.

No.	Attached to/from	Seal type(s)	No.	Attached to/from	Seal type(s)
5c(?)	—	P	275	shrine-shaped chest	K
36e	shrine 37(?)	L(?)	279	wooden box	K
38a	shrine-shaped box	L	280–282	shrine-shaped chests	L
40c	calcite box(?)	N, ?	283	square wooden chest	N
44	gilded and inlaid box	N	290–303	shrine-shaped chests	L
68c	painted wooden box(?)	?	304	shrine-shaped chest	Q
119c	cloth bag	O	305	shrine-shaped chest	L
179	reed and papyrus boxes 178–178a	P	315	plain wooden box	I, O (?)
			317	plain wooden box	J
237a	second gilded shrine	I, J	317a	outer coffin, first foetus	J
238a	third gilded shrine	I, J	317b	outer coffin, second foetus	J
261q	linen wrapping of jewellery(?)	L	318	*shabti* box	L
266b	canopic chest	J	320	miniature coffin	K
267	ivory and ebony casket	N	320d	miniature coffin with hair of Tiye	N
268	ornamental casket	N	322–329	*shabti* boxes	L
269	cartouche-shaped casket	N	418	*shabti* box	L
270	painted wooden box	N	496	*shabti* box	L
271	ornamental casket	M, N	514	*shabti* box	L
272	wooden box with vaulted lid	M, N	605	*shabti* box	L
			611	*shabti* box	L

The Robberies

The replastered and sealed hole in the outer doorway had forewarned Carnarvon and Carter that, whatever the nature of this underground chamber, its contents would not be intact. The disorganized state of the deposit, the damage sustained by several objects and the discernible lack of solid metalwork, bedding, glass, oils and unguents were marks of the ancient Egyptian tomb robber. The Annexe was the worst affected: 'One [robber] – there would probably not have been room for more than one – had crept into the chamber, and had then hastily but systematically ransacked its entire contents, emptying boxes, throwing things aside, piling them one upon another, and occasionally passing objects through the hole to his companions for closer examination in the outer chamber. He had done his work just about as thoroughly as an earthquake.'

The excavators' first inclination was to date the disturbance to the late 20th dynasty, when the Theban west bank was being plagued by a serious spate of tomb robbery. It was a conclusion they soon had to revise. Breasted 'reminded Carter that the tomb of Thutmose [Tuthmosis] IV . . . had after a robbery been restored by Tutenkhamon's almost immediate successor, King Harmhab [Horemheb]. . . . If another royal burial had suffered robbery soon after Tutenkhamon's death, might not the same robbers . . . also have entered *his* tomb?' The argument for a near contemporary plundering of the tomb was compelling, and one for which the evidence offers considerable support.

The first robbery

There can be little doubt that the entrance corridor was empty at the time the first illicit entry was made. The earlier breach in the entrance blocking was positioned too low to have allowed a passage to have been successfully burrowed through the mass of loose chippings in the corridor beyond. Moreover, the original plastered surface of the inner doorway, unlike the replastered hole, was unmarked by the pressure of the chipping fill, suggesting that the main plaster coating had been long dry when the rubble was introduced. Carter recovered from beneath the fill a number of fragments of objects which appear to have been stored in the corridor at the time of the first break-in. This material had evidently included the king's embalming refuse and remains of the so-called 'funerary meal' discovered by Davis in 1907, packed in a series of large ceramic storage jars in Pit 54 where they had been reburied

at the time of the first reclosure of Tutankhamun's tomb (p. 38).

A number of objects was recovered from within and beneath the corridor fill, including stone jar lids, splinters of gilded wood, fragments of gold, a bronze arrowhead, razors and a gilded bronze staple (p. 189). These pieces, it seems, had been dropped at the tomb entrance by the first band of robbers, and were later gathered up with the rubble employed to fill the corridor. Where it can be identified, this material appears to have come exclusively from the Antechamber: the gold elements originated from the 'corslet' found in box 54 (p. 190); the bronze staple had been wrenched off the semicircular box no. 79 + 574, while the arrowhead is conceivably one of those broken from the arrows in the Antechamber. Although Carter had concluded that the first band of robbers had had access to the entire tomb, the second to the Antechamber and Annexe only, the evidence would seem to indicate the opposite sequence.

Carter's view that the first group of thieves were interested primarily in metal would seem to be borne out by the materials which may be associated with

The king's white-painted bow-box (no. 370) as found on the floor at the southern end of the Annexe, still showing what Carter identified as the dirty footprints of one of the tomb-robbers.

Drawing of the tomb showing the holes made by the ancient robbers to gain access to the different chambers.

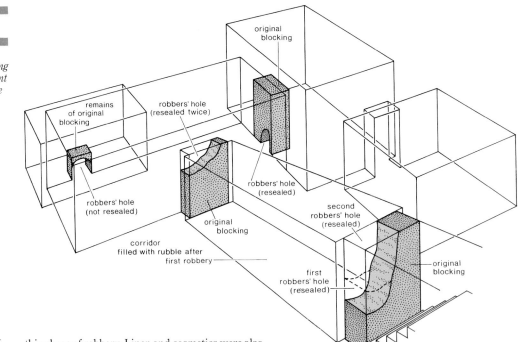

original blocking

remains of original blocking

robbers' hole (resealed twice)

robbers' hole (not resealed)

robbers' hole (resealed)

original blocking

second robbers' hole (resealed)

corridor filled with rubble after first robbery

first robbers' hole (resealed)

original blocking

(Below) Twisted linen scarf (no. 44b) into which one of the second band of robbers had wrapped eight elaborate gold rings (right) ready for carrying off. The robber had evidently been caught in the act, and the rings tossed back into the tomb by the necropolis guards.

this phase of robbery. Linen and cosmetics were also on the robbers' shopping list. The intruders' interest in the latter commodity clearly indicates that the entry could not have occurred many years after the king's burial: Egyptian cosmetics were fat-based and in the hot Egyptian climate their life-span will have been limited.

The second robbery

The available evidence would suggest that the second period of theft was more extensive than the first, if equally brief. It will have presented far more of a challenge than the first entry: Carter estimated that a chain of men passing back baskets of rubble would have taken some 7–8 hours to dig a tunnel through the newly installed chip-fill of the corridor. Once in, the robbers appear to have had access to all parts of the tomb, though their activity within the Treasury appears to have been restricted to removing the lids of the king's jewel caskets and unsealing one of the black varnished shrines containing gilded funerary figures (which proved to be of little interest). Carter was able to estimate, from inventory

dockets scribbled at the time of the funeral, that some 60 per cent of the jewellery originally contained in the Treasury caskets had been stolen, together with a whole series of precious-metal vessels.

A knotted scarf of linen containing 'a handful of solid gold rings' had been tossed casually into one of the boxes in the Antechamber. 'We are almost forced to the conclusion that the thieves were either trapped within the tomb, or overtaken in their flight – traced, in any case, with some of the plunder still upon them.' If so, the second group of robbers had stolen from the burial on more than the one occasion, since so very much of the jewellery from the Treasury was gone. The fate of the captured robbers will probably have been that of their later Ramessid counterparts: the bastinado, followed by impalement on a sharpened stake.

The officials responsible for resealing the tomb – perhaps led by Maya, who undertook restoration of the Tuthmosis IV burial (Tomb 43) in Year 8 of Horemheb, and whose assistant, Djehutymose, scribbled his name on a calcite jar stand found by Carter in the Annexe – 'seem to have been in almost as great a hurry as the thieves, and their work of reparation was sadly scamped'. Perhaps they were fearful of drawing attention to the tomb. The restoration party succeeded in restoring a superficial order to the burial, though none of the boxes or shrines broken open by the thieves was resealed. The breaches in the Burial Chamber and Antechamber blockings were reclosed, plastered over and stamped with the necropolis seal – the jackal over nine bound captives. The hole dug through the Corridor fill was packed anew, and the dismantled portion of the Corridor blocking made good and resealed. The seal employed was again that of the necropolis administration. It was the same seal as that which had been employed following the first break-in, an indication that the two separate instances of theft were not far apart in time. There seems little doubt, therefore, that Tutankhamun's burial had been robbed, on both occasions, by the subjects of one of his immediate successors – members, perhaps, of the very party which had buried him.

(Above left) Calcite vessel (no. 435), as seen from above, with marks of the robber's fingers still visible in the decayed cosmetic.

(Above top) The king's jewel-caskets lined up within the entrance to the Treasury. The seals had been broken in antiquity, the contents ransacked. The restoration party repacked what was left, replacing the lids to achieve a semblance of order.

(Above) The ultimate fate of tomb-robbers and enemies of the state: impalement on a stake, as represented in this hieroglyph.

(Below left) Hieratic graffito in the tomb of Tuthmosis IV (No. 43), dating from the restoration carried out under Horemheb and recording the name of the necropolis scribe Djehutymose. This same man had scribbled his name on a jar stand (no. 620: 116/122) in the tomb of Tutankhamun (below right).

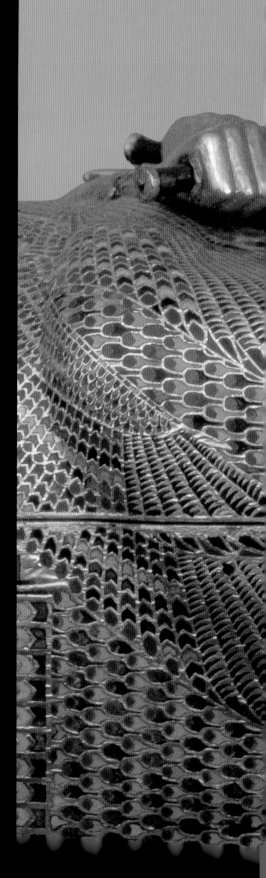

The realization that the tomb had been robbed in antiquity was tempered by the discovery that the robbers had not penetrated beyond the outermost gilded shrine: Tutankhamun still reposed within his sarcophagus and coffins, just as the priestly burial party had left him thirty centuries before.

Egyptologists had a shrewd idea of what to expect: a papyrus in Turin preserved a plan of the burial of Ramesses IV in position, his stone sarcophagus surrounded by five shrines and a linen pall; while a document (Papyrus Amherst) dating from the 20th dynasty provided a graphic description of a king's mummy lavishly adorned with jewels and accompanied by his weapons (p. 111).

In an interview with *The Times* on 18 December 1922, Lord Carnarvon gave free rein to the ultimate archaeological fantasy. 'I shall expect [the sarcophagus] to be of alabaster . . . I expect it will be filled with flowers and will contain the royal regalia. In the sarcophagus I shall first expect to find the ordinary wooden coffin. Inside there will probably be a second coffin of thin wood, lined with finely chased silver. Inside this, again, there will be a coffin of thin wood, richly gilt. Then we shall find the mummy. It will be, I conjecture, encased in sheet gold about the thickness of the tin used for making tobacco-boxes. The mummy will have gold bracelets at the wrists, gold rings at the ankles, a gold collar and breastplate, and a gold plate on the side where the abdomen was opened. His fingernails and toenails will be inlaid with gold. Enclosed with him in the coffins will probably be other precious royal objects. I shall also expect to find the richly ornamented vessels in which the heart and other internal organs are preserved, and it will, no doubt, have a finely worked portrait of the king on the lid.'

No one could have guessed how much reality, for once, would exceed even the wildest speculation.

Tutankhamun's gilded and richly inlaid second coffin (no. 254).

IV Pharaoh's Burial

The Shrines
and Sarcophagus

❛ The [second] shrine was intact, its doors bore their original seal uninjured, indicating that the robbers had not reached him. Henceforth, we knew that, within the shrine, we should be treading where no one had entered, and that we should be dealing with material untouched and unharmed since the boy king was laid to rest nearly three thousand three hundred years ago. We had at last found what we never dreamed of attaining – an absolute insight into the funerary customs followed in the burial of an ancient Pharaoh. ❜

Howard Carter

(Above) Carter and Mace, perched on scaffolding, carefully roll back the brown linen pall (no. 209) which lay over a gilded framework (no. 208) erected between the first and second outermost shrines.

(Right) The Divine Cow and attendant deities: an image modelled in sunk-relief on the inside back panel of the first (outermost) shrine (no. 207).

Immediately behind the blocking of the Burial Chamber entrance, Carter and his colleagues were confronted by what appeared to be a wall of gilded wood inlaid with brilliant blue faience. This wall proved to be the outermost of a nest of floorless shrines of carefully joinered wood. The larger sections were of cedar, held together by tenons of oak, Christ's Thorn wood and bronze. Each shrine, copper-bound at its lower edge, was fitted at its eastern end with double folding doors. The doors were held shut by ebony bolts sliding within massive, silver-coated copper staples; two further staples on each door had been intended to receive a cord binding and seal. On the outermost shrine neither cord nor sealing was in evidence, though on the second and third shrines, these corded seals were present and intact (seal types I and J); the doors of the fourth (innermost) shrine had never been sealed.

Now terrifyingly fragile, their gilded gesso surfaces having in places parted owing to shrinkage of the base wood, the shrines so closely filled the confines of the hot and stuffy chamber that the disassembly into their 51 sections (weighing between a hundredweight and half a ton) and removal from the tomb proved no easy task. As Carter records, 'We bumped our heads, nipped our fingers, we had to squeeze in and out like weasels and work in all kinds of embarrassing positions.' But by the end of the second season, after 'eighty-four days of real manual labour', employing only the most primitive of lifting-gear, the work of dismant-

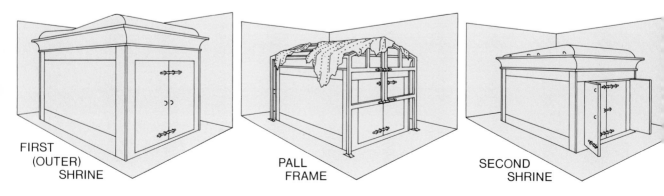

FIRST (OUTER) SHRINE

PALL FRAME

SECOND SHRINE

ling had been completed: the wall panels lay propped against the walls of the Burial Chamber, their roof sections in the Antechamber. Conservation began in 1928, using up over half a ton of paraffin wax; two seasons later the shrines were strong enough to be transported to the Cairo Museum where they could be properly examined.

The outermost shrine (no. 207)

The outermost of the four shrines measures 5.08 by 3.28m (16ft 8in by 10ft 9⅛in) and 2.75m (9ft) high. Constructed from heavy panels of 32mm (1¼in) thick cedar, the surfaces both inside and out are gessoed, gilded and inlaid. In shape, this outermost shrine, with its battered walls and double-sloping roof, bears a close resemblance to the *sed*-festival pavilion in which the king achieved rejuvenation and rebirth. In Carter's view, the shape had been chosen as much for aesthetics as ritual requirement: 'owing to the great depth of the shrine, a single sloping roof would have necessitated its elevated curved front to have been in height far out of proportion with the rest of the structure.'

The sides and rear panel of the shrine are decorated with double *tyet*-knot amulets of Isis and *djed*- ('stability') hieroglyphs of Osiris, set, to dazzling effect, against a brilliant blue faience background. A pair of protective *wedjat*-eyes decorate what was intended to be the shrine's north side, but as erected these eyes actually faced south. The two doors each carry a rectangular panel with a representation in sunk relief: that on the left a headless and pawless leonine creature; that on the shrine's right door panel a seated divinity with twin-feather headdress, grasping an *ankh* or 'life' sign. In contrast with the exterior, the inside surfaces of the shrine are heavily inscribed, with extracts from Book of the Dead spells 1, 134 and 141–2, and from the Book of the Divine Cow (the legend of the Destruction of Mankind). The inside of the roof (the middle section of which was put on the wrong way around) is decorated with winged solar discs and 13 vultures.

The linen pall (no. 209)

Between the first and second outermost shrines had been erected a poorly constructed nine-piece gabled framework (no. 208) of gessoed, varnished and gilded wood – 4.32 by 2.93m (14ft 2in by 9ft 7⅜in) and 2.78m (9ft 1½in) high. Over this had been crookedly spread a coarsely woven, dark brown linen pall (no. 209), 5.5 by 4.4m (18ft ½in by 14ft 5¼in), made up of several widths of material sewn together, decorated with large – 4.7cm (1⅞in) in diameter – marguerites of gilded bronze which had been sewn on to the fabric at intervals of 19.5 and 22cm (7⅝ and 8⅝in). To the American Egyptologist J.H. Breasted, this pall was 'like a night sky spangled with stars.' Although the excavators expended a great deal of time and ingenuity on the preservation of this extremely fragile item, which had torn apart from the weight of its bronze sequins, it suffered irremediable damage through having been left out in the open during the period Carter and his team were locked out of the tomb and laboratory (p. 66):

'Mr. Carter's agitation on discovering the condition of the precious object was intense, but he contented himself with the remark, "Well, anyway, it's your pall, not mine, and it's the only one in the world."'

Professor Newberry and his wife unroll the fragile linen pall (no. 209) after its removal from the tomb, preparatory to conservation.

(Below) The complex of closely nested shrines filling the Burial Chamber: (left to right) the outermost shrine (no. 207); the framework and pall (nos. 208–209); the second, third and fourth shrines (nos. 237–239); and the quartzite sarcophagus (no. 240).

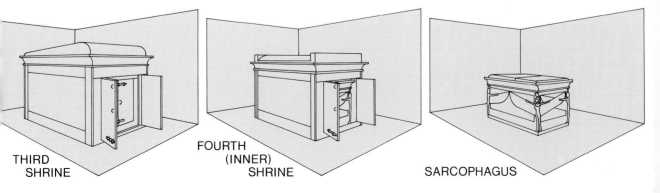

THIRD SHRINE

FOURTH (INNER) SHRINE

SARCOPHAGUS

(Right) Isis and Nephthys, the divine kites, spread their wings protectively over the interior end panel of the third shrine (no. 238).

(Far right) Isis presents Pharaoh to Osiris, lord of the Underworld: a detail from the outer left-hand door of the second shrine (no. 237).

(Below) Osiris of the Horizon: a detail from the left-hand outer door panel of the inlaid first (outermost) shrine (no. 207). An orientation mark, 'north', may be seen in black directly above the god's figure.

The second outermost shrine (no. 237)

The second shrine differed from the first in both size – 3.74 by 2.35m (12ft 3¼in by 7ft 8½in) and 2.25m (7ft 4⅝in) high – and appearance. Unlike that of the outermost shrine, the second shrine had a sloping roof which reached its maximum height above the entrance doors. The shrine imitates, in its basic form, the shape of the *Per-wer*, the ancient shrine of Upper Egypt.

Constructed from 16 heavy wooden sections, most surfaces, both inside and outside, had been gessoed and covered with a layer of gold leaf; the roof was covered with thick black resin divided into squares by gilded bands of incised decoration. The exterior surface of each door carries a superbly modelled representation of the king before Osiris (left) and Re-Horakhty (right), executed in sunk relief. At the rear of the shrine stand Isis and Nephthys, who as the sisters of Osiris would have been the principal mourners at the god-king's funeral. The remainder of the outer surface is decorated with texts and vignettes from various funerary compositions, including Book of the Dead spells 1, 17, 26, 27 and 29, and a unique cryptographic funerary book which has as its theme the triumph of light.

The interior of the second shrine is dominated by a figure of the winged sky-goddess Nut standing upon the hieroglyph for 'gold' which, together with five vultures with outspread wings, decorates the ceiling. Flanking the goddess are spells from the Pyramid Texts and the Book of the Dead. The inner surface of the right-hand door carries a representation of a donkey-headed herald and a ram-headed guardian of the underworld; that of the left door panel carries a similar underworld guardian and a human-headed figure wearing a close-fitting cap. Above is a text taken from spell 144 of the Book of the Dead, invoking the keepers of the gates of the underworld. The right and left side panels of the shrine are decorated with sunk-relief vignettes illustrating Book of the Dead spell 148 (the seven celestial cows, the bull of heaven, and the four rudders of heaven). Another vignette illustrates spells 141–2, with additional texts from spells 130, 133, 134 and 148. The back panel of the shrine is inscribed in finely delineated hieroglyphs with Book of the Dead spell 17, a statement of the solar doctrine.

One interesting feature of this shrine is that it has been reinscribed. The more brilliant gilding of the cartouches reveals that the nomen 'Tutankhamun' was written over an original name, a component part of which, according to Carter, was '-aten'.

The third shrine (no. 238)

The third of Tutankhamun's shrines is of similar design to the second, with a sloping roof and somewhat smaller dimensions – 3.40 by 1.92m (11ft 1⅞in by 6ft 3⅝in), with a maximum height of 2.15m (7ft). It again reproduces the form of the *Per-wer*.

The structure is made from 10 separate sections. Like the second shrine, the third shrine is gilded over its entire surface and decorated in sunk relief with vignettes and extracts from Egyptian religious texts. The roof of the shrine carries a winged solar disc and a vertical row of eight spread-winged birds four vultures, two mythical serpent-headed vultures, and two falcons. The sides of the shrine are inscribed with abridged versions of the second and sixth divisions of the Book of What Is in the Underworld (the Amduat). The outer faces of the doors and back panel of the shrine are inscribed with extracts from spell 148 of the Book of the Dead, and carry representations of four ram-headed guardian figures and four heralds, each grasping one or two knives and variously represented as human-headed, antelope-headed or crocodile-headed.

The design on the roof exterior is balanced on the inside ceiling with a similar decoration, comprising a winged disc, five vultures, a serpent-headed vulture, a sixth vulture and a falcon. The inner walls of the shrine are decorated with processions of various gods, while on the inside door panels and end are shown Isis and Nephthys, their wings again outspread to protect the occupant.

The innermost shrine (no. 239)

The innermost of Tutankhamun's four shrines measures 2.90 by 1.48m (9ft 6⅛in by 4ft 10¼in), and 1.90m (6ft 2⅘in) high, and was constructed from five separate sections. A representation in miniature of the prehistoric 'Palace of the North', the *Per-nu*, its

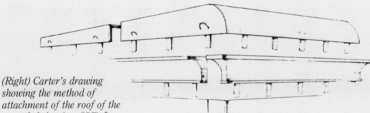

(Right) Carter's drawing showing the method of attachment of the roof of the second shrine (no. 237). In dismantling the shrines, Carter found a wide variety of jointing techniques – including the square or smooth joint, the rebated glued joint, the plain mitre, the tenon and mortise, pairs of single tenons, stub tenons and the joggle joint. Carter noted that the wood had been supplied in more or less standard cuts – balks, planks, deals, battens and strips.

(Above right) One of the many assembly marks (centre of photograph) on the shrines.

Construction

The space available in the Burial Chamber was so restricted that the shrines had been introduced in sections and placed in order against the walls for erection innermost first and outermost last. More than 150 joiners' marks had been either scratched into the metal or painted on in black, intended to show not only how the various sections fitted together but also their correct orientation. For practical reasons, perhaps, the correct orientation was ignored, and the doors of all four shrines positioned at the east rather than the west end of the chamber, where, by the Treasury doorway, there was more space for manoeuvring. Even so, the erection of the shrines had proved no easy matter. Serious difficulties had been encountered when it was found that the sarcophagus was slightly out of true: even after chopping away the inner surface of the innermost shrine at strategic points, the fit continued to be tight and joints between the side and end sections had to be left gaping. Problems with the third shrine were resolved by brute force, with hammer blows still in evidence on the gilded corners.

roof is barrel-vaulted, decorated in bas relief with kneeling figures of Isis, Nephthys, Selkis and Neith, alternating with *wedjat*-eyes, recumbent Anubis dogs and vultures, each on a pylon. The right and left side panels carry respectively a procession of Imsety, Anubis, Duamutef and Geb, and of Hapy, Anubis, Qebhsenuef and Horus between figures of Thoth supporting the sky; the end panel and outside door panels carry protective images of the winged Isis and her sister Nephthys.

The ceiling of the innermost shrine is decorated with a magnificent representation of the goddess Nut, again with outspread wings, flanked by the falcon-headed Horus. Isis and Nephthys again guard the doors, while the interior wall panels carry the text of spell 17 from the Book of the Dead.

The sarcophagus

'The decisive moment was at hand! An indescribable moment for the archaeologist! What was beneath and what did that fourth shrine contain? With intense excitement I drew back the bolts of the last and unsealed doors; they slowly swung open, and there, filling the entire area within, effectually barring any further progress, stood an immense yellow quartzite sarcophagus, intact, with the lid still firmly fixed in its place, just as the pious hands had left it. '

Howard Carter

'When Carter and I opened the doors of the third and fourth shrines and beheld the massive stone sarcophagus within, I felt for the first time the majesty of the dead Pharaoh's actual presence '

James Henry Breasted

Some 2.74 by 1.47m (9ft by 4ft 9⅞in) and 1.47m (4ft 9⅞in) high, the king's golden-yellow sarcophagus (no. 240), carved from a single block of the hardest quartzite, was supported at each corner upon a block of calcite. The sloping lid, with its winged sun disc at the head end and three vertical columns of incised hieroglyphs, was of red granite, painted to match the yellow of the sarcophagus box. Carter suggested that it was perhaps a replacement for the intended lid, which had not been ready in time for the funeral. The lid had been cracked across the centre, owing perhaps to some accident at the time of its hurried installation. This crack had been filled with gypsum, which was itself touched up to blend in with the new colour of the lid.

The decoration of the sarcophagus is dominated by the four tutelary deities Isis, Nephthys, Selkis and Neith, carved in high relief to the traditional proportions of the pre-Amarna, 18-square grid and delicately picked out in colours. They stand at each of the corners of the monument, their winged arms outstretched to envelop the box in a protective

embrace. A cavetto cornice at the top edge of the box is balanced at the bottom by a dado of double *tyet*- and *djed*-amulets. Each long side of the sarcophagus is decorated with one horizontal and six vertical columns of deeply incised hieroglyphs, and, at its westernmost end, an incised *wedjat*-eye. The east and west ends of the box are similarly inscribed with a single horizontal band of text and a further 14 verticals.

As Carter records, 'the crack greatly complicated our final effort, the raising of [the sarcophagus] lid.' But, by passing angle irons beneath the long edges of the lid, permitting 'it to be raised by differential pulleys as one piece', the difficulty was resolved. On 12 February 1924 the tackle was brought into play: the ropes tightened and the ton and a quarter granite lid slowly lifted into the air. The supreme moment was at hand.

The mis-matched granite lid of the rectangular quartzite sarcophagus (no. 240) as first revealed, with the crack running across the middle.

The west or head end of the beautifully modelled sarcophagus (no. 240), towards which the faces of the four tutelary goddesses – here Isis (left) and Nephthys (right) – are turned.

The Coffins

The face of the second coffin (no. 254), of wood overlaid with thick gold foil and richly inlaid with faience, glass and semi-precious stones.

' The sarcophagus lid trembled, began to rise. Slowly, and swaying uncertainly, it swung clear.
' At first we saw only a long, narrow, black void. Then across the middle of this blackness we gradually discerned fragments of granite which had fallen out of the fracture in the lid. They were lying scattered upon a dark shroud through which we seemed to see emerging an indistinct form.... '

James Henry Breasted

The outer coffin (no. 253)

As the broken lid of the stone sarcophagus was slowly raised by means of Carter's elaborate pulley system the shrouded form of the dead king came into view. There was an audible gasp from the crowd of assembled dignitaries as the two sheets of covering linen (nos. 252 and 252a) were rolled back to reveal a magnificent anthropoid coffin, its golden surface shimmering in the heat of Burton's arc lamps. How different from the battered hulks recovered by Brugsch 40 years before from the royal cache at Deir el-Bahri! And its size suggested that this was merely the first of several such coffins, contained one within another like so many Russian dolls. But the excavators had to be patient. Conservation demands on objects already removed from the tomb meant that it would be another year and a half before work on opening the coffins could begin.

The exposed coffin, 2.24m (7ft 4⅜in) long, its head to the west, rested on a low leonine bier (no. 253a) still intact though straining at the ton and a quarter weight it had had to endure for more than 3,200 years. Fragments adzed from the toe of the coffin lid at the time of the funeral – a crude attempt to rectify a design error and allow the sarcophagus lid to sit properly – were found in the bottom of the sarcophagus. These revealed that the structure of the coffin was cypress, modelled in relief with a thin layer of gesso overlaid with gold foil. The gold varied in thickness from heavy sheet for the face and hands to the finest gold leaf for the curious *khat*-like headdress. The metal covering also varied in colour, the paler alloy of the hands and face conveying, in Carter's words, 'an impression of the greyness of death'.

The surfaces of both lid and base were covered with *rishi* – or feathered – decoration, executed in low relief. Superimposed upon this feathering, on the right and left sides, were two finely modelled images of Isis and Nephthys with their wings extended, their protective embrace alluded to in one of the two vertical lines of hieroglyphs running down the front of the lid. The underside of the foot carried a further representation of the goddess Isis, kneeling upon the hieroglyph for 'gold'. Below this are 10 vertical columns of text.

The lid itself had been modelled in high relief with a recumbent image of the dead king as Osiris, wearing a broad collar and wristlets modelled in low relief, his arms crossed on the chest to clutch the twin symbols of kingship, the crook and the flail, in his left and right hands. From the forehead of the king rose the 'Two Ladies', Wadjit and Nekhbet – the divine cobra of Lower Egypt and the vulture-goddess of Upper Egypt. A small wreath tied around the pair was composed of olive leaves and flowers resembling the blue cornflower, bound on to a narrow strip of papyrus pith. The olive leaves had been carefully arranged to show alternately their green front and silver back surfaces.

The second coffin (no. 254)

The original design of the outermost coffin's lid had included four silver handles – two to each side – to enable it to be safely lowered in position. Now, on 13 October 1925, three millennia later, these same handles would be employed to raise it. According to Carter, 'It was a moment as anxious as exciting.' But the lid was lifted without great difficulty, and the anticipated second anthropoid coffin revealed.

Here again the surface was concealed beneath a decayed shroud of linen (no. 254b), itself obscured by floral garlands (no. 254a) not dissimilar to those found by Davis in Pit 54 (p. 38). Around the protective deities on Pharaoh's brow, over the shroud, was a small wreath of olive leaves, blue lotus petals and cornflowers (no. 254a (1)).

Before the linen covering was drawn back, Carter and his team decided to remove both the delicate lower half and contents of the outermost coffin from the sarcophagus. The delicacy of the gessoed and inlaid surface necessitated that this be achieved with as little handling as possible – by inserting steel pins through the inscribed tenons of the outermost coffin and employing pulleys. It was, as Carter records, a task 'of no little difficulty'. But it was carried through without incident, and the coffin was deposited upon trestles resting upon the rim of the sarcophagus box.

The second coffin was in due course revealed as even more magnificent than the first, 2.04m (6ft 8¼in) long. Constructed from a still unidentified wood, the surface was again found to be overlaid with gold foil. The use of inlays, however (which had suffered from the presence of damp and showed a disconcerting tendency to fall out), was far more extensive than on the outermost coffin. Details, such as the stripes of the *nemes*-headcloth, eyebrows, cosmetic lines and beard were inlaid with lapis-blue glass (the inlays of the headcloth somewhat decayed). The uraeus on the forehead was of gilded wood, with a head of blue faience and inlays of red, blue and turquoise glass; the head of the vulture, Nekhbet, was also of gilded wood and, like the image of the outermost coffin, with a beak of dark black wood (probably ebony) and eyes of obsidian. The symbols of divine kingship, the crook and the flail (held in the left and right hands respectively), were inlaid with lapis-blue and turquoise glass and blue faience. A broad 'falcon collar' picked out with inset pieces of brilliant red, blue and turquoise glass showed at the king's throat, with two similarly inlaid bracelets modelled at the wrists.

The entire surface of the body was decorated in *rishi*-pattern, though here, unlike the outermost coffin, the feathers were each inlaid with jasper-red, lapis-blue and turquoise glass. The places of Isis and Nephthys were taken by the winged vulture goddess Nekhbet and the winged uraeus, Wadjit; here again the figures were inlaid with pieces of red, blue and turquoise glass.

The third coffin (no. 255)

Unlike the outermost coffin, the lid of the second coffin had not been furnished with handles, and its removal was further hampered by the fact that the 10 gold-headed silver nails holding it in place could not be fully withdrawn while it lay in the close-fitting outer shell. Carter faced the task with the sang-froid he reserved for his Egyptian endeavours. The pins of the second coffin were withdrawn sufficiently for 'stout copper wire' to be attached; 'Strong metal eyelets' were then screwed into the edge of the outer coffin and the two separated by lowering the outer shell into the sarcophagus while the inner hung suspended. The removal of the fragile second coffin's lid was accomplished in a similar fashion: eyelets were screwed into the edge

The breathtaking mask of Tutankhamun's innermost coffin (no. 255), the most magnificent ever brought to light, beaten from sheet gold and embellished with chasing and inlay.

of the lid at four points, the silver pins securing the 10 inscribed silver tenons removed, and the coffin lid, after some initial flexing, was lifted effortlessly into the air.

Removal of the lid revealed a third anthropoid coffin, a covering of fine linen in place above the *nemes*-headdress, the body tightly tucked in from neck to feet with a shroud of red linen, folded three times (no. 255b). The face had been left exposed, the breast decorated with an extremely fragile broad collar of blue glass beads and various leaves, flowers, berries and fruits (including *Punica grana-*

tum (pomegranate) and *Salix* sp.) sewn onto papyrus backing (no. 255a).

'Mr. Burton at once made his photographic records. I then removed the floral collarette and linen coverings. An astounding fact was disclosed. The third coffin . . . was made of solid gold! The mystery of the enormous weight, which hitherto had puzzled us, was now clear. It explained also why the weight had diminished so slightly after the first coffin, and the lid of the second coffin, had been removed. Its weight was still as much as eight strong men could lift.'

The initial appearance of the metalwork was very far from gleaming, however. Removal of the linen shroud and papyrus collar revealed that the coffin had been covered 'with a thick black pitch-like layer

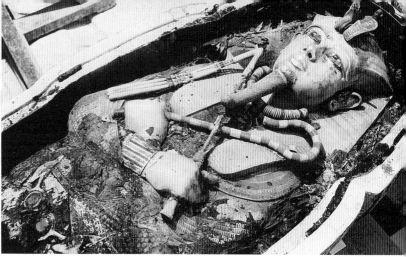

which extended from the hands down to the ankles'. Carter estimated that two bucketfuls of this anointing liquid had been poured over the coffin, filling in the whole of the space between it and the base of the second coffin, setting solid and causing them to stick firmly together. The removal of this resinous layer proved extremely difficult:

'This pitch like material hardened by age had to be removed by means of hammering, solvents and heat, while the shells of the coffins were loosened from one another and extricated by means of great heat, the interior being temporarily protected during the process by zinc plates – the temperature employed though necessarily below the melting point of zinc was several hundred degrees Fahrenheit. After the inner coffin was extricated it had to be again treated with heat and solvents before the material could be completely removed.'

The coffin measures some 1.88m (6ft 2in) in length. The metal, beaten from heavy gold sheet, varies

(Above, left to right) Steps in the salvage of a priceless treasure: Carter delicately brushes away the decayed remains of the linen shroud which covered the face of the second coffin (no. 254); the second coffin is removed from the outermost coffin shell (no. 253) by means of an elaborate pulley system; Carter patiently chips away at the hardened black unguents poured liberally over the innermost, gold coffin (no. 255).

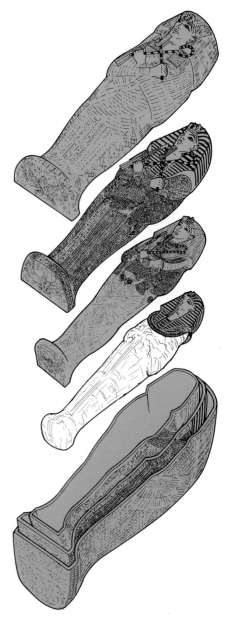

(Right, top to bottom) Tutankhamun's coffins, varying slightly in size, were accommodated one within another around the gold-masked mummy.

(Left) The physiognomy of the second coffin (no. 254), shown centre, differs markedly from that of the first (no. 253), shown far left, and the third (no. 255), shown left, and there is every reason to believe, as with other objects from the burial furniture, that Tutankhamun was not its intended owner.

from 0.25–0.3cm in thickness. When the coffin was eventually weighed in 1929 it tipped the scales at 110.4kg (296lb troy); its scrap value alone would today be in the region of £1 million, or $1,700,000.

The image of Tutankhamun on this innermost coffin is today oddly ethereal, owing to the decomposition of the calcite whites of the eyes. The pupils are obsidian, the eyebrows and cosmetic lines lapis-lazuli coloured glass. Tutankhamun's beard, fashioned separately and attached to the chin, is inlaid with lapis-coloured glass. As with the second coffin, the headdress is the *nemes*, though here the pleating is indicated in relief rather than by inlays of coloured glass. When found, patches of gold foil concealed the fact that the ears, cast separately, were pierced – a reminder that the wearing of ear-rings by males was at this period an affectation discarded at puberty. At the neck of the coffin had been placed two heavy

necklaces of disc beads fashioned from red an[d] yellow gold and dark blue faience, threaded on wha[t] looked like grass bound with linen tape. Each strin[g] had lotus flower terminals inlaid with carnelia[n], lapis and turquoise glass. Below these necklace[s] was the falcon collar of the coffin itself, agai[n] fashioned separately from the lid, inlaid with 1[?] rows of lapis, quartz, carnelian, felspar and tu[r]quoise glass imitating tubular beadwork, with a[n] outer edge of inlaid drops.

As on the first and second coffins, the king's arm[s] are shown crossed upon the chest, with she[et] bracelets inlaid in a similar fashion to the collar wit[h] lapis, carnelian and turquoise-coloured glass. Th[e] crook and the flail are held in the left and righ[t] hands, overlaid with sheet gold, dark blue faienc[e,] polychrome glass and carnelian. Most of the deco[-]ration of the flail's shaft had decayed through th[e] application of the thick black resin with which th[e] coffin had been so liberally anointed.

Below the hands the goddesses Nekhbet an[d] Wadjit, fashioned from gold sheet and inlaid wit[h] red-backed quartz and lapis- and turquoise-coloure[d] glass, spread their wings protectively around th[e] upper part of the royal body. Both the lid and base o[f] this coffin are further decorated with richly chase[d] figures of the winged goddesses Isis and Nephthy[s] on a *rishi* background, protecting the lower right an[d] left sides respectively. Two vertical columns of tex[t] are chased down the front of the coffin lid from th[e] navel to the feet, with the usual figure of Isi[s] kneeling upon the hieroglyph for 'gold' (*nub*) chase[d] upon the soles of the feet.

The lid of the innermost coffin, like the oute[r] coffin, was fitted with handles, and was attached t[o] its base by means of eight gold tongues, four on eac[h] side, which dropped into sockets in the shell an[d] were retained by gold pins. Since the available spac[e] between the two coffins was so narrow, these pin[s] had to be removed piecemeal; then, at long last, 'Th[e] lid was raised by its golden handles and the mumm[y] of the king disclosed.'

(Below) An image of the winged goddess Isis, chased with supreme delicacy and skill beneath the foot of Tutankhamun's innermost gold coffin (no. 255).

(Below right) One of the ten inscribed silver tenons attaching the lid and base of the second coffin.

> ' We opened their sarcophagi and their coffins in which they were, and found the noble mummy of this king equipped with a falchion; a large number of amulets and jewels of gold were upon his neck, and his head-piece of gold was upon him. . . . '
>
> Extract from the confession of an ancient tomb robber

> ' Before us, occupying the whole of the interior of the golden coffin, was an impressive, neat and carefully made mummy, over which had been poured anointing unguents as in the case of the outside of its coffin – again in great quantity – consolidated and blackened by age. In contradistinction to the general dark and sombre effect, due to these unguents, was a brilliant, one might say magnificent, burnished gold mask or similitude of the king, covering his head and shoulders, which, like the feet, had been intentionally avoided when using the unguents. '
>
> Howard Carter

The Gold Mask and Trappings of the Mummy

the outer as well as the inner angles. As on the coffins, the lapis-lazuli outline of the eyes reproduces the distinctive *kohl* eye make-up, originally applied to protect against the sun's glare but increasingly employed for its beautifying effect. Additional personal embellishment is alluded to in the pierced ears, which were covered with discs of gold foil when found.

(Below) Profile of the awesome mask of inlaid sheet gold (no. 256a).

(Below left) The sheet-gold hands (no. 256b(1)) which were sewn on to the mummy bandages; between them is black-resin scarab no. 256b.

Superbly modelled, the king's portrait mask (no. 256a) stands without parallel as a masterpiece of the Egyptian metalworker's craft. Beaten from two separate sheets of gold, remarkably consistent in thickness and joined by hammering, the mask was subsequently embellished by chasing, burnishing, and by the addition of inlay work. It measures some 54cm (1ft 9¼in) in height and weighs 10.23kg (22½lb).

The mask represents the young king as Osiris, wearing the *nemes*-headcloth with bound queue, or pigtail, falling down at the back, inlaid with opaque blue glass in imitation of lapis lazuli. On the brow sit the vulture and cobra, Nekhbet and Wadjit, the latter poised to spit fire at Pharaoh's enemies. Each of these fittings has been fashioned from solid gold, inlaid with blue faience, glass, carnelian and lapis lazuli, with eyes of translucent quartz backed with a touch of red pigment (the eyes of the vulture are missing). The eyes of the king are made from quartz and obsidian, and convey a distinctly life-like impression; as so often in Egyptian art, they mistakenly show red discoloration (caruncles) on

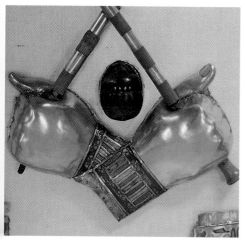

Ornaments of the Mummy

(material: gold, unless otherwise stated)

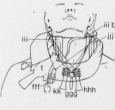

*The king's mummy (no. 256)
as first revealed, with the gold
mask, floral collar, crook,
flail, mummy-bands and
other exterior trappings in
position.*

Object group no. 256

a	gold mask		yy	scarab bracelet
b	external trappings		zz	*wedjat*-eye bracelet
c	Y-shaped amulet		aaa	*wedjat*-eye bracelet
d	oval plaque		bbb	finger-ring
e	vulture collar		ccc	finger-ring
f	vulture and uraeus collar		ddd	disc bracelet
g	uraeus collar		eee	tail
h	falcon collar		fff	*tyet*-knot amulet
i	two falcon collars		ggg	*wadj*-sceptre amulet
j	apron		hhh	*djed*-pillar amulet
k	dagger		iii	double-leaf amulet
l	girdle		iii bis	serpent amulet
m	T-shaped amulet		jjj	leaf amulet
n	bracelet		kkk	amuletic knot
o	faience broad collar		lll	uraeus collar
p	falcon collar		mmm	vulture collar
q	resin scarab		nnn	vulture and uraeus collar
r	uraeus from 4o		ooo	scarab pectoral
s	vulture head from 4o		ppp	vulture pectoral
t	falcon collar		qqq	scarab pectoral
u	circlet		rrr	faience *wedjat*-eye
v	circlet		sss	beads
w	circlet		ttt	falcon collar
x	vulture bracelet		uuu	falcon pectoral
y	beads		vvv	*wedjat*-eye pectoral
z	falcon collar		www	bracelet
aa	two falcon collars		xxx	Anubis amulet
bb	beadwork		yyy	falcon-headed amulet
cc	circlet		zzz	serpent-head amulet
dd	iron dagger		4a	Thoth amulet
ee	girdle		4b	*wadj*-sceptre amulet
ff	five finger-rings		4c	bead
gg	falcon collar		4d	chain
hh(1)	bracelet with lapis barrel-bead		4e	five pectoral clasps and pendants
hh(2)	bracelet with iron *wedjat*-eye amulet		4f	human-headed winged uraeus amulet
hh(3)	bracelet with carnelian barrel-bead		4g	double uraeus amulet
ii	funerary papyrus?		4h	vulture amulet
jj	four circlets		4i	vulture amulet
kk	*djed*-pillar amulet		4i bis	vulture amulet
ll	sandals, toe- and finger-stalls		4j	vulture amulet
mm	wire bracelet		4k	uraeus amulet
nn	beadwork of eee		4l	vulture amulet
oo	*wedjat*-eye bracelet		4m	bead collar
pp	*wedjat*-eye bracelet		4n	two fibrous fillets
qq	scarab bracelet		4o	diadem
rr	barrel-bead bracelet		4p	temple band
ss	scarab bracelet		4p bis	linen headdress
ss bis	disc bracelet		4q	uraeus insignia of 4p bis
tt	amuletic knot		4r	vulture insignia of 4p bis
uu	bracelet with carnelian swallow		4s	temple band
vv	three finger-rings		4t	beaded linen skull-cap
ww	barrel-bead bracelet		4u	conical linen pad
xx	beaded bracelet		4v	iron headrest amulet

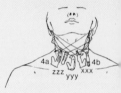

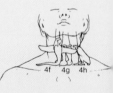

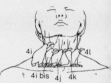

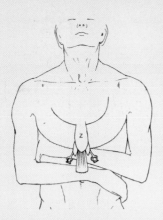
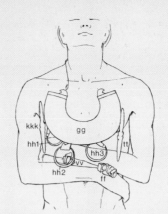

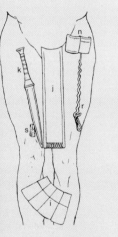
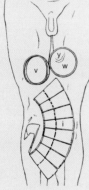
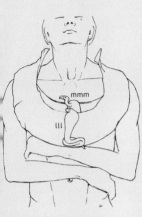
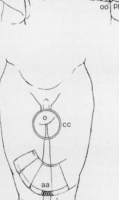

(Left) Carter's unpublished series of drawings (with new lettering added) recording the jewels and amulets that had been bandaged in with the royal mummy. (Far left) The crook-winged Nekhbet-vulture pectoral no. 256ppp. At least one authority has suggested this may be one of the earliest examples of enamelling.

The bead-work cap (no. 256 4t) found in position on the king's head. The cartouches contain a variant form of the early Aten name.

Tutankhamun's blackened left hand, detached for photography, with sheet-gold finger-stalls (no. 256 ll) and heavy signet rings (nos. 256 bbb and 256 ccc) in position.

*(Above) Part of the inscribed
gold framework or 'mummy
bands' (no. 256 b(3))
enclosing the royal corpse,
inlaid with coloured glass and
semi-precious stones.*

*(Above right) A radiograph
of the gold mask (no. 256 a)
showing the remarkable
consistency in the thickness of
the metal. The only
unevenness which may be
detected is on the left cheek.
The superstitious have not
been slow to point out that a
lesion was detected by Derry
at this very point on the
surface of the king's mummy
– and that Carnarvon's
untimely death had been
caused by a cut to the cheek.*

*(Opposite) A detail of the gold
mask.*

The broad collar, with its falcon-headed terminals, is inlaid with lapis lazuli, quartz, green felspar,
obsidian and coloured glass. Over it was hung a
separate necklace of three strands with lotus flower
and uraeus terminals: the top and bottom strands of
this collar were composed of large disc beads of
yellow and red gold and dark blue faience, while the
beads of the centre strand were of yellow gold alone.
A divine beard, again of gold, is attached beneath
the chin, its plaits indicated by inlays of faience
which have decayed to a grey-blue colour.

The back of the mask is chased with a series of
texts containing a version of spell 151b of the Book
of the Dead. The text identifies the component parts
of the mask with a succession of deities (Anubis,
Horus, Ptah-Seker, and others) who were each to
play a crucial role in the protection of the king
against the manifold dangers of the underworld.

Other ornaments

The mask, perhaps the best-known image from the
tomb, is in fact but one element in the outer
ornamentation of the royal mummy. A scarab of
black resin, its base inscribed with Book of the Dead
spell 29b, hung suspended from the neck on a

decorative gold band made up from odd trappings
originally prepared for Ankhkheprure (no. 256b).
Beneath, a pair of burnished gold hands (no.
256b(1)), sewn directly onto the mummy wrappings
clasped the decayed crook and flail. Below them,
barely visible through the unguents, was a large
gold *ba*-bird (no. 256b(2)) surmounting a flexible
framework of one vertical and four horizontal inlaid
gold bands (nos. 256b (3)–(4)). These had again been
prepared for Ankhkheprure, and were only subsequently taken over for use by Tutankhamun by
cutting out some of the original names. Each element
numbered on the back, the trappings had been made
to fit their original owner; Tutankhamun was
evidently a rather different shape, and the framework had had to be adapted by cutting out and
piecing together.

As the wrappings of the mummy were gradually
removed, a further 150 magnificent items of jewellery, superb amulets and other objects were brought
to light (nos. 256c–4v). Fashioned and positioned
according to the dictates of the Book of the Dead,
they would ensure the king's transformation from
death to true immortality – if in a rather different
way from that originally envisaged.

The Royal Mummy

' The youthful Pharaoh was before us at last: an obscure and ephemeral ruler, ceasing to be the mere shadow of a name, had re-entered, after more than three thousand years, the world of reality and history! Here was the climax of our long researches! The tomb had yielded its secret; the message of the past had reached the present in spite of the weight of time, and the erosion of so many years. '

Howard Carter

Fitting closely into his anthropoid case, some 1.85m (6ft 1in) in height, the head protected by its magnificent portrait mask (no. 256a) (p. 111) and the curves of the body skilfully reproduced by means of

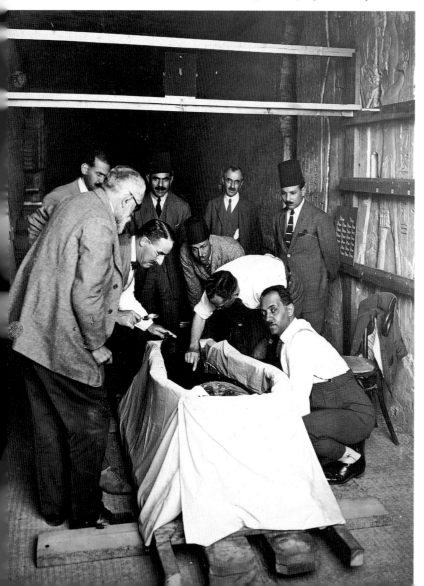

Autopsy by committee: Douglas Derry makes the first incision in the wrappings of the royal mummy (no. 256), watched by Lacau, Carter, Lucas, Saleh Bey Hamdi and other interested parties.

padding, the king (no. 256) appeared truly to ha[ve] achieved his goals of health, strength, vigour a[nd] eternal life. A second glance indicated that t[he] reality was otherwise: the outer shroud, held in pla[ce] by linen bands (five (?) transverse and one longitu[d]inal), had suffered greatly from the resin-bas[ed] libations liberally poured over the corpse short[ly] before the mummy and coffins had been rough[ly] lowered into the sarcophagus. Owing to the fr[ee] application of these same resins (which were st[ill] viscid in places), both body and mask were found [to] have stuck fast to the interior of the coffin – with t[he] result that the excavators had little choice but [to] examine the mummy where it lay.

The unwrapping of the king

The autopsy began on 11 November 1925 in t[he] outer corridor of the tomb of Sethos II (No. 1[5]) undertaken by Douglas E. Derry, Professor [of] Anatomy at the Egyptian University in Cairo, a[nd] Dr Saleh Bey Hamdi of Alexandria, in the presen[ce] of Carter, Alfred Lucas, Harry Burton, and vario[us] Egyptian and European officials and dignitarie[s]. The brittle surface of the shroud was first coate[d] with a layer of paraffin wax. Derry then made [a] longitudinal incision down the middle, allowing t[he] decayed wrappings to be turned outwards an[d] gradually removed in large pieces. Slowly, patientl[y] the unwrapping proceeded, though with an eve[r] increasing sense of foreboding.

The blackened, carbonized appearance of t[he] outer shroud had been a sad augury of things [to] come; Carter's hope that they might find t[he] wrappings in better condition after several thic[k]nesses had been removed proved vain. Except f[or] one or two areas where the linen was somewh[at] better preserved, the inner wrappings had be[en] reduced to the consistency of soot – according [to] Lucas, the chemist, the result of 'some kind of slo[w] spontaneous combustion in which, almost certainl[y] fungoid growth plays a part'. As a result, no reliab[le] record could be made of the system of binding th[e] corpse. It was evident that all the fingers and toe[s] had been individually wrapped, as indeed had all th[e] limbs; the front of the body had been packed wit[h] sheets of linen which reached down as far as th[e] knees and were held in place by transverse ba[n]dages, while more elaborate methods of bindin[g] were observed in the perineum (between the anu[s] and scrotum) and over the thorax. All in all, th[e] technique appeared to conform to 'the mode [of] binding . . . usually practised upon mummies of th[e] New Empire'.

The body

The first parts of the mummy to be complete[ly] divested of their wrappings were the shrunken an[d] attenuated lower legs. By 15 November the team ha[d] progressed as far as the neck. The king's sexu[al]

By 16 November the body had been dismantled to allow its removal from the coffin for closer examination. Now, at last, the excavators were able to turn their attention to the problem of the head – stuck 'so firmly' into the mask, in Carter's view, 'that it would require a hammer and chisel to free it'. Fortunately, such extreme measures were not to prove necessary: 'Eventually we used hot knives for the purpose with success', and the king's 'beautiful and well formed features' were finally revealed.

While the poorly preserved skin of the body was greyish-white in colour, the face proved to be somewhat darker, though equally brittle and with a cracked surface further disfigured by spots of natron (hydrated sodium carbonate residue from the embalming process). The head was cleanly shaven, the skin of the scalp covered with what appeared to be a whitish fatty acid, and the ears pierced with holes some 0.75cm ($\frac{3}{10}$in) in diameter. A rounded lesion of uncertain origin but perhaps associated with the embalming process was noted on the left cheek in front of the ear lobe. The nose had been flattened by the pressure of the bandages employed to wrap the head, while the nostrils themselves, like the eyes, had been plugged with resin-soaked fabric; resin had similarly been applied to seal the lips. The skull itself was empty, save for a small amount of resinous material introduced through the nose by breaking down the ethmoid bone.

The findings – and the second autopsy

From his examination, Derry was able to suggest that Tutankhamun had been a slightly built youth, 2.54cm (1in) or more taller in life than the 1.63m (5ft 4$\frac{1}{8}$in) yielded by direct measurement of his remains. This estimate, which was essentially confirmed by a re-examination of the body undertaken in 1968 (see below), is precisely the height of the two 'guardian figures' (p.128) positioned at the entrance to the Burial Chamber. The extent of union of the epiphyses (growth plates at the ends of the long bones that seal at full growth) suggested to Derry that Tutankhamun had died aged between 17 and 19, and in all probability at 18. A series of X-rays made in 1968 by a team led by Professor R.G. Harrison of the University of Liverpool was able to confirm Derry's dating ('within the early part of the age-range 18–22 years') – an estimate which F. Filce Leek, a member of the Harrison team, later sought to reduce to 16 or 17 years on the basis of the state of eruption of the third molars (the wisdom teeth). Doubtless the last word on the subject has yet to be said.

Another feature noted by Derry and again confirmed by the Harrison team's radiographic examination is the similarity between the shape of Tutankhamun's skull and that of the body from Tomb 55 in the Valley of the Kings (p. 20). Other anatomical similarities have been noted between these two bodies, including a common blood-group

rgans had been revealed, the penis bound in the rect position and the scrotum flattened against the erineum; no pubic hair was visible, and it could not e established whether or not the king had been ircumcised. A ragged embalming wound 8.6cm ⅜in) or more in length was visible, uniquely ositioned 'parallel to a line drawn from the mbilicus to the anterior superior iliac spine [i.e. avel to hip bone] and an inch above it'; no mbalming plate was in evidence. The arms were exed at the elbow, the forearms arranged in parallel ne to the other, the left above the right.

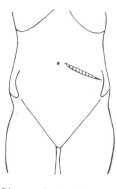

Diagram showing the peculiar positioning of Tutankhamun's embalming wound, running from the navel to the hip-bone on the left-hand side of the body.

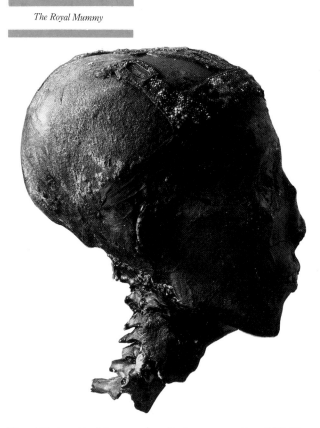

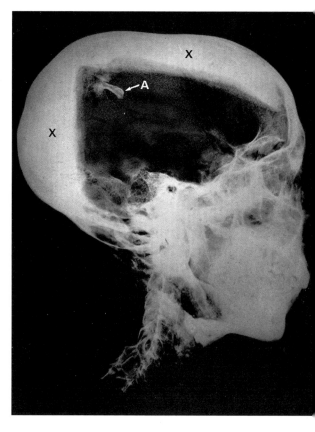

(Above) Photograph of the royal skull (left) taken in 1925/26, and in a radiograph (right) made in 1968. The areas marked 'X' represent resin introduced during the embalming process. 'A' is a small fragment of bone.

(Opposite left) The king's canopic shrine (no. 266). (Opposite above) Detail of the inlaid uraeus frieze. (Opposite below) The gilded wooden figure of Isis, with an orientation mark in black.

A_2 with the serum antigen MN. The conclusion that the two were closely related seems inescapable.

Two distinct levels of radiopaque resins visible in the 1968 X-rays of Tutankhamun's skull indicate that the embalmers treated the head on two separate occasions: once with the top of the skull downwards, and again with the back of the skull in the downward position. The X-rays further confirmed that the sternum and much of the rib cage had been removed by the embalmers, presumably at the time the internal organs were extracted for separate embalming and subsequently replaced with bundles of cloth.

Derry's inability to offer a suggestion as to the possible cause of the young king's death was a great disappointment to Carter, though hardly surprising in view of the poor state of preservation of the corpse. X-rays of the vertebrae made in 1968 revealed that the epiphysial plates were intact, and that Tutankhamun had not died as a result of consumption (tuberculosis), as some had previously speculated. Another feature revealed by Harrison's examination was the presence of a small fragment of bone within the skull, initially misidentified as a piece displaced from the nasal cavity. Sadly Harrison did not live to publish fully his thoughts on this feature, and it is not clear whether he believed the damage to have been sustained before or after death, accidentally or intentionally. That the king was murdered, however, seems increasingly likely.

Herodotus on mummies and mummification

The peculiar Egyptian practice of mummification was described by Herodotus, writing in the fifth century BC, in Book Two of his *Histories*. He noted that there were three qualities available: good, bad, and indifferent. Tutankhamun's mummy, although embalmed several centuries before the time of which the Greek historian was writing, had evidently been treated according to a version of the most elaborate:

'. . . as much as possible of the brain is extracted through the nostrils with an iron hook, and what the hook cannot reach is rinsed out with drugs; next the flank is laid open with a flint knife and the whole contents of the abdomen removed; the cavity is then thoroughly cleansed and washed out, first with palm wine and again with an infusion of pounded spices. After that it is filled with pure bruised myrrh, cassia, and every other aromatic substance with the exception of frankincense, and sewn up again, after which the body is placed in natron, covered entirely over, for seventy days – never longer. When this period, which must not be exceeded, is over, the body is washed and then wrapped from head to foot in linen cut into strips and smeared on the underside with gum, which is commonly used by the Egyptians instead of glue. In this condition the body is given back to the family, who have a wooden case made, shaped like the human figure, into which it is put. . . .'

One thing in particular . . . simply knocked us all of a heap . . . I think it is the most beautiful thing I've ever seen anywhere. . . . Round [the canopic shrine] were four statues of goddesses, most un-Egyptian in attitude, and beautifully modelled. One simply couldn't take in what one saw; it was so wonderful we all came out dazed.

Arthur Mace to his wife Winifred

The Canopic Shrine

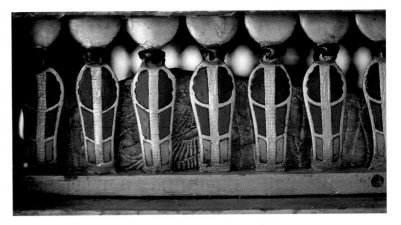

Dominating the middle of the Treasury's east wall, west-facing, its summit barely clearing the ceiling of the chamber, was a large gilded shrine mounted on a sled (no. 266), which held the embalmed internal organs of the young king – it is, as Carter observed, 'a monument not easily forgotten'. The outer canopy of this shrine (no. 266a), 1.98m (6ft 6in) high, some 1.53m (5ft) long and 1.22m (4ft) wide, consisted of four square corner posts supporting a cavetto cornice surmounted by a continuous frieze of uraei inlaid with coloured glass and faience. Between the posts, on each of the shrine's four sides, stood an elegant guardian goddess of gilded wood – Isis, Nephthys, Neith and Selkis, each identified by the hieroglyph upon her head and all modelled on the Amarna 20-square grid. Each figure stands feet inwards, arms outstretched in a gesture of protection, with the head gently inclined to either right or left – breaking the rule of frontality which is basic to Egyptian art. Within this outer framework was a

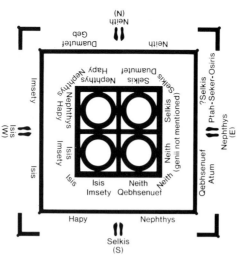

(Right) Diagram (after Carter) showing the relative positions of the tutelary goddesses and genii.

(Below left to right) The multi-layered protection accorded the royal viscera: removal of the outer portion of the gilded canopy (no. 266a) revealed a gilded wooden shrine, which in turn protected a linen-draped calcite chest (no. 266b). Within the canopic chest were four cylindrical compartments, each fitted with a human-headed stopper (nos. 266c–f) and containing an inlaid gold coffinette (no. 266g) holding a carefully wrapped canopic package.

second layer, the shrine proper, each of its gilded walls decorated in sunk relief with one of the four guardian goddesses facing one of the four canopic genii, and its own cavetto cornice decorated with a second cobra frieze.

The canopic chest

Work on dismantling the shrine could not be undertaken until clearance of the Treasury had been completed in 1926/7. When the gilded outer casing had been removed, the canopic chest itself (no. 266b) stood revealed, draped with a dark linen sheet 1.5 by 4.5m (4ft 11in by 14ft 9⅜in) folded over three times.

Although examples of such chests had been encountered before, the pristine beauty now exposed was something quite new. With the shroud removed, it could be seen that the chest had been carved from a single block of delicately veined and semi-translucent calcite, picked out in contrasting dark blue pigment and with a gilded dado of double *djed-* and *tyet-*symbols. It stood upon a second wooden sled, gessoed and gilded in the usual manner and fitted at its northern and southern sides with four huge staples of silver-sheet covered bronze intended to serve as handles. Its sloping lid, which separated from the box below the cavetto cornice, was decorated at the front with the winged solar disc of Horus-of-Behdet. It was attached to the chest by means of cords passing through four pairs of gold staples, two pairs to either side, sealed with the ubiquitous jackal and nine captives motif. The chest itself, shrine-like and with inward-sloping sides, was decorated at its four corners with images of Isis (southwest corner), Nephthys (northwest), Selkis (northeast) and Neith (southeast), sculpted in high relief to the traditional proportions, while the front was dominated by a second winged disc surmounting six vertical columns of text spoken by the goddesses positioned to either side; further invocations are present on either side and the rear of the chest.

With the lid of the canopic chest removed, four human-headed stoppers were exposed (nos. 266c–f), arranged in pairs, those on the east facing west and the lids on the west facing east. Exquisitely modelled in calcite, each lid represents the king wearing the *nemes-*headcloth with separately modelled vulture head and uraeus. All four are hollowed out underneath and carry a symbol painted in black on the shoulder to identify the compartment for which they were intended. The facial features are carefully picked out with black, with dabs of red for the lips.

These detachable lids concealed four cylindrical hollows, the king's canopic 'jars', drilled into the

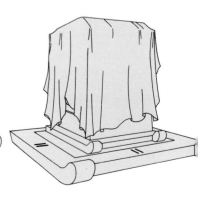

matrix of the chest proper. Each hollow contained a single linen-wrapped and resin-smeared coffinette of beaten gold (no. 266g), all four closely similar in design to the second coffin (see p. 107), inlaid in *rishi*- or feathered-pattern with coloured glass and carnelian; these coffinettes contained the embalmed and carefully wrapped viscera of the dead king. On each of these coffins, which are 39cm (1ft 3⅜in) high, is inlaid the name of the appropriate protecting genius with whom the king's internal organs were identified – Imsety the liver, Hapy the lungs, Duamutef the

stomach, and Qebhsenuef the intestines – the four 'sons of Horus'. Over them, perhaps before their introduction into the tomb since the canopic lids were displaced slightly, had been poured the black resin already encountered on the king's coffins and mummy. According to Carter, 'There was . . . sufficient evidence to show that the anointing commenced with the south-east coffin, thence to the south-west coffin, the north-west coffin and ending by the north-east coffin, when a very little of the unguent was left.'

(Above) Exterior and interior views of one of the four elaborately decorated gold coffinettes which contained Tutankhamun's embalmed viscera. This coffinette (no. 266g), holding the King's wrapped intestines, was under the protection of Qebhsenuef.

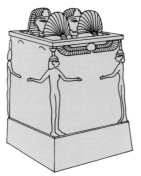

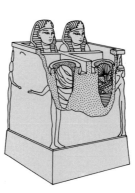

The same lack of care noted in the arrangement of the large gilded shrines was evident in the canopic equipment also. The positions of the free-standing gilded deities Nephthys and Selkis had been transposed, and a similar mistake had been made in the placement of two of the inlaid coffinettes. A heap of wooden chips, detached during the fitting of the gilded wooden canopy, had been abandoned on the Treasury floor.

Intended for another?

As with other objects from the king's burial furniture, there are indications that certain elements of the canopic assemblage had not originally been prepared for Tutankhamun, but were surplus items left over from the unused funerary equipment of a predecessor. In the case of the calcite canopic lids, the grounds for doubting the attribution are stylistic: quite simply, the portraits do not resemble those of the boy king, though such a resemblance has been claimed. In the case of the canopic coffinettes (the lid to at least one of which Carter believed differed in workmanship and offered a poor fit to the box), the evidence is more substantial: the inscriptions chased on the interior gold linings have had the owner's cartouches altered from those of Ankhkheprure – presumably Nefernefruaten, the enigmatic coregent of Akhenaten (p. 18), of whom the coffinette masks perhaps offer a likeness.

(Above) The elegant canopic chest of banded calcite (no. 266b), with details picked out in dark blue and a gilded dado, mounted on a gilded wooden sledge. The sealed cords which originally held the lid in position may be clearly seen.

(Right) Removal of the chest lid revealed four finely modelled calcite heads (nos. 266 c-f), their facial and other features picked out in black, facing one another in pairs.

> ' . . . had one of those babes lived there might never have been a Rameses. '

Howard Carter

Among the shrines and chests piled up in the Treasury was an undecorated wooden box (no. 317), some 61cm (just over 2ft) long, the lid of which, originally tied in position and sealed with the jackal and nine captives motif (type I: p. 94), had been removed in antiquity. Within were two miniature anthropoid coffins, 49.5cm (19½in) and 57.7cm (22$\frac{7}{10}$in) long, placed side by side, head to foot.

The toes of the larger coffin (no. 317b) had been roughly hacked away in order to allow the lid of the box to close. The outer surfaces of the coffins had been painted with the usual black resin, relieved by gilded bands of inscription referring to each occupant simply as 'the Osiris', with no name specified. The lids were attached to the coffin bases in the usual way, by means of eight flat wooden tenons. Bands of linen had been tied around the coffins beneath the chin and around the waist and ankles, and applied to each of the bands was a clay seal, again impressed with the jackal and nine captives motif (type I).

When these linen bands had been detached and the lids pulled away, the coffins were each found to contain a second coffin (nos. 317a(1), 317b(1)), differing from the first in having the entire surface covered with gold foil. Within these second coffins were two tiny mummified foetuses.

The first mummy (no. 317a(2)) measured less than 30cm (1ft) in height. It was preserved in almost perfect condition, with large sheet swathings held in place with five transverse and two triple longitudinal bands down the front, back and sides. Upon the head had been placed a well-modelled mask of gilded cartonnage, with the facial details picked out with dabs of black paint. Though the mask was quite small, similar in size to the masks sometimes employed for packets of canopic contents, it was nevertheless far too large for the foetus.

The second mummy (no. 317b(2)), in outward appearance less well preserved than the first, was somewhat larger (39.5cm (1ft 3½in) overall) though wrapped in a similar fashion with a triple longitudinal band over the front, back and sides and four transverse bandages. It wore no mask, although one had evidently been prepared for it: when the embalmers found that it was too small to fit over the head of the wrapped bundle, this mask had been consigned to the embalming debris stored in the entrance corridor, later reburied in Pit 54 where it was brought to light by Davis in 1907 (see p. 38).

The autopsies

The examination of the mummies was entrusted to Douglas Derry in 1932. The bandages of the first mummy had been removed by Carter, and Derry

Pharaoh's Children

was able to record little more than a badly ordered mass of linen some 1.5cm (⅝in) in thickness, with pads placed over the chest, legs and feet to give the bundle its form. Beneath he found the body of a prematurely born child with grey, brittle skin through which the arrangement of the bones could clearly be discerned. Neither eyebrows nor eyelashes were in evidence, and the eyelids were nearly closed. There was no abdominal incision, and it was not apparent how the body had been preserved. The limbs were fully extended, with the hands arranged flat to the thighs. According to Derry, the foetus (which preserved a portion of its umbilical cord, still in a low position) was probably female. It measured a mere 25.75cm (about 10in) from head to toe, and in the anatomist's view could have been of no more than five months' gestation.

The gilded cartonnage mask discovered by Theodore Davis in Pit 54, originally intended for the elder foetus (no. 317b(2)).

The second mummy Derry unwrapped himself. Beneath the linen shroud, held in place by the transverse and longitudinal wrappings, he found a further series of transverse bandages which in turn revealed a second shroud. Beneath this shroud, which covered the whole of the front of the body, was a layer of transverse and criss-cross bandaging and a series of pads which had been inserted for stiffening and shape. The sides, legs and chest of the mummy were built out with further pads, again held in place by transverse bandaging. The removal of several large, transversely wound and somewhat charred covering sheets revealed a final layer of delicate linen. Beneath this covering lay the body of a child, 36.1cm (about 1ft 2¼in) in length and again probably female, the age of which Derry put at about seven months' gestation.

Rather less well preserved than the first, this child's limbs were fully extended though with the hands placed beside rather than upon the thighs. The skin was again a uniform grey colour, with remains of downy hair upon the scalp. Eyebrows and eyelashes were visible, the eyes open and still containing the shrunken eyeballs. Unlike the first mummy, the method of embalming was easily determined. The skull had been packed with salt-soaked linen inserted through the nose, and Derry noted a tiny embalmer's incision, little more than 1.8cm ($\frac{7}{10}$in) in length, immediately above and parallel to the inguinal ligament (i.e. the groin). This cut, through which further salt-soaked linen had been introduced into the abdominal cavity, had been sealed with what Derry took to be resin, but which Lucas identified as altered animal tissue. The child had probably died at or shortly after birth: the umbilical cord, which appears to have been cut off close to the abdominal wall, had not dried up as it would have done had she survived for any length of time after birth.

When this second foetus was re-examined more recently by a team led by the late Professor R.G. Harrison of the University of Liverpool, radiography revealed evidence to suggest that the child had a condition known as Sprengel's deformity, with congenitally high right scapula, spina bifida and scoliosis. The age suggested by this X-ray examination was eight or nine months' gestation.

Whose were these children? Although more involved, 'ritualistic' hypotheses have been proposed, the most likely answer is, Tutankhamun's own, and presumably by Ankhesenamun since he is not known to have had any other wife. Several 18th dynasty parallels may be cited of royal children, predeceasing their father, being buried in the king's tomb: Webensenu, a son of Amenophis II, buried in Valley Tomb 35; and Tentamun, Amenemhat and another, unidentified offspring in the tomb of Tuthmosis IV (No. 43).

(Opposite) The outer and inner wooden coffins, bandaged mummies and unwrapped corpses of Tutankhamun's two baby daughters (nos. 317a-b).

(Below left) X-ray of the second foetus (no. 317b (2)), now in the Department of Anatomy of the University of Cairo. The abnormally high left scapula and accentuated curvature of the left clavicle may be clearly seen.

(Below right) The painted wooden box (no. 317) containing the two coffined foetuses, as found stacked in the northeast corner of the Treasury.

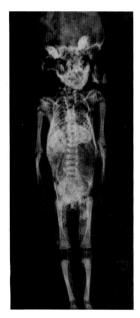

Despite the richness of previous finds and the evidence of the tomb-robbery papyri, the opulence and sheer quantity of the funerary furniture buried with Tutankhamun were difficult for the excavators and the world at large to take in. The broken scraps recovered from the robbed and dismantled burials of other 18th dynasty royals were a poor preparation for the riches Tutankhamun had in store.

Tutankhamun, in life the embodiment of Horus, was in death identified with Osiris, lord of the hereafter, the various aspects of whose presence pervade the tomb. He was, at the same time, 'son of Re', the sun-god, with whom he travelled in his barque through the sky from dawn until dusk, continuing his circuit through the 12 hours of the night – the underworld – to be reborn again each morning. The dangers of this journey were manifold; and here, in his tomb, smothered in gold leaf and inlay-work of semi-precious stones and coloured glass, were the ritual figures and amulets upon which Pharaoh could depend for his future well-being.

But the king was also a man, whose needs after death would mirror those of his lifetime. And so we find the tomb stocked with ample supplies of clothing and shoes, regalia and jewellery, perfumes and cosmetics; a treasured lock of hair from the head of his grandmother, Queen Tiye; the beds, headrests, chests, chairs and stools upon which Pharaoh could take his ease; writing equipment and game-boards; chariots, weaponry and hunting paraphernalia, and sticks, staves and fans; lamps and vessels of pottery, stone and metal; jars and baskets containing wines and provisions.

The tomb, in short, was a microcosm of the hopes, beliefs and aspirations of an Egyptian king more than 3,000 years ago. By the discovery of his burial, Carnarvon and Carter had caused the name of Tutankhamun to live once again; here, among his treasures, was material to flesh out the boy's skeleton, to breathe air into his shrivelled lungs, and establish personality, taste and affections.

The lion-goddess from the first of the gilded ritual couches (no. 35).

V   Treasures of the Tomb

The Guardian Statues

When he shone his torch through into the Antechamber, among the first things which caught Carter's eye, their gilded details reflecting in the light, were two large, blackened portrait statues of the king, their ancient linen shawls still hanging in tatters from their shoulders. Standing opposite one another, upon papyrus mats, in characteristic pose left leg forward, holding a staff in the left hand and mace in the right – these two figures guarded the entrance to the Burial Chamber. Slightly off-set on their pedestals, 1.9m (*c.* 6ft 3in) high overall, the statues focused their penetrating gaze on anyone who threatened to enter.

Carved from wood, jointed, and with any unevenness made up with plaster, the flesh parts of the statues had been painted directly on to the wood with a shiny black resin, the headcloths, broad collars, kilts and other details overlaid with gold on a base of linen and gesso. The forepart of a gilded bronze uraeus had been attached to each statue's brow, and the eyes (showing double caruncles) inlaid with indurated limestone and obsidian set in frames of gilded bronze. Although closely similar, the figures are not a matching pair: the most notable difference is the headgear, the statue on the west of the doorway wearing the *khat* (no. 29), that on the east the *nemes* (no. 22).

(Left) The life-sized guardian statue (no. 29) positioned to the west of the Burial Chamber blocking.

(Right) Arthur Mace and Alfred Lucas at work conserving the second guardian figure (no. 22).

The front of the triangular kilt of each figure is
inscribed with the names and titles of Tutankhamun; the figure wearing the *khat* headdress carries
the additional information that it represents the
royal *ka*, or spiritual double of the king.

Fragments of other life-sized figures have been
recovered from several royal tombs of the New
Kingdom. Three of the best preserved are in the
British Museum (EA 854, 882, 883), and in one of
these (EA 882) the kilt has been hollowed out from
beneath to a depth of 20cm (7⅞in), probably to
receive a papyrus roll. Both of Tutankhamun's
guardian statues show evidence of a similar feature,
with the hollow stopped up by means of an irregular
piece of stone plastered in position, and gilded over –
precisely the way in which the 'magic bricks' of the
Burial Chamber were sealed in place (p. 85). These
statues represent less the guardians of the Burial
Chamber, perhaps, than the guardians of Tutankhamun's final secret: the hiding place of his missing
religious texts (p. 167).

*The uneven undersurface of
each of the guardian figures
is suggestive of a limestone
flake plastered in position
over an aperture – seen at
one stage as the hiding-place
for Tutankhamun's 'missing'
papyri. Sadly, recent X-ray
examination of the statues
has shown each to be solid,
with no indication of the
postulated hollow.
Tutankhamun's papyrus
rolls, if they ever existed,
remain to be found.*

*Detail of the second guardian
figure (no. 22). The flesh
parts are painted directly
onto the wood with a thick,
black resin, the* nemes-
*headdress, broad collar and
pectoral, armbands and kilt
richly gilded on a base of
gesso. The uraeus is of gilded
bronze, as are the eyebrows
and the frames of the
limestone- and obsidian-inlaid
eyes.*

Ritual Figures
and Magical Objects

‘ We will now turn to those sinister black chests and boxes that were stacked along the whole of the south side of the room. . . . ’

Howard Carter

The collection of hardwood figures buried with Tutankhamun (35 in total) was divided between the Antechamber, the Burial Chamber and the Treasury. The figures are of two principal types: images of the king himself; and that class of figure belonging to what, in the Turin plan of the tomb of Ramesses IV, is referred to as 'the divine ennead which is in the netherworld', positioned close to the sarcophagus. Painted representations of such ritual figures are found on the walls of the tomb of Sethos II (No. 15), while further, usually fragmented, examples have been recovered from a number of kingly burials, including those of Amenophis II, Tuthmosis IV, Horemheb, Ramesses I, and Sethos I. One figure, from the tomb of Amenophis II, had been hollowed out in order to contain a rolled funerary papyrus (Cairo CG 24619 and 24742). Unlike Tutankhamun's divine images, the majority of which are gessoed and fully gilded, the fragmentary

material recovered from elsewhere in the Valley generally painted with a thick, black resin varnis From the ritualistic point of view, the efficacy w have been the same, black and gold being equall associated with regeneration and rebirth; but th overall effect of the varnished figures is far le striking.

The greater number of Tutankhamun's ritu figures was recovered from the Treasury, whe they had been crammed into 22 double-doore shrines of resin-coated wood, 90.5cm (2ft 11½in) hig 27cm (10⅞in) deep, and 26.5cm (10¹¹⁄₁₆in) wid mounted on sleds and with sloping roofs; thre figures (nos. 283a–c) had been placed within docketed, flat-topped box 67.5cm (2ft 2½in) hig 51cm (1ft 8in) deep and 62cm (2ft ⅟₁₆in) wide. Tw further shrines were located in the Antechamber o the tomb, and a resin-coated goose-figure was foun in the Burial Chamber. The doors of only one of th Treasury shrines (no. 289) had been opened by th tomb robbers; the seals of the remainder ha survived untouched since the day of the funeral. Th seal impressions were predominantly of the jacka and nine captives type (in two versions, Carter's and L); one shrine (no. 304) was sealed with th Golden falcon motif (type Q) formerly read as th nomen of Horemheb (p. 94), while the seal impres sion affixed to another (no. 283) was of Carter's typ N, which, as well as appearing elsewhere in Tutankh amun's burial, had earlier been found among th floor debris of Tomb 55 (p. 20).

According to Carter, the figures themselves ha each been wrapped in a linen shawl which left onl the face revealed; some figures wore wreaths o

(Below left) One of the shrines (no. 275) from the Treasury, in the process of being unpacked by the excavators. The linen shawls worn by the ritual figures when found may be clearly seen.

(Below right) The 'odd' striding image of Tutankhamun wearing the white crown (no. 296b).

sprouting barley grains, or garlands made up from olive, willow and pomegranate leaves and blue cornflowers sewn on to a strip of papyrus pith. The eyes of all but Qebhsenuef and the Duamutef from shrine no. 304, 55 and 58cm (1ft 9¾in and 1ft 10¾in) high respectively, which are simply painted in black, are framed in bronze and inlaid with glass or semi-precious stone. The fittings, including the objects they carry and their sandals, are of gilded copper-alloy. The bases of the majority are inscribed in yellow with the king's prenomen, Nebkheprure, beloved of' the appropriate deity.

The same carelessness evident elsewhere in the tomb may be discerned among the figures. The base of the Sakhmet statuette (no. 300a), 55.2cm (1ft 9¾in) high, for example, has been roughly sawn off to allow it to fit into its shrine. Moreover, the collection – which may be incomplete (a striding figure of the king appears to be lacking) – is something of an *ad hoc* assemblage. One figure (no. 289b), 85.6cm (2ft 9¾in) high, which shows Pharaoh standing upon the back of a leopard, differs in a number of important respects from its 'pair' (no. 289a) of similar height: Amarna influence notwithstanding, the figure's prominent breasts and low hips would seem to indicate that it had originally been made for a woman. According to Carter, all the figures were wrapped in linen shawls carrying dockets dating from as early as Year 3 of Akhenaten; the texts of only three of these dockets are recorded (nos. 281a, 291a, 300a). If the linen marks date the figures, these had evidently been prepared for Akhenaten's projected Theban tomb (perhaps No. 25 in the West Valley), abandoned at the time of his break with the

Ritual figures – Conspectus

Type of figure	Number found	Where found	Seal type on shrine	Object number
King				
— striding	3	Treasury	K	275b, 275d,
			L	296b
— harpooning	2	Treasury	K	275c, 275e
— on leopard	2	Treasury	K	289a, 289b
Deities				
— Atum	1	Treasury	L	290a
— Duamutef	2	Treasury	L	302a,
			Q	304b
— Geb	1	Treasury	L	299a
— Gemehsu falcon	1	Treasury	N	283c
— goose	1	Burial Chamber	—	176
— Happy	1	Treasury	L	301a
— Haroeris	1	Treasury	L	293a
— Horus of Letopolis	1	Treasury	L	298a
— Ihy	2	Treasury	K	275a,
			K	289c
— Imsety	1	Treasury	L	280a
— Isis	1	Treasury	L	295a
— Kheperiu	1	Treasury	L	297a
— Mamu	1	Treasury	L	281a
— Menkeret	1	Treasury	L	296a
— Nephthys	1	Treasury	L	305a
— Netjerankh serpent	1	Treasury	N	283a
— Ptah	1	Treasury	L	291a
— Qebhsenuef	1	Treasury	Q	304a
— Sakhmet	1	Treasury	L	300a
— Sendet	1	Treasury	L	294a
— serpent standard	2	Antechamber	L?	37a,
			L	38b
— Shu	1	Treasury	L	282a
— Sopdu	1	Treasury	N	283b
— Tata	1	Treasury	L	303a
— Tatenen	1	Treasury	L	292a

(Left) *Pharaoh standing upon a leopard (no. 289b), one of two such figures found, each designed to a different scheme of proportions.*

(Centre) *Menkeret carrying the mummified king (no. 296a).*

(Below) *The serpent Netjerankh (no. 283a).*

old religion, and pulled out of storage and reinscribed for the burial of his son.

Carter recorded his own impressions of the tomb's
ritual figures. Of those of Tutankhamun:

'The statuettes of the king show the influence of the El
Amarna school. In the modelling of these particular
figures, even though they be of repeated traditional type,
there is a direct and spontaneous feeling for nature. The
feeling here exhibited is beyond the formalized
conventions learnt by rote; they show both energy and

*(Above) Detail of the gilded
wooden Menkeret figure (no.
296a).*

*(Left) Tutankhamun as
Horus, one of two similar
images from shrine no. 275.
The king's arm is raised to
spear the hippopotamus of
Seth – which, for magical
reasons, is excluded from the
composition.*

grace, in fact, the divine and the human have been brought in familiar touch with one another.'

Of the figures of the gods, Carter wrote:

'These comparatively inartistic figures of strange gods are valuable to us as a record of myths and beliefs, ritual and custom, associated with the dead. That they were supposed to be potent for good or evil, or have some form of magic inherent in them, is evident, although their exact meaning in this burial is not clear to us.'

The Anubis Shrine

The main focus of attention in the Treasury was a large sled-based pylon of gilded wood with long (273.5cm (8ft 11⅜in)) carrying poles, upon the top of which lay a life-sized image of the black Anubis dog, guardian of the Burial Chamber and of the king's canopic equipment (no. 261). Around the dog's shoulders when found was wrapped a delicate linen shawl, 'while fastened around his neck was a long leash-like linen scarf . . . adorned with a double fillet of blue lotus and cornflowers woven upon strips of pith, twisted into a bow at the back of the neck' (nos. 261b–d). Over the whole thing had been wrapped a linen shirt (no. 261a) inscribed in ink with a docket dated to Akhenaten's seventh regnal year.

Carved from wood and with a covering of black resin, picked out around the ears and the collar in gold leaf, the Anubis dog has inlaid eyes of calcite and obsidian set into gold surrounds, and nails of solid silver. The cavetto-corniced shrine upon which the 95 by 37cm (3ft 2⅛in by 1ft 2⅝in) and 54.3cm (1ft 9⅜in) high dog lies is made of gessoed and gilded wood, its long sides decorated with two rows of double *djed*- and *tyet*-symbols, a palace-façade dado and one horizontal and two vertical bands of text. Its inner compartments, four small and one large, contained a curious array of materials which, in Carter's view, 'seem to signify the perpetuation of, or belong to, the ritual of mummification'. These

(Left) Ptah, god of Memphis, divine patron of artists and craftsmen: a figure (no. 291a) of gilded wood with blue faience cap and gilded bronze scepter.

(Below) Large carrying-shrine of gilded wood (no. 261), surmounted by the elegant Anubis dog, guardian of the Treasury and the king's canopic equipment.

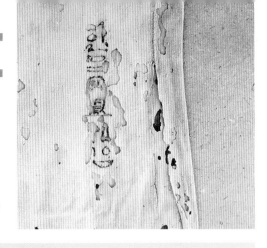

(Right) Ink docket from the linen shirt (no. 261a) found wrapped around the shoulders of the Anubis dog, dated 'Year 7 of the lord of the two lands, Nefer-[kheprure-waenre], who gives life every day.'

(Below right) The gilded cow head (no. 264), after cleaning and conservation.

included four bovine forelegs of blue faience, two small mummiform figures of wood, blue faience figures of Thoth and a falcon-headed god (perhaps Re-Horakhty), a papyrus sceptre of blue faience, resin, and a calcite dish containing a mix of resin, sodium chloride, sodium sulphate and natron (sodium carbonate). A further compartment contained eight large pectoral ornaments (p. 150), originally wrapped in linen and sealed, which 'possibly comprise the god's jewellery, or perhaps . . . were worn by the eight priests who carried him in procession to the tomb'. Between the dog's paws had been placed an ivory palette inscribed for Meritaten, Tutankhamun's half-sister (p. 24).

Gilded Cow Head

The splendid cow head (no. 264), 91.6cm (3ft) high overall, of gessoed wood, partially gilded and partially covered with a black resin varnish (perhaps obliterating a decorated base), represents Hathor, goddess of the west. The inlaid eyes, which are probably of glass or indurated limestone with obsidian (?) pupils, are set in surrounds of blue-black glass, and the long, elegant horns are of wood covered with thin copper sheeting. Positioned between the Anubis shrine and the canopic shrine on the floor of the Treasury, facing towards the west, the neck and the base were wrapped in linen so that only the gilded portions of the head proper were exposed to view.

Figures of Tutankhamun

Object number	Figure of king	Crown	Inscription	Other
275b	striding	red	yes	curved staff, flail
275d	striding	red	yes	straight staff, flail
296b	striding	white	yes	curved staff, flail
275c	harpooning	red	no	
275e	harpooning	red	no	
289a	on leopard	white	yes	straight staff, flail
289b	on leopard	white	yes	straight staff, flail

Figures of gods

Object number	God	Type	Inscription	Other
290a	Atum	mummiform	yes	
302a	Duamutef	dog-headed	yes	
304b	Duamutef	dog-headed	no	
299a	Geb	mummiform	yes	
283c	Gemehsu	falcon	yes	on standard
176		goose	yes	
301a	Hapy	mummiform	yes	
293a	Haroeris	falcon-headed	yes	
298a	Horus of Letopolis	falcon-headed	yes	
275a	Ihy	youth holding sistrum	no	
289c	Ihy	youth holding sistrum	no	
280a	Imsety	mummiform	yes	
295a	Isis	mummiform	yes	
297a	Kheperiu	mummiform	yes	
281a	Mamu	mummiform	yes	
296a	Menkeret	mummiform king on head	yes	king with red crown
305a	Nephthys	mummiform	yes	
283a	Netjerankh	serpent	yes	
291a	Ptah	mummiform	yes	
304a	Qebhsenuef	falcon-headed	no	
300a	Sakhmet	lioness-headed, on throne	yes	
294a	Sendet	mummiform	yes	
37a		serpent	yes	on standard
38b		serpent	yes	on standard
282a	Shu	mummiform	yes	triple plumes
283b	Sopdu	falcon	yes	on standard
303a	Tata	mummiform	yes	white crown
292a	Tatenen	mummiform	yes	

Magical Objects

... a system of defense against human imaginations.
Howard Carter

The tomb of Tutankhamun included a whole range of what may, for the sake of convenience, be classified as 'magical objects'. Their form is frequently as obscure as their significance. A selection is listed here.

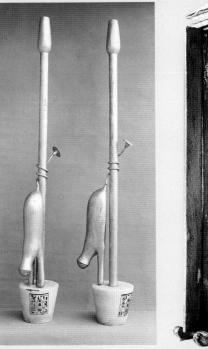

(Far left) From the Burial Chamber: a black-varnished ritual object (no. 181) in the form of a varnished hes-vase between two pylons.

(Centre left) The two 'Anubis fetishes' (nos. 194 and 202), from the northwest and southwest corners of the Burial Chamber.

(Left) Narrow wooden shrine (no. 487), found empty in the Annexe. Carter believed that it had originally contained a metal cubit-rod, carried off by the tomb robbers.

(Below left) Wooden frame in the shape of Osiris (no. 288a), from the Treasury. Filled with silt from the Nile, such 'Osiris beds' were planted with corn seed which would germinate in the tomb to symbolize the resurrection of both god and deceased.

Object number	Description	Findspot	Dimensions (centimetres)
181	varnished wooden *hes*-vase between twin pylons	Burial Chamber	ht. 44.5
182–92	wooden oars	Burial Chamber	l. 76–83
193	*pesesh-kaf* emblem between twin varnished shrines containing resin and natron	Burial Chamber	ht. 36
194	Anubis fetish	Burial Chamber	ht. 167
196	model *res*-hieroglyph	Burial Chamber	l. 111
198a	clay troughs for nos. 196, 199–201	Burial Chamber	l. 7.5
199–201	model *res*-hieroglyphs	Burial Chamber	l. 111
202	Anubis fetish	Burial Chamber	ht. 167
212	palm rib	Burial Chamber	l. 155.5
215	palm rib	Burial Chamber	l. 159.5
250	*djed* pillar	Burial Chamber	ht. 56
257	'magic brick' with Osiris figure	Burial Chamber (east wall)	ht. 20.5
258	'magic brick' with Anubis figure	Burial Chamber (west wall)	ht. 14.5
259	'magic brick' with *shabti*-like figure	Burial Chamber (north wall)	ht. 15.1
260	'magic brick' with *djed*-pillar	Burial Chamber (south wall)	ht. 10.6
261e (2–3)	faience forelegs	Treasury	l. 12
261f (1)	wooden *shabti*-like figure	Treasury	ht. 10.5
261f (2–3)	faience forelegs	Treasury	l. 12
261f (4) + 261f (7)	faience Horus figure	Treasury	ht. 12.1
261f (5)	wooden *shabti*-like figure	Treasury	ht. 11
261f (6)	faience papyrus sceptre	Treasury	l. 8.5
261g (2)	faience Thoth figure	Treasury	ht. 8
263	'magic brick' with reed torch	Treasury	ht. 13.2
288a	Osiris bed	Treasury	l. 190
367q–r	33 faience forelegs	Annexe	l. 12.3
487	attenuated wooden shrine	Annexe	ht. 65

The Shabtis

Shabti figures were a common feature of most la[rge?]
Egyptian burials, first appearing singly in tombs [of?]
the late Middle Kingdom as substitutes for [the?]
deceased. By the 18th dynasty, the *shabti* h[ad?]
become the dead man's deputy, charged w[ith?]
working on his behalf in the next world on a[ll?]
menial agricultural tasks that needed to be carri[ed?]
out as part of the national corvée. This new role w[as?]
reflected in the implements with which, from [the?]
mid-18th dynasty on, such figures are common[ly?]
represented or provided – a pick, a hoe, and one [or?]
more baskets. The extract from spell 6 of the Book [of?]
the Dead, which often appears painted or incised [on?]
the figure in a more or less abbreviated form, refle[cts?]
the *shabti*'s new function:

'O *shabti* allotted to me [i.e. the owner]! If I be summon[ed?]
or if I be detailed to do any work which has to be don[e?]
in the realm of the dead, . . . you shall detail yourself f[or?]
me on every occasion of making arable the fields, of
flooding the banks, or of conveying sand from east to [the?]
west: "Here am I", you shall say.'

The typical private burial of Tutankhamun's d[ay?]
was provided with one or perhaps two *shabti* figur[es?]
With the boy-king were buried a staggering 413 –
total which has been broken down as: 365 workm[en?]
(one for each day of the year); 36 overseers (one f[or?]
each 10-day week); and a supplementary series of [12?]
monthly overseers. Of the total number of figur[es?]
found, only 29 were inscribed with a more or less f[ull?]
version of the *shabti* formula; the remaining 3[84?]
carried little more than the king's name and title[s.]

Only one *shabti* came from the Antechamb[er,]
compared with 176 found in the Treasury and [a?]
further 236 specimens in the Annexe (of which t[he?]

(Opposite and above, left to right) 'In the finer specimens, by their own symbolism is expressed the perfect serenity of death'. Details of large and finely carved shabti-figures (nos. 110, 330a, 330c, 318a, 330j).

(Below) Tutankhamun recumbent upon a lion-bier (no. 331a), in its black-varnished wooden box-coffin. The figure had been furnished with a set of copper agricultural implements, and was evidently related to the king's shabtis. Each of the two long sides of the image carries an incised band of text recording that it had been presented to the king's burial by the high official Maya.

(Above and right) Three large wooden shabti-figures (nos. 318b, 325b, 458), and (right above) three of the resin-coated wooden 'kiosks' (nos. 318, 322, 325) in which the shabtis were found. As with other elements of the funerary equipment, there are indications that not all of the shabtis buried in the tomb had originally been made for the king. The facial features of the third specimen (no. 458), wearing the nemes-headcloth, are quite different from those of the boy-king; more significantly, the hips are positioned low, and suggest that the figure had originally been made to represent a woman.

(Bottom row) Selection of the king's less elaborate shabtis in faience, limestone and quartzite, (nos. 324j, 323l, 327b, 330n, 322e, 605a, 605b).

Antechamber specimen was a stray). The materials employed were of several sorts: wood (carved, painted and/or gesso-gilt); quartzite; calcite; limestone (white, yellow, and the indurated variety); black granite; and a range of coloured faience. The largest, of wood, measured over 0.5m (1ft 7in) in height. Quality ranged from the spectacular to plain run-of-the-mill. The iconography of the figures varies enormously. Eight different types of headdress are represented (see table), with and without uraeus and/or vulture, the most frequently occurring type being that wearing the 'archaic' or tripartite wig, of which some 286 specimens were noted. The least frequent was the double crown, of which only one example was recovered. Carter noted eight variations in the objects held in each figure's hands, variously combined with headdress types and materials as shown in the table. The *reis* or overseer *shabtis* were identified by Carter as those shown holding 'the ribbon and flagellum'.

The *shabti* figures had been housed originally in 24 boxes, 10 recovered from the northeast corner of the Treasury and 14 from the Annexe. Twenty-three of these were resin-painted, sloping-roofed 'kiosks' resting on sledges (no. 318, for example, measuring

Tutankhamun's Shabtis – Headdress Types and Distribution

Headdress	Antechamber	Treasury	Annexe	Total
nemes	1	10	16	27
blue crown	—	1	1	2
white crown	—	1	1	2
red crown	—	4	—	4
double crown	—	1	—	1
khat	—	16	40	56
Nubian wig	—	18	17	35
tripartite wig	—	125	161	286
Total	1	176	236	413

Tutankhamun's Shabtis – Headdress and Hand Types

Head-ress ype	Hands holding:							
	crook & flail	two flails	djed, flail & bandage	ankh & flail	two ankhs	flail & bandage	hoes & baskets	empty
Quantity ound	Ant. 1 Tr. 39 Ann. 32	Tr. 1 Ann. 1	Ann. 1	Tr. 6 Ann. 4	Tr. 23 Ann. 21	Tr. 9 Ann. 36	Tr. 33 Ann. 46	Tr. 66 Ann. 95
emes	w(c), q, l, w(gg)	c	—	—	—	—	—	l(i), q
lue rown	w(c)	—	—	—	—	—	—	l(y)
white rown	w(gg)	—	—	—	—	—	—	l(y)
ed rown	w(gg)	—	—	—	—	—	—	—
ouble rown	w(gg)	—	—	—	—	—	—	—
hat	w(c)	—	—	c	c	c, w(gg), f(v), f(b), f(t), w(pg)	—	q, c
Nubian vig	w(c), w(gg)	w(pg)	w(pg)	c	c	w(gg), f(v), c, w(pg)	—	w(gg)
ripartite vig	q, g, l	—	—	—	w(p), w(gg), f(t), f(b), w(lpg)	—	w(p), w(lpg), w(gg)	w(p), f(b), f(v), f(t), f(w), l(y), l(i), w(gg), g(bk)

Key:
w = wood (c, carved; gg, gessoed and gilded; lpg, linen and painted gesso; p, painted; pg, painted and gilded;
f = faience (b, blue; t, turquoise; v, violet; w, white)   l = limestone (i, indurated; y, yellow)
c = calcite   q = quartzite   g = granite (bk, black)

(Below) Drawing by Carter of one of the faience model implements (group no. 459h) included in the tomb for the use of Tutankhamun's shabti-figures.

25cm (9⅞in) wide, 21.5cm (8½in) deep, and 61.5cm (2ft ½in) high. One (no. 330, from the Treasury) was a lime-washed rectangular box, 70.5 by 50cm (2ft 3¾in by 1ft 7⅝in) and 46cm (1ft 6⅛in) high. Their lids had originally been tied down by means of a cord wrapped around the knobs protruding at top and side, and sealed with the simple jackal and nine captives motif (seal type L).

The most interesting of the king's *shabti* figures are six of the larger specimens, finely carved in wood, which, according to the short hieroglyphic inscriptions incised beneath the feet, had been presented to the king's burial by the high officials Nakhtmin (five – nos. 318a, 318c, 330i–k) and Maya (one – no. 318b) (p. 31).

Associated with the *shabtis* were 1,866 miniature agricultural implements – hoes, picks, yokes and baskets – made of copper, faience and wood. Of these model *shabti* tools, 793 were found in the Treasury; the greater proportion, 1,073, in the Annexe.

The Little Golden Shrine

(Right) The Little Golden Shrine (no. 108).

Details of the right and left sides: (below) Tutankhamun supported by Ankhesenamun, and a scene of fowling in the marshes from a papyrus skiff; (bottom) Tutankhamun pours liquid into the cupped hand of his queen, and a touching representation of Ankhesenamun fastening a collar around her husband's neck.

❛ These are charming scenes and full of the kindliness which it pleases us to consider modern. ❜

Howard Carter

This small shrine (no. 108), one of the most elegant objects from the tomb, appears in Burton's photographs of the Antechamber immediately behind the hippopotamus couch, a position to which it had perhaps been moved, to allow access to the Annexe, during Carnarvon and Carter's initial survey of the tomb in November 1922 (p. 55). Measuring some 50.5cm (1ft 7¾in) high, 26.5cm (10½in) wide and 32cm (1ft ½in) deep, its sloping roof identifies it as the *Per-wer*, the ancient shrine of the goddess Nekhbet of Elkab. Mounted on a silver-encased sledge, the silver-bolted, double-doored shrine is constructed of wood overlaid with thick gold foil (that on the inside left door panel having been removed since the time of the discovery) on a linen-covered plaster base.

(Above) The Weret-heqau amulet (no. 108c). (Below) The interior of the shrine, showing the statue plinth (no. 108a) and inlaid corslet.

140

Within the shrine was an ebony pedestal, 24.8cm (9¾in) high, with gilded, round-topped back-pillar, lightly incised with the royal titulary – on its outward-facing surface, the king's nomen; on its back surface, his prenomen. Two small, depressed sandal-prints on the top surface of the base indicate the original position of the statuette which must once have stood upon it; this, as Carter suggests, had probably been carried off by the robbers. All that was left within were fragments of a corslet, the major portion of which was recovered from box no. 54 (p. 193), and a large (14cm (5½in) high), gilded wooden pendant strung with beads of carnelian, felspar, glass and gold and carefully wrapped in linen. In this amulet, the serpent-goddess Weret-heqau, given great prominence in the shrine's framing texts, is shown suckling the king who stands before her.

The shrine is decorated on its roof with two columns of seven Nekhbet vultures. The inner and outer surfaces of its doors and the outer surfaces of its sides and back carry a series of 18 embossed and chased scenes of touching intimacy representing Ankhesenamun as the perfect wife and queen –

A detail of the shrine's vulture-decorated roof.

scenes in which some have recognized a sexual metaphor, or even an allusion to the coronation. Given the maternal role of Weret-heqau, 'Great-of-Magic', an epithet associated with several goddesses with whom the queen could on occasion be identified, the scenes more probably emphasize the vital role played by Ankhesenamun in the continued existence and sustenance of her husband in the hereafter.

Tutankhamun, hunting birds with a bow, is kept supplied with arrows by his queen, Ankhesenamun: a detail from the right-hand side of the Little Golden Shrine.

Wooden Funerary Models

(Below) The model boat (no. 336) in place against the west wall of the Treasury.

(Opposite, first and second from top) A primitive papyrus skiff, still in use on the upper Nile in the 1930s, and a model of the same type of craft from the tomb of Tutankhamun (no. 313).

(Opposite, third and fourth from top) Two of the king's fleet of 'lunar' (no. 312) and 'solar' (no. 311) model barques.

Boats

' Among these craft we find models to follow the voyage of the sun; canoes for hunting the hippopotamus and fowling in the Hereafter, symbolizing the mythical pastimes of Horus in the marshes; vessels for the holy pilgrimage to and from Abydos; and craft to render the deceased independent of the favours of the "*celestial ferrymen*" to reach the "*fields of the blessed*", that are surrounded by seething waters difficult to traverse. '

Howard Carter

Model boats seem to have been a standard feature of 18th-dynasty royal burials, and that of Tutankhamun, which had been equipped with 35 craft, ranging in length from less than 1m (*c.* 3ft) to over 2.5m (*c.*8ft), was no exception. Of these vessels, 18 were found in the Treasury: 16 placed upon the 2? chests positioned against the south wall, and tw(with rigging and sails in the southwest and north east corners, all with their bows turned to the wes1 two other boats were recovered from the north sid(of the room, overturned during the robbery. Seven teen additional boat models, unfortunately mucl damaged, were found thrown higgledy-piggledy into the Annexe.

The boat models fall into two distinct groups ritualistic barques, and practical, river-going craft The ceremonial craft from the tomb include tw('lunar barques', four 'solar barques', and two simpl(canoes of reed-float design (nos. 313, 464). Th(former (nos. 308 and 312), of very simple and graceful form, display inward-turning lotus prow and stern-posts; one of the vessels is fitted with tw(steering oars. The four solar barques (nos. 285–6 307, 311), with vertical, lotiform prows and charac teristic indented stern-posts, are each fitted with a gilded throne and a pair of steering paddles.

The river-going boats divide into craft with on(steering oar, and those with two. Twelve simpl(decorated examples of the latter type, with spoon shaped hull, cleft stern and single square sail (nos 375, 460, 462–3, 481, 491, 556, 581, 609–10, 612, 617)

all come from the Annexe and have been identified as ordinary fishing, cargo or transport boats; four further specimens, two with a single chequered cabin (nos. 334, 597) and two with cabin and forward kiosk (nos. 437 + 598, 513 + 572), may be seen as an elaborated form of the same type. The class of boats with double steering paddles is represented by seven barges without mast (nos. 273, 284, 287, 306, 309–10, 314) and one craft with mast and sail (no. 352); all have a central roofed cabin and a kiosk at either end, with protruding prow and stern posts.

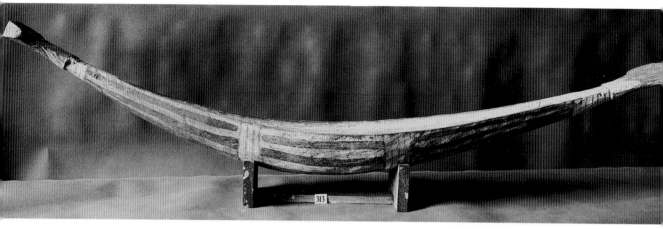

(Opposite above) Model
granary (no. 277) of white-
painted wood.

(Opposite below) The granar[y]
as found in the Treasury,
supporting a model sailing
boat (no. 276).

*(Above) Brightly painted
barge (no. 309), with
rectangular, stepped central
cabin, prow and stern kiosks
and two steering oars.*

*(Below) The masted boat of
Tutankhamun's viceroy: a
detail from the Theban tomb
of Huy, King's Son of Kush
(No. 40). The official's horses
may be seen in their stall in
front of the central cabin.*

The tomb's three large sailing boats (nos. 276, 321 and 336) were found in the Treasury, and are characterized by their flattened, papyriform sterns. Each has a stepped central cabin and mast, and two steering oars. The linen sails (madder dyed) and rigging of nos. 276 and 336 are preserved intact, and closely resemble the rigging of the Punt ships of Hatshepsut reproduced on the walls of the queen's mortuary temple at Deir el-Bahri.

The basic construction of each of these models is the same: the hull adzed from a single block of wood – or from a number of joined pieces of wood – (in a[t] least one instance, probably of acacia), which was then elaborated by the addition of fittings such as masts, gessoed, painted (often carelessly), and sometimes gilded. The smooth finish of the models reproduces well the surface of the carvel-built hull (i.e. with the planks of the hull laid edge to edge, rather than overlapping).

For details concerning the boat-shaped calcite 'centre-piece', see p. 199. For the 'ritualistic oars', see pp. 83, 85, 135.

The granary

One of the model sailing boats (no. 276) from the south end of the Treasury was supported upon a rectangular structure of white-painted wood (no. 277). This object was, in fact, the model of a granary, 74 by 65cm (2ft 5⅛in by 2ft 1⅝in), and 21.5cm (8½in) high,

'showing a doorway to an enclosure with entrance yard and sixteen separate compartments for cereals, which were found filled to the brim with grain and seeds. Large "*Shunas*" of this kind, built of sun-dried mud bricks, are the mode for storing cereals in Egypt to-day. Their external architectural details are precisely the same as this very model of thirty-three centuries ago.'

Models of this sort had been buried in Egyptian tombs since the First Intermediate Period and were intended to provide the deceased with an inexhaustible supply of sustenance for their new life in the hereafter.

The Ritual Couches

> ' The immense crowd surrounding the tomb on all side waited patiently under the remorseless rays of the sun for several hours ... shortly before noon, [Mr Carter] emerged from the tomb with his assistants bearing a grotesque elongated cow built on the lines of a dachshund. ...
>
> "What is it – calf, donkey, goat, deer, or rocking horse?" ejaculated the crowd.
>
> "It is an Egyptian cow, 3,350 years old", explained Mr. Carter, with a smile. "It has guarded King Tutankhamen throughout his 33 centuries' sleep." '

Yorkshire Pos

Despite the interest which the three ritual couche aroused, they were not in fact a new class of objec splintered fragments had been brought to light b Giovanni Belzoni and Theodore Davis in a numbe of wrecked tombs in the Valley (e.g. British Museur EA 61607), while painted representations of simila couches were depicted on the walls of the tomb c Sethos II (No. 15), which the Tutankhamun tear were employing as a laboratory. What singled ot

(Above) The head of Ammut, 'the devourer', of gilded wood with ivory teeth and a red-stained ivory tongue: a detail of the third ritual couch (no. 137). Ammut was a composite goddess of a sort popular with the Egyptians: part hippopotamus, part crocodile and part lioness.

(Right) The Ammut couch (no. 137), partially cleared, in position in the Antechamber. The breached entrance to the Annexe may be seen between the creature's legs.

ese couches for comment was their magnificent
ate of preservation and the gleam of their gold.

The couches had been positioned in the Ante-
hamber, arranged nose to tail, facing north, along
e west wall. All are constructed in the same way, in
ur parts – the couch proper, with footboard at the
il end and two supporting animal side-sections
lotting into a stout rectangular base-frame with
mitation mesh mattress – of gessoed and gilded red
ardwood, held together with hooks and staples and
ngle pieces of copper alloy.

The first couch (no. 35), with lion (or leopard)
ides and high, curling tails enclosing a footboard
rnamented with *djed*-pillars and *tyet*-knots, mea-
ires 1.8m by 0.91m (5ft 10⅞in by 2ft 11⅞in) and
.56m (5ft 1⅜in) high. The animal's features are
ighlighted to good effect with elaborate inlay work:
ose, eye frames and 'tear drops' of blue glass, and
yes of crystal, painted on the back for the detail to
how through. There are two construction marks in
lack on the right-hand animal, at the neck, and

remains of a third on the neck of the left; the couches
had clearly been brought into the tomb in sections to
be assembled, as they were disassembled, on site.
The rail connecting the two creatures is inscribed
with an extended cartouche containing the king's
prenomen preceded by the epithet 'the Osiris'
(indicating that this couch had been prepared for the
tomb), and a reference to the goddess Mehetweret,
'the great flood'. As others have pointed out, this
inscription is better suited to the cow-goddess of the
second couch than to the lioness supports present
here – while the text of the goddess Isismehtet of the
cow couch is more appropriate to this. There was
clearly some confusion at the time the component
parts of the two couches were inscribed.

(Above) The cow-goddess of the second gilded couch (no. 73), which is evidently to be recognized as an image of Mehetweret, 'the great flood'. The blotches of the cow-hide are represented by trefoils of opaque blue glass.

The second couch (no. 73), at 2.21m (7ft 2¾in), was longer than the first but somewhat less in height, measuring just under 1.5m (4ft 11in). It differed significantly from the lion couch only in its supporting animals, each of which here took the form of a cow, her body inlaid with trefoils of blue glass and the base of the tail picked out in red paint. The cosmetic lines and eyebrows are similarly of blue glass, as is the iris of the eye, with whites picked out with gypsum and red caruncles.

The third couch in line (no. 137), 2.37m (7ft 9¼in) long and (4ft 4¾in) 1.34m high, was that of the composite goddess Ammut, 'the devourer', ide[ntif]ied by the cartouched text at the head-end of [the] mattress frame. Hippopotamus-headed (her o[pen] mouth sporting a perfect set of ivory teeth and a r[ed]-stained ivory tongue), she is shown with a crocod[ile] tail and feline legs.

The Book of the Divine Cow, a version of whic[h is] inscribed upon the interior of the first (outermo[st]) shrine protecting the sarcophagus, suggests that [the] Mehetweret couch was a solar barque which wo[uld] speed the king from this world to heaven. The rit[ual] purpose of the other beds is still unclear.

(Below) The second ritual couch (no. 73), as re-erected in the Cairo Museum. The head would have been supported at the raised front-end, on a gilded wooden headrest, with the feet against the tail-end footboard.

Removal from the tomb

As Carter records, the dismantling of these couches was no easy task:

'. . . after three thousand years the bronze hooks had naturally set tight in the staples, and would not budge. We got them apart eventually, and with scarcely any damage, but it took no fewer than five of us to do it. Two supported the central part of the couch, two were responsible for the well-being of the animals, while a fifth, working from underneath, eased up the hooks, one after the other, with a lever.'

Nor was their removal any less stressful. The fragile sections were manoeuvred, with difficulty, up the corridor and into the daylight, where the excavators, 'sweating with the physical exertion and awesome responsibility of their task, were greeted with acclamations and a perfect tornado of camera clicks'.

For the three headrests of gilded wood (nos. 21c, 47–8) perhaps to be associated with these couches, see p. 183.

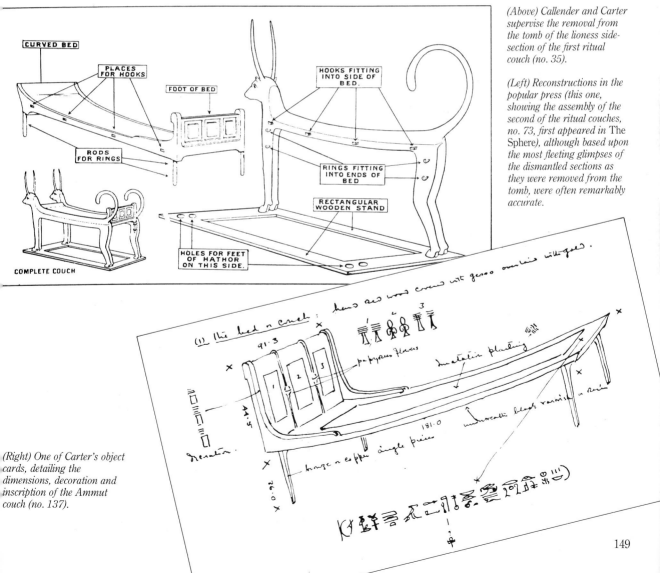

(Above) Callender and Carter supervise the removal from the tomb of the lioness side-section of the first ritual couch (no. 35).

(Left) Reconstructions in the popular press (this one, showing the assembly of the second of the ritual couches, no. 73, first appeared in The Sphere), although based upon the most fleeting glimpses of the dismantled sections as they were removed from the tomb, were often remarkably accurate.

(Right) One of Carter's object cards, detailing the dimensions, decoration and inscription of the Ammut couch (no. 137).

149

Jewellery, Amulets and Regalia

(Above) Drawings by Carter of a selection of faience rings recovered from the floor of the Annexe (no. 620:66 (part)).

(Right top) Solid gold pendant of a squatting king (no. 320c) – usually identified as Amenophis III, but more probably an image of Tutankhamun himself. A string of glass beads is tied around his neck, and the whole is suspended on a loop-in-loop chain of heavy gold.

(Right) Flexible scarab bracelet (no. 256qq) from the right arm of the king's mummy. The various elements of the design spell-out the king's prenomen, Nebkheprure.

' . . . in many ways these New Empire specimens do not exhibit the same perfection of finish as we find in the workmanship of their Middle Kingdom predecessors. There is shown, however, by the Theban jewellers, excellent skill in execution, a marked decorative sense, and much inventiveness in symbolical device. '

Howard Carter

Jewellery and amulets

Tutankhamun had been buried with many more jewels and amulets than those Carter found upon the king's mummy (p. 112), but, to judge from the ancient dockets detailing the contents of the jewellery boxes (p. 190), a good proportion of the more precious pieces had been carried off by the tomb robbers (p. 95); indeed, Carter estimated that perhaps as much as 60 per cent of the best 'loose' jewellery was missing. What was left – well over 200 items, including 20 pectoral ornaments of precious metal and five counterpoises – represented a substantial addition, nonetheless, to the range of pieces then known, both in terms of quantity and quality.

Major and minor items of jewellery were recovered from: the tomb entrance (obj. no. 1a); the corridor (including nos. 12a, c, d, f and k); the Antechamber (boxes, baskets, shrines and vessels 21, 25, 40, 43, 44, 46, 50, 54, 56, 63, 79, 92, 97, 101, 108, and individual obj. nos. 53a–b, 138, 147b, 153a); and

the Annexe (including box nos. 547, 585, 587, a individual obj. nos. 525, 619, 620:38–49, 620:66a– 620:94). The remains of one or more collars wi falcon terminals, the left of gold, the right electrum (no. 172), were found on the very thresho of the Burial Chamber, 'hanging on the jagged edg of the stones' behind the resealed robbers' hole. T largest number of pieces, however, came from t Treasury, where many of the king's valuables see originally to have been deposited; they were found the Anubis shrine (no. 261) and in two caskets (no 267 and 269) on the north side of the room; vario

(Left, centre, above and below) Earrings and ear-studs (top, no. 269a(5), flanked by no. 269a(3); bottom, no. 269a(2) flanked by no. 269a(6)) from Tutankhamun's youth. Made of inlaid and granulated gold-alloy, they were found in a small jewel box (no. 269a) in the Treasury. The design of no. 269a(3) incorporates a version of the king's prenomen.

(Left) Two lavish pectoral ornaments of gold from a jewel box (no. 267) in the Treasury, the outer face of each inlaid with coloured glass and semi-precious stones, the reverse with chased decoration. In the top specimen (no. 267a) the motif of the scarab pushing solar disc has been elaborated to form the king's prenomen, Nebkheprure. The bottom pendant (no. 267m(1)) takes the form of a falcon with outspread wings, clutching in its talons the shen- ('eternity') and ankh- ('life') hieroglyphs.

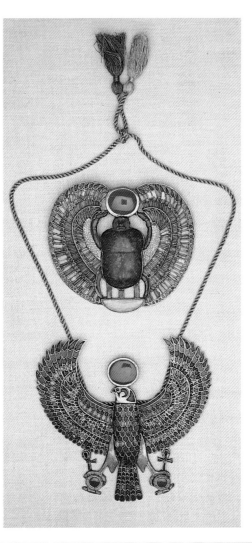

other items of jewellery were found in boxes 270, 271, and within the miniature coffin no. 320b.

Tutankhamun's jewels ranged in type from bead jewellery of the most elaborate sort, fashioned from precious metal and inlaid with semi-precious stones, to the plainest of stone hoop jewellery. The various classes represented included a large assortment of pectoral ornaments, pendants, collars, necklaces, ear-rings (discarded by the king at puberty), finger-rings, bracelets and armlets, and scarabs. The metals employed in fashioning these pieces included gold (employed pure, or deliberately alloyed to vary

Re-used pieces

As with many classes of the king's funerary equipment, much of the jewellery buried with Tutankhamun seems to have been produced under his predecessors.

Some objects, such as the faience bangles of Akhenaten and Nefernefruaten recovered from the floor of the Annexe (nos. 620:40–42), still carry the names of these kings; with a number of the precious jewels, the cartouches have been altered. In the pectoral ornament on the right, above (no. 261j), the hieroglyphs of Tutankhamun's prenomen, with the epithet 'image of Re', have been clumsily set into the oval of a cartouche originally intended to accommodate a much longer name; their orientation is reversed, though, as a pectoral of Ramesses II from the Serapeum at Saqqara suggests, this was perhaps intentional.

Incorrectly orientated hieroglyphs may be noted on a second pectoral from the same box (no. 261p(3)) (left), though the presence of the epithet 'the good ruler' could indicate that this was a piece originally prepared for Akhenaten, as another jewel, no. 261p(1), certainly was.

With the third pectoral (right, below) (no. 261i), the difference in technique between the inlaid names of the two goddesses, Isis and Nephthys, and the chased signs of the king's prenomen and nomen, suggest that this too is likely to be an appropriated piece.

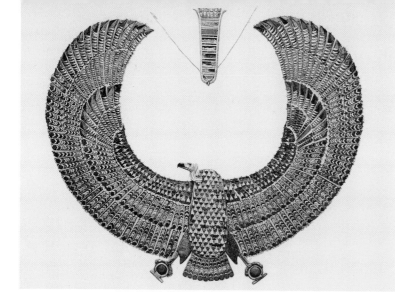

(Below) Detail of an ivory bracelet (no. 585q) from the Annexe, delicately carved with running animals (here a horse, a gazelle and a hare).

(Above) Nekhbet collar and counterpoise of gold (no. 256mmm), made up of 250 glass-inlaid sections.

(Right) Drilling and threading beads to produce a broad collar: from the tomb of Sobkhotep at Thebes (No. 63).

(Below and bottom right) A faience broad collar (no. 53a), as reconstructed (below) and as found, with a 'pad' of faience finger-rings (no. 53b).

the colour), electrum, silver, bronze, and iron. Stones chosen for the richness of their colours, included amethyst, calcite, carnelian, green felspar, lapis lazuli, quartz, serpentine, steatite and turquoise. Resin and shells were also used, as well as the artificial materials 'Egyptian blue' (calcium-copper silicate), Egyptian faience, and glass (both coloured and clear varieties). The various floral garlands from the coffins (p. 106) and the tomb's gilded figures (pp. 130–31) in the Treasury, might also be mentioned, as well as the broad collars recovered by Theodore Davis from Pit 54 which had originally been stored in the corridor of the Tutankhamun burial (p. 38). Decorative techniques ranged from basic threading for beads to the use of repoussé, chasing, granulation and tinting for the gold, and the extensive use of inlays. This latter technique is commonly termed 'cloisonné work', despite the fact that the inlays seem normally to have been introduced in a solid form and not fused within the cell.

As Carter remarked, the design of many of the jewels is remarkably vibrant and fresh, individual pieces showing much subtlety in their composition. The iconography would seem to indicate that many of the king's more elaborate jewels had been prepared solely for funerary use. However, evidence of wear noted on some pieces (such as the pectoral no. 256ppp, recovered from the mummy), taken in conjunction with the box dockets (p. 190), would indicate that other pieces of jewellery had actually been worn in life.

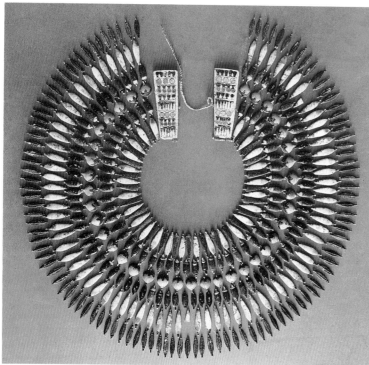

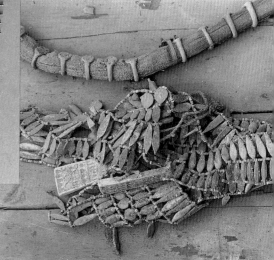

(Left) Four gold and gold-mounted jewellery elements from the Annexe: a heart amulet (no. 620:67); a 'tooth' amulet (no. 620:68); and two papyrus-sceptre amulets (nos. 620:72, 620:73).

(Right) The crook and flail (nos. 269h and 269e), concrete expressions of the divine kingship. The butt-cap of the crook is chased with the king's two cartouches, the nomen in its later, -amun form.

(Below) The flexible gold corslet, much of which was recovered from box no. 54 in the Antechamber, as first reconstructed by Carter and Mace.

Regalia

The most awe-inspiring of the jewels buried with Tutankhamun were the several and varied symbols of his mortal kingship. Of these, the most familiar are the Osirian crook (*heqa*) and flail (*nekhakha*). Three examples of the crook were recovered – (nos. 44u (33.5cm (13¼in) long), from the Antechamber, and 269d (43cm (16⅞in) long), and 269h (43.5cm (17⅛in) long) from the Treasury. Two flails, nos. 269e (43.5cm (17⅛in) long) and 269f (33.5cm (13¼in) long), both came from the Treasury. They are the only kingly examples of such regalia to have come down to us. The odd crook is uninscribed, the two smaller and larger sets of regalia from the Treasury inscribed upon their butt-caps for Tutankhaten and Tutankhamun respectively. The construction of each is similar: cylindrical sections of dark blue glass, obsidian and gold mounted upon a copper-alloy rod; the long, pendant beads of the flail are of gilded wood.

Another sceptre (no. 577), perhaps an *aba* (54cm (22¼in) long) was found in the Annexe. Fashioned from wood and overlaid with sheet gold, one face of this object is decorated in repoussé with five registers of offerings; the opposite side carries a vertical inscription in blue faience and gold: 'The good god, the beloved, one glittering of face like the Aten when he shines, son of Amun, Nebkheprure, living forever' – which, as Carter notes, 'is of interest, as it suggests a compromise between the Aten and Amen creeds'.

An object which should also be classed with the royal regalia is the king's elaborate 'corslet', the greater part of which was recovered from box no. 54 in the Antechamber, with other fragments scattered among the corridor fill (nos. 12a, 12c), the Antechamber floor, the little golden shrine (no. 108) and the boxes 101 and 115. The costume (40cm (15¾in) high; 85cm (33½in) wide overall) consists of a broad collar with pendant pectoral ornament (showing Tutankhamun before Amon-Re, Atum and his consort Iusaas behind) and counterpoise-clasp, and the corslet proper with its *rishi*-ornamentation and shoulder suspension straps. Fashioned from gold and richly inlaid with coloured glass and semi-precious stones, the corslet is incomplete, several

pieces having evidently been carried off at the time of the robberies. As now reconstructed, it differs slightly from the arrangement first suggested by Carter, Mace and Lucas, having its slide fasteners positioned on either side of the body (rather than down the centre), and on each shoulder.

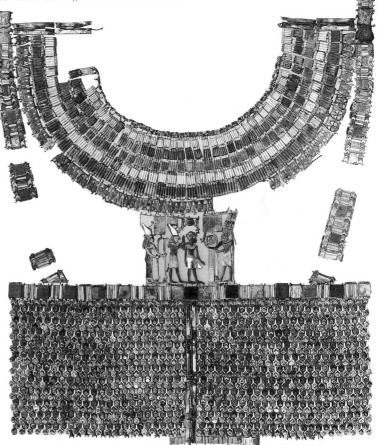

(Right) A detail of the royal diadem (no. 256: 4o), the circlet found in place on the head of the mummy, the detachable vulture-head and uraeus recovered from lower down on the body. The base material is gold, with inlays of glass and semi-precious stones.

The king's mummy, naturally enough, had been embellished with several familiar items of regalia, including the ritual tail, and the elegant diadem of gold and cloisonné work, with its pendant ribbons and uraei, which is of a type familiar from wall decorations and sculpture. Even more exciting, perhaps, was evidence of a decayed headdress of 'a fine cambric-like linen', of which, sadly, no more than the pigtail could be recovered. In Carter's view this was a unique example of the *khat* or bag-shaped wig-cover, with its gold temple band (256p). To its brow had been sewn the flexible uraeus-serpent of inlaid gold, with, to the back, a delicately chased sheet gold vulture, its outspread wings offering protection to the royal head.

Although these symbols of Pharaonic power evoked a considerable sense of awe among the excavating team, the absence of further items of regalia, particularly headgear, was keenly felt. Had a part of the crown jewels been taken by the robbers? Or had the principal emblems of Tutankhamun's earthly rule perhaps been retained by his successor to establish the legitimacy required to exercise his sway?

Cryptography

It was not uncommon, for ritual and other reasons, for the Egyptians to assign to particular hieroglyphs new and obscure values. The practice is particularly well illustrated in the tomb of Tutankhamun on the second shrine and on the king's jewels where various obscure or elaborated writings, especially of the king's prenomen, Nebkheprure ('Lordly-manifestation-of-Re'), are in evidence. Substitutions include the festival sign *heb* for *neb*, 'lord', and the lunar disc and crescent for the solar disc *re*; while the beetle-sign *kheper* plus three plural strokes (*khepru*, 'manifestation') is on occasion replaced by a squatting figure or 'manifestation' of the king. (See also p. 158.)

On the topmost element of one pectoral from the tomb of Tutankhamun (no. 267d) (below), and on a number of sealings of Amenophis III from Tomb 55 and elsewhere, the *neb* hieroglyph is replaced by a figure of the ibis-headed god Thoth – perhaps because of the basic similarity in shape between the *neb*-basket and the god's lunar crescent; the supporting figures on the Tutankhamun pectoral – a falcon-headed deity and a standing figure of the king – are evidently to be construed as cryptographic writings of *re* and *khepru* respectively.

Colour

Colour was always used with care in Egyptian composition, and it is generally significant. Our understanding of ancient usage, however, is complicated by the fact that the Egyptians appear not to have classified colours in the same way as we do today.

Light blue, for example, seems to have been associated with green or white rather than seen as a shade of dark blue, which the Egyptians evidently related to black. This difference in perception may explain the use of light blue for the flesh of the normally green-skinned god Ptah in this pectoral ornament (above) from the Treasury (no. 267q) – and similarly the use of black for both the blue crown of the king and the god's close-fitting cap. For the black face of the king, see the double-cartouche unguent box, p. 158.

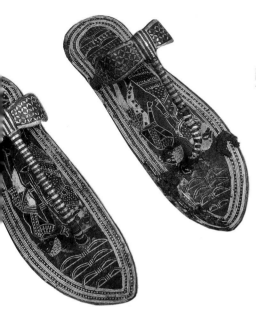

Clothing and Textiles

' We have some fearful problems at the tomb. Just now we are working on a box which contains garments and shoes all covered with beadwork. The cloth is so rotten you can hardly touch it, and the beads drop off the shoes if you look at them '

Arthur Mace to his wife Winifred

(Left) Pair of marquetry-veneered sandals (no. 397). The upper surface of each sole is decorated with two bound captives – a Nubian and an Asiatic – and nine bows, symbolizing the traditional enemies of the Egyptian state. They would be crushed underfoot with every step Tutankhamun took.

' The most novel, perhaps, among all the antiquities seen to-day was a wooden dummy upon which it is believed Tutankhamen tried his tunics and other vestments, after the fashion of a modern dressmaker. Mr. Henry Burton, of the New York Metropolitan Museum of Art, who is an enthusiastic member of Mr. Carter's staff, advanced the opinion that Tutankhamen was a man of fashion, scrupulously exact in the fit and hang of his garments. . . . '

Manchester Guardian

Whether the delightful image of a dapper Tutankhamun conjured up by Harry Burton had any basis in fact is now difficult to assess. Clearly, much linen was in evidence in the tomb, despite the depredations of robbers (p. 95); but full details of the collection seem now to have gone for good. Unlike most classes of the tomb's funerary equipment, the textiles were but poorly documented at the time of the clearance; many bundles Carter and his team seem never to have unwrapped at all, either because of their unpromising appearance or their poor state of preservation due to humidity and mould. While 'Cloth in some cases is so strong that it might have come fresh from the loom, . . . in others it has been reduced by damp almost to the consistency of soot.' And the inexorable process of deterioration has continued.

(Below left and right) The gessoed and painted wooden 'mannequin' (no. 116), a portrait figure in Carter's opinion 'probably used either for the king's jewellery or robes'.

155

(Above) Gold sequins (no. 46gg), once attached to garments from Tutankhamun's decayed wardrobe.

Garments

Sheets and bed-linen appear to have been carried off by the robbers. Tutankhamun's clothes, however, remained, and the range of his wardrobe is clear. His clothing was linen throughout, much of it of the finest quality, consisting of tunics, shirts, sashes, kilts, triangular loincloths, scarves, caps, head-dresses, and gloves, several items of which (especially those recovered from the Painted Box no. 21 (p. 157)) had clearly been worn by the king as a small child. The most striking feature of the costume is the form and variety of its decoration. This ranged from simple fringing to the king's plain linen shirts to overgarments boasting a veritable carpeting of gold spangles and sequins or exquisite beadwork; other items of clothing displayed magnificently embroidered borders and panels, originally present-ing a brilliant contrast of colours – blue, green, red, yellow, white, and black – though now for the most part darkened to a black-brown. Each of these garments had originally been folded with care and rolled up for storage. Unfortunately, the same attention to detail had not been given by those who tidied up the tomb following the chaotic period of the thefts; interested in achieving only the most superfi-cial order, the officials simply stuffed the dishevelled textiles into whichever box came to hand. This slovenliness was to have dire consequences when, three millennia later, Carter came to unpack them.

Carter's notes record the presence of linens in varying quantities throughout the tomb, though the bulk of the material appears to have been stored in the Antechamber, within eight boxes (nos. 21, 43, 4 46, 50, 54, 79, 101); see also the box dockets, p. 19(Other scraps and fragments were recovered from th wrappings of the mummy (p. 116), and from th Treasury and Annexe. Many of the textiles from th Treasury consisted of 'shawls' and other garment some docketed (p. 86), employed to wrap the variou divine figures. These were found still in positio precisely as the original burial party had left them

As well as everyday clothing, the tomb containe a number of garments of a more specialized natur including several leopard-skin *setem*-priest outfit (including nos. 44q, 46ff, etc.) and a leather cuiras (no. 587a) (p. 176).

Gloves

'I made a strange find among the king's robes today – a child's glove of cloth, belonging to a child I should say three or four years old. I imagine it must have been one of his own. . . .'

Arthur Mace to his wife Winifre

At the time of their discovery, Tutankhamun' gloves aroused an enormous amount of interes among glove-makers – and for good reason, sinc they are said to exhibit a type of stitch no introduced into the modern industry until th eighteenth century. In all, some 27 gloves wer found in the tomb: 23 from the Antechamber (c which 13 were recovered from boxes); and a furthe

(Above) Tutankhamun's first aid kit, found in box no. 79 in the Antechamber, included what Carter described as a sling bandage, several other bandages of various sizes, and the finger stall (no. 79q) shown here.

(Left) The celebrated 'dalmatic' (no. 367j): a superb tunic made from a single length of linen folded in two, sewn down the selvedges, supplemented with tapering sleeves of a finer material and embellished with woven decorative bands. The character of much of the decoration is decidedly Syrian; the detailed drawing (far left) of the applied, ankh-shaped neck opening gives an impression of the quality of the work. When worn, perhaps with a waist sash, the garment would have reached to just below the knee.

(Right) The king's underwear: a triangular linen loincloth (no. 50b) from the Antechamber.

two pairs from separate boxes in the Annexe. One of the finest pairs, 38.4cm (just over 15in) long, recovered 'neatly folded' from box no. 367 in the Annexe, is tapestry-woven on both sides with a *rishi*-pattern, and has tape for securing at the wrists; entirely modern in design, like all those found, Carter believed that the gloves 'were possibly intended to go with' the 'dalmatic robe' no. 367j.

(Below left) Ay shows off his red gloves, a gift from the king and a mark of honour: a scene from Ay's Amarna tomb (No. 25).

Sandals

'When these sandals have been restored, they will be among the most wonderful articles in all the mass of extraordinary works of art, and I fully expect that in a few years' time we shall see our smartest ladies wearing footgear more or less resembling and absolutely inspired by these wonderful things.'

The Times

Carter recorded 93 items or fragments of footwear: 17 from the Antechamber, of which 10 were found scattered between boxes 21 and 54; a pair of sheet-gold sandals on the mummy itself (no. 256 ll), 29.5cm (11½in) long; a pair of 'sandal-like' slippers of leather from a box in the Treasury (no. 270), 28cm (11in) long; and a range of sandals (including 32 pairs, 'of basketwork' – nos. 620:119 – 21.5–31cm (c. 9–12in) long) scattered throughout the debris of the Annexe. The types varied from undecorated specimens of rush and papyrus to elaborate examples of wood with marquetry veneer (no. 397). Several elegant sandals of leather (on one occasion calf-skin), partially melted, like all the leather from the tomb, were sumptuously patterned with bead-work or gold (in particular, no. 85a, 20.5cm (c. 8in) long). One large papyrus sandal from the Annexe floor (group 620:119) Carter describes as having 'a design in linen and needle-work upon the sole representing African and Asiatic prisoners above the tie of Upper and Lower Egypt'. Each time the king took a step, he crushed them underfoot.

(Above) An elaborate sandal (no. 85a) of multi-coloured beadwork, from the floor of the Antechamber.

(Left) One of the tapestry-woven gloves from box no. 367.

Contents of the Painted Box (no. 21) as found

a–b	rush and papyrus sandals
c	gilt headrest
d	ceremonial robe
e	cloth
f–g	decorated sandals
h–i	leather sandals
j	beadwork sandal
k–l	decorated shoes
m	remains of tapestry woven garment
n	wooden label
o	collar band from shirt
p–r	garments decorated with gold and faience sequins
s	cap or bag of beadwork
t	leopard-skin cloak
u	collar of faience beads and pendants
v	parts of garment of tapestry-woven cloth
w	cap or bag of beadwork
x	pieces of tapestry-woven garment
y	two-string collar
z	child's glove of fine linen
aa	collar of shirt
bb	pieces of similar garment
cc	tapestry-woven garment
dd	necklace of resin beads
ee	pieces of two or more tasselled belts
ff	two ends of tasselled belt
gg	tapestry-woven belt or scarf
hh	several small bundles of cloth
ii	large linen tassel
jj	gold sequins
kk	belt(?)
ll	tasselled belt of plain cloth
mm	shawl(?)
nn	loin-cloth
oo–pp	rolls of fine linen
qq	10 rolls of bandage of fine linen
rr–uu	pads of linen
vv	gauntlet
ww–xx	boards of wood covered with gesso and painted blue
yy	gold pendant

The unpacking of box no. 21. The sandals in the first shot were in perfect condition; the beaded robe next to them, visible in both photographs, crumbled at a touch.

Cosmetic Objects

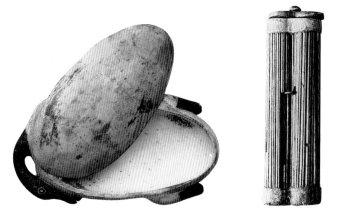

An ivory cosmetic box with swivel lid (above left), carved in the form of a trussed duck (no. 54s), and a double kohl*-tube (above right) of wood, glass and ivory (no. 46jj).*

Like all good Egyptians, Tutankhamun was careful to take to the grave with him the implements and preparations necessary for maintaining his appearance. While some of these had evidently been used in life, others were clearly prepared solely with the hereafter in mind.

(Right) Ointment container (no. 240 bis) of gold, inlaid with coloured glass and semi-precious stones. Each face is decorated with a pair of opposed cartouches containing a rebus of the prenomen, Nebkheprure, each cartouche differing slightly to reflect the stages in the king's transformation from royal child to ultimate rebirth.

Boxes, spoons and containers

A small ivory cosmetic box in the shape of a trussed duck, hollowed out to contain salve or a similar substance and fitted with a swivel lid, 8.5cm (*c.* 3⅜in) long overall, was found in box no. 54 in the Antechamber of the tomb. The head, neck and lower part of the bird's legs are stained black. Two identical boxes were in Carter's possession at the time of his death. Other cosmetic objects formerly in the Carter collection included a magnificent grasshopper box of stained ivory, its lid in the form of a pair of movable wings, and a delicately carved ointment spoon of stained ivory, with swivel-lidded pomegranate bowl.

Ancient Egyptian *kohl*, or eye-paint, was usually composed of either malachite (hydrated copper carbonate) or galena (lead sulphide), ground into powder and applied in the form of a paste by mixing it with water or, perhaps, with gum. Tutankhamun had been buried with several lumps of both materials (e.g. the galena pieces no. 456b, from the Annexe, originally tied up in a linen bag), presumably with this use in mind. The four 'paint slabs' from box no. 32 might have been intended for grinding the mineral.

Remarkably few *kohl* containers were recovered, and all of these from the Antechamber: a pot of dark serpentine, 3.2cm (*c.* 1¼in) high, was found in box no. 32, a container which held a number of small stone cosmetic vessels and related objects; a tiny tube (4.6cm (1⅞in) long) and *kohl* sticks bound together with strips of cloth came from the gilded and inlaid casket no. 44; and a double *kohl* tube of wood, glass and ivory, 12cm (4¾in) long, was found among group no. 46. Two gold *kohl* sticks are mentioned in the hieratic docket of box no. 575.

A particularly important ointment container, though of ritualistic rather than everyday use, was the gold box no. 240 bis, 16cm (*c.* 6¼in) high, of a type frequently seen being offered by Akhenaten to the solar disc. Although Carter places this object within the sarcophagus, there is little doubt that it had originally been discovered within the doors of the outermost shrine; its original number was probably 220. This box, which takes the form of a double cartouche with high-plumed lid, still held the remains of its original unguent, decomposed to a 'bad smelling' brown colour. Both faces of the box are inlaid with a cryptographic writing of Tutankhamun's prenomen, Nebkheprure. The *khepru* element, normally written with the scarab beetle *kheper* and three plural strokes, has here been replaced with a squatting figure of the king in two variations. The colour progression in the face inlays – orange-red black-orange – has been interpreted as reflecting the different stages or *khepru* in the king's transformation from royal child, through to adult king, dead king and ultimate rebirth.

For the series of stone vessels containing the king's oils and unguents, see p. 198.

Mirrors and mirror-cases

Although clearance of the Treasury produced two elaborate mirror-cases of gilded wood (nos. 269b and 271c–d, each 27cm (10¾in) high), the mirrors themselves were not present; the inscribed ivory handle from that of no. 271c–d was found in box no. 54 in the Antechamber, its mirror disc wrenched off by the robbers for the sake of its metal – probably silver or gold.

The mirror-cases were each made in two halves. The first of the cases (no. 269b) takes the form of the hieroglyph for 'life' (*ankh*), an appropriate funerary play on the Egyptian word for mirror which was also *ankh*. The central part of its lid is decorated with the king's prenomen picked out in coloured glass and semi-precious stones, while bands of hieroglyphs in raised relief on the gilded surface of the case reproduce the standard titulary. The interior of the case is lined with silver. The second mirror-case is fashioned after the god Heh, who is shown kneeling, a cartouche before and behind his head, with palm branches held in either hand surmounting frog- and *shen*-hieroglyphs. The exaggerated disc upon his head is decorated in gilded relief, again with versions of the king's prenomen. The entire composition may be understood as conveying the simple wish that Tutankhamun's years of renewed life might be without number. This case is lined with foil of brilliant beaten gold.

Shaving equipment

Razors in Egypt were employed not only to shave the face but other parts of the body also, including the head. A hieratic docket scribbled in ink on the white-painted box no. 68 from Tutankhamun's tomb records that it had originally contained 'The equipment of His Majesty life! prosperity! health! when he was a child. Contents: copper handled-razors, knife-razors, and ewers; linen.' – i.e. the royal shaving tackle. When found, the box contained nothing more than two cloth 'pads', a bundle of cloth and a clay sealing; it had evidently been emptied by thieves, who carried off for their metal content all but one knife-razor which Carter recovered from the Annexe floor (no. 620:53, 18cm (*c.* 7in) long). A further group of razors (no. 12g), which may or may not be associated with the equipment of this particular box, was found in the fill of the tomb's entrance corridor.

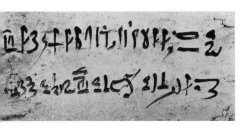

(Left) The lid of the second mirror-case (no. 271c-d). The interior of the case is hollowed out to receive the mirror today represented by the handle no. 54ddd (3) (below), incised in black with Tutankhamun's Horus name. The mirror disc, perhaps of gold or silver, had been carried off by robbers in antiquity.

(Below) The first mirror case (no. 269b) as found in the cartouche-shaped box no. 269 in the Treasury. No trace was found of the mirror it had once contained.

(Far left) Hieratic docket on the lid of a whitened box (no. 68), containing the king's shaving equipment.

Games and Game-Boxes

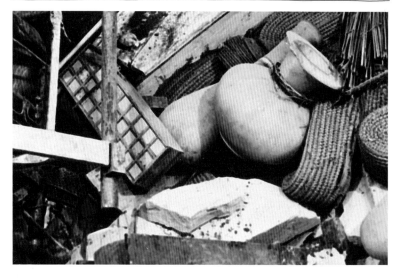

The ancient Egyptians were exceedingly fond o[f] board games, and sets of the 30-square (*senet*) an[d] 20-square game are not infrequently found amon[g] the grave-goods of the more prosperous dead.

Tutankhamun's tomb contained four comple[te] game-boards (nos. 345 + 383 + 580, 393, 585r, 593[)] with portions of one and perhaps two others. Th[e] original presence of six boards is supported by th[e] fact that six sets of knucklebones were recovered. I[n] addition, some 56 playing pieces (called *ibau*, o[r] 'dancers') of 'pawn' and 'reel' forms were found i[n] the tomb, together with two sets of fou[r] casting-sticks.

Of the game boards, only one odd drawer (no. 46u[) and a fragment of ivory veneer (no. 46v) wer[e] recovered from the Antechamber; all the complet[e] boards came from the Annexe. The Annexe, sim[i]larly, produced the larger number of playing piece[s;] strays were found in the entrance passageway an[d] Antechamber. The casting sticks were found in th[e] Annexe, as were at least seven of the knucklebone[s;] two (and perhaps three) other knucklebones wer[e] found in the Antechamber. The Annexe, in shor[t,] appears to have been the original home of Tutankh[-] amun's gaming equipment, from which it had bee[n] partially displaced (and partially plundered, t[o] judge from the homeless drawer) at the time of one o[r] other of the robberies.

The Game of Senet

The senet *board developed over the years from an ordinary item of funerary equipment, included in the tomb as an amusement for the dead, to a curious allegory of the final judgment. In the game played by the nobleman Amenmose (right), the adversary was Fate, and the stake immortality.*

In the 30-square game of *senet*, each player had an equal number of playing pieces, distinguished from those of the opposition by the form, which was generally 'pawn'-like or 'reel'-shaped. Movement of the pieces, lined up along the two longer edges of the board, was dictated by the throw of the knucklebones or of the casting-sticks (the 'score' of the latter dependent upon the fall of the black and white surfaces). Movement has been characterized as

'a pathway of 30 steps, shaped like a backward S, along which the pieces wound their way single file toward the five final squares of the board, which were usually marked in some way.' The aim was to remove all of one's pieces from the board before those of the opposing player. The marked squares were clearly advantageous to the player (those marked with the hieroglyph *nefer*), or hazardous (such as those marked with the water hieroglyph). According to Carter, 'The contest was obviously an early form of, and allied to, the modern game called "*El-Tab-el-Seega*", played almost universally in the Near East. . . .'

The Game of 20 Squares

This game, often (but erroneously) called *tjau*, was perhaps of Western Asiatic origin. It possessed none of the religious overtones of *senet*. Many of the details are uncertain, but each player was evidently allotted five pieces, perhaps entered individually onto the board. Moves were made by throwing knucklebones or casting-sticks. The object of the game seems to have been for a player to remove all his pieces from the board along the central row of

squares, avoiding his opponent's pieces and any 'unlucky' squares which might lie in his path.

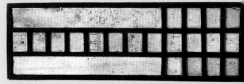

The ebony game-box and stand (no. 345 + 383 + 580)

The ebony game-box (44.4cm (17½in) long), found dismantled into its three component parts (board, drawer and stand) at the south end of the Annexe, is one of the most elegant objects from the tomb. Now somewhat warped, so that the bolted drawer will not fit the box, which now no longer sits squarely on the partially gilded and ivory-clawed feline legs of its sledge, its fine appearance belies its actual construction. The surface is merely a veneer, applied to a core of poor quality wood, and though conventionally identified as 'ebony' may well be some other wood to which a dark stain has been applied. Both the upper and lower surfaces of the box are veneered with ivory, to which raised strips have been glued to divide each surface for either the 30-square (*senet*) or 20-square games (see opposite), with five and three of the squares incised with one or more hieroglyphic symbols. The sides of the box, as well as the ends, are inscribed with large, yellow-filled hieroglyphs which expound the royal titulary and leave no doubt as to the game's ownership.

When found, the drawer was empty, Carter in print taking the view that the original playing-pieces 'were probably of gold and silver and consequently stolen in ancient times'. This is arguable. Eight faience playing pieces of a suitable size for this game were recovered from elsewhere in the tomb, and it is possible that they, together with a pair of knuckle-

bones and set of ivory and ebony casting-sticks, formed part of the set as buried.

The two ivory boxes (nos. 393, 585r)

Although one of the ivory game-boxes was found broken on the floor of the Annexe, close to the doorway, Carter believed that it had originally been stored with its 'pair' in the box 585. Both game-boxes, each some 13.5cm (5⅓in) in length and extensively inscribed with extracts from the royal protocol inlaid with blue pigment, are carved from a single block of ivory, with the squares for the 20- and 30-square games cut directly into the upper and

(Top) The elegant ebony game-box and stand (no. 345 + 383 + 580). The top and bottom surfaces of the board itself (seen on the opposite page in position in the Annexe) were each laid out for one of the principal games (left).

(Above) The two pairs of ivory and ebony casting-sticks associated with the ebony game-box no. 345 + 383 + 580.

161

(Above) Ivory-veneered game-box (no. 593) from the Annexe, with its 'pawn'- and 'reel'-shaped playing pieces of red-banded ivory and twin knucklebones. The ivory fragment no. 46v, from the Antechamber, may at one stage have formed part of this box.

(Below) Two pairs of ivory casting-sticks (no. 620:110) found broken on the Annexe floor, taking the form of Nubian and Asiatic captives. Carter wished to associate these sticks with game-box no. 593, though they are too long to fit the drawer and are of inferior quality.

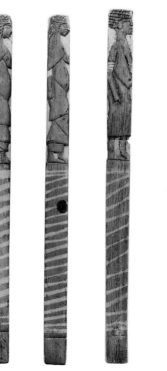

lower surfaces. There are no specially marked squares. A small bolted drawer, also carved from a single piece of ivory, is fitted at one end of each box. The opposite end of one of the boxes (no. 585r) carries an incised representation of Tutankhamun, seated on a block throne, wearing the blue crown and clutching the *heqa*-sceptre, receiving a lotus from Queen Ankhesenamun, who stands before him; their names (his the prenomen) are inscribed above in cartouches.

Carter associated nine ivory playing-pieces and a single knucklebone with the first box, and the full set of 10 ivory playing-pieces and two knucklebones with the second.

The wood and ivory game-box (no. 593)

This charming game-box, 27.5cm (10⅞in) in lengt 'had suffered much from rough usage on the part the thieves' but, with the exception of the drawe which have now warped and do not fit, the box ha now been reassembled. It was found in the soutl west corner of the Annexe, in the same pile as th sled-mounted box, with one of its two bolte drawers some distance away. Veneered with carve and black- and red-stained (or heat-treated) ivor the decoration on each side consists of five alterna ing lotus and poppy motifs with a decorative borde The effect is closely similar to that of the large, ivor veneered casket no. 540 + 551 described on p. 19 The core of the game-box, as with the first bc described, is of poor quality local wood. The uppe surface is divided by means of gilded 'stucco' rit into 30 squares, with the lower surface similar divided for the 20-square game. Five squares of th last surface still retain traces of hieroglyphic mar ings; they would originally have been highlighte with gold foil.

Carter associated 20 black- and red-banded ivor playing-pieces with this box, as well as a pair (ivory knucklebones. He also proposed that the tw pairs of ivory casting-sticks taking the form (Asiatic and Nubian captives (no. 620:110) 'probabl belong to this game', although they are too large t fit into either one of the box's drawers.

The odd drawer (no. 46u) found in the Ant chamber of the tomb evidently came from a gam box similar in size to this ivory-veneered specime and conceivably its pair. One of the two sets (playing-pieces which Carter associated with th wood and ivory board might well have bee intended for this missing object.

The 'musical instruments' recovered by Carter from the tomb are few in number and conservative in type: a pair of ivory clappers; two trumpets; and a pair of sistra. Eighteenth-dynasty Egypt had far more to offer than this, and it may be suspected that the presence in the tomb of these objects owes more to their ritual function than to any desire that Tutankhamun should have pleasurable musical accompaniment in the next life.

The ivory clappers (no. 620:13)

Found on the floor of the Annexe, these arm-shaped clappers measure some 15.7cm (6⅛in) in length. Holes at the proximal end of each clapper were intended for the insertion of a cord linking the two together in the manner of castanets – though, as tomb scenes apparently show, the noise would have been produced by shaking rather than by controlled percussion. Each arm is rather crudely incised on its polished outer surface with an elongated cartouche associating Queen Tiye with her granddaughter, Meritaten: 'The great royal wife Tiye, may she live; the king's daughter Meritaten'. Precisely why granddaughter and grandmother should have been linked in this way is uncertain. The clappers' presence in the tomb of Tutankhamun is similarly obscure.

(Right) Pair of ivory clappers inscribed for Tiye and Meritaten, pierced at one end and with hands carved at the other.

(Below) Similar clappers in use: a scene from the 12th-dynasty tomb of Inyotefiqer at Thebes (No. 60).

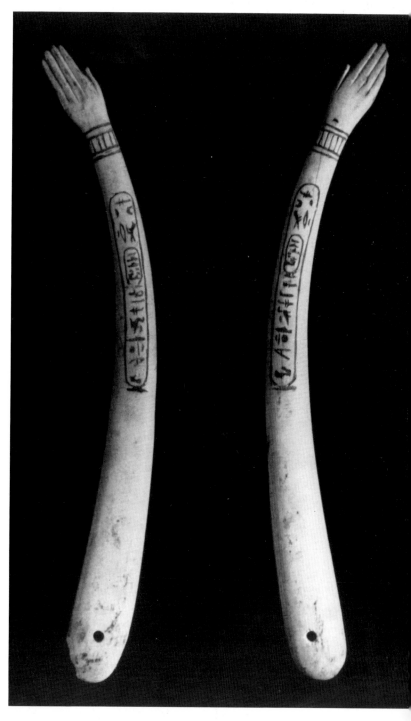

163

The trumpets (nos. 50gg, 175)

Tutankhamun's military trumpets – one (no. 175) of beaten silver, with bell-rim and rolled mouthpiece of gold, the other (no. 50gg) of copper or bronze and gold-alloy (electrum?) overlaid in part with sheet gold – were recovered from the Burial Chamber wrapped in reeds, lying on the floor in the southeast corner, and from the Antechamber with the contents of the long wooden box no. 50. Each trumpet was furnished with a gessoed and painted wooden core, perhaps intended to protect the thin metal from accidental damage or distortion when the trumpet was not in use.

The bell and tube of the silver trumpet were fashioned in two pieces from hammered sheet metal, the edges cut in square taps, folded over and joined by silver solder to give an overall length of 58.2cm (*c.* 23in); the finished diameter of the bell itself is a mere

(Below left) Tutankhamun's silver and copper-alloy trumpets, flanked by their gessoed and painted wooden cores.

(Below right) The scene chased upon the bell of the silver trumpet (no. 175) compared with that incised upon the bell of the copper-alloy trumpet (no. 50gg).

8.2cm (3¼in). According to Carter, the gold decoration at the mouth of the bell and the mouthpiece had been beaten into position. The lotiform decoration on the bell is chased, with vertical cartouches containing the king's prenomen and nomen alternating in the sepals (the leaves surrounding the flower bud). Subsequently, perhaps following Tutankhamun's death, a rectangular frame was superimposed upon the lotus decoration containing a scene of Amon-Re and Re-Horakhty before Ptah – representatives of the entire Egyptian pantheon.

The copper-alloy trumpet was fashioned from sheet metal (0.2–0.25mm thick), with a brazed meander joint running the whole length of the tube and a four-rivet join between tube and electrum(?) bell concealed by means of a gold sleeve. The mouthpiece consists of a simple electrum(?) ring brazed on a scarf joint, passed over the end of the trumpet tube and brazed into position. With a length of around 50cm (*c.* 20in), the trumpet is shorter than the silver specimen; the diameter of the bell, however, is slightly larger, at about 9cm (3½in). The bell itself is plain, except for a chased panel similar to that on the silver trumpet, which shows the blue-crowned Tutankhamun, the god Ptah behind,

receiving the *ankh* ('life') from Amon-Re, behind whom stands the falcon-headed Re-Horakhty.

The physical differences between the trumpets indicate that, though two in number, they are not a pair. As became apparent on the two occasions they were played in modern times – the silver trumpet during the BBC broadcast of 1939 (by Bandsman Tappern, with a modern mouthpiece inserted), when it shattered; the copper (or bronze) trumpet in 1939 and 1941 (on the last occasion without a modern mouthpiece) – both instruments are tuned differently. The noise they produced was characterized by the musicologist Hans Hickman as 'raucous and powerful', recalling 'rather the timbre of a medieval trombone or primitive horn than that of a trumpet or cornet'. In the case of both trumpets, the higher range was achieved with such difficulty that it is unlikely ever to have been used, while the lower range is decidedly poor both in quality and strength. One may conclude, with the musicologist Jeremy Montagu, that the middle range achieved during the experiments was that for which the trumpets had been designed – and from this that 'the Egyptian military trumpet signal code was a rhythmic one on a single pitch'.

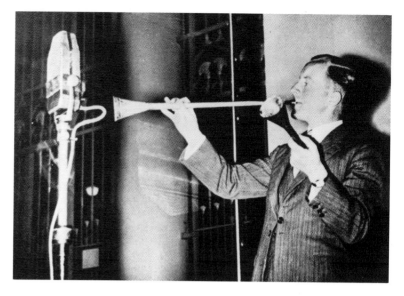

The sistra (nos. 75–6)

The two arched sistra, or ritualistic rattles, though differing slightly in size (51.5 and 52cm (20¼ and 20½in) high), clearly represent a pair. Each has a wooden grip of facetted section, surmounted by a cube-like 'capital' into which slots the shaker-loop with its three serpentine rods and three sets of three square jangles. The heaviness of this unique design is relieved, though only marginally, by the gold leaf applied to the gessoed wooden grip.

That the two sistra were functional instruments and not merely funerary models is indicated by wear on the inside of the arch. The sistrum is predominantly a female instrument, with little relevance to the burial of a king. It is possible, therefore, that the sistra from the tomb of Tutankhamun were not part of the funeral equipment proper, but instruments employed during the burial ritual and abandoned on the Hathor couch at the time the tomb was closed.

(Above) Bandsman Tappern playing the silver trumpet moments before it shattered during the BBC broadcast of 1939.

(Left) The gilded sistra of wood and copper alloy (nos. 75–6). These had perhaps been used in the ritual associated with the closing of the tomb in 1323 BC.

(Below) A scene from the small gilded shrine (no. 108), showing Ankhesenamun presenting her husband with a broad collar, to the accompaniment of a shaking sistrum.

Writing Materials and Equipment

(Right above) The red-stained ivory 'water dish' (no. 271f), part of the king's personal writing equipment.

(Below left) From box no. 271: two scribal palettes (the left of ivory, the right of gilded wood), an ivory and gold papyrus burnisher, and an elaborate pen-case of gilded and inlaid wood.

(Below right) Detail of a scene in the Memphite tomb of Horemheb, showing two scribes at work with papyrus roll, writing palette and rush pen.

According to the Pyramid Texts, the king in death became scribe to the sun-god. This helps to explain, at least in part, why so much writing equipment had been buried with Tutankhamun. Fifteen palettes were noted by Carter (nos. 262, 271b, 271e(2), 3671–n, 442c, 585bb, 620:89–93, 620:114, but see p. 169), a fine pen case (no. 271e(1)), two writing horns (nos. 387, 398), and a burnisher (no. 271g), as well as various pigments (black, white, red, yellow, blue), contained in shells (nos. 620:79–81, 85) or in lumps and cakes (nos. 620:82–83, 85–87), and four indurated limestone paint slabs (no. 32o). An *ad hoc* paint container made from a potsherd (no. 175d) may also be noted, from the Burial Chamber; while no. 147e, a small piece of shaped sandstone, perhaps served as a scribal 'eraser'.

Palettes and paints

The palettes were of the traditional Egyptian type: a length of wood or some other material, rectangular in section, with a slot in the top surface to receive the rush pens and brushes with their sharply cut or gently chewed ends. Although several of the palettes were solid funerary models, including an example produced in glass (no. 367n, 42.1cm (16⅜in) long) Carter believed that one group of writing implements recovered from the Treasury was 'actually the private property of the king'. This group, from box no. 271, included a small (30.3cm (11$\frac{9}{10}$in)) palette bearing the king's name in its earlier, -aten, form, and another of identical length in ivory bearing the name Tutankhamun – 'The colours, red and black, in both cases show evidence of having been used'. The writing assemblage includes a spectacular rush case of gilded and inlaid wood, 30cm (*c.* 1ft) in length, a lollipop-shaped 'papyrus burnisher', 16.5cm (6½in) long, of ivory and gold, and what Carter identified as a water-dish of ivory (diameter 16.3cm (6⅜in)). Belonging to this same outfit, and from the same chest, was a rectangular box of papyrus decorated both on its top and frontal panels with scenes of the king in the presence of Amon-Re and Re-Horakhty, and Ptah

nd Sakhmet. The box carries an impression of seal-pe N (p. 94); '. . . one hoped, upon opening it, to find me writing, perhaps a specimen of the boy's alligraphy; but it was void . . . of any form of ocument'.

nscriptions

he tomb, in fact, was void of any significant ocument written on papyrus. In the early days of ne discovery, hopes had been high that 'among the ocuments which are expected to be found in 'utankhamen's tomb will be some that will afford n explanation of his reconversion to Amen worhip, determine the length of his reign at Thebes, nd reveal the real reason for the inveterate hatred vhich his successor, Horemheb, displayed towards im . . . .' Great excitement was caused by the ighting, in the Antechamber, of a 'box of papyri', in vhich the fevered imaginations of the Egyptologists t once saw significant historical documents and nknown literary works; the excitement turned to ismay when the box was opened, and it was iscovered that the 'papyri' were nothing more than iscoloured rolls of linen', described by the *Daily Mail* (with some relish) as 'simply folded table apkins'. But hope continued to be expressed that,

with the unwrapping of the royal mummy, 'at least an example of the "Book of the Dead" will be discovered'. The closest that the excavators came were traces on the mummy of a small and very fragmentary 'ritual . . . written in white linear hieroglyphs' (perhaps no. 256ii). Although this was 'too decayed and disintegrated to allow of practical conservation, . . . here and there names of gods, such as Osiris and Isis, were with difficulty decipherable.' It proved the final disappointment: Tutankhamun's papyri were written off as a dream, and Egyptologists abandoned the chase. Had no papyri been buried with the king? Or had Carter and his team simply misdirected their search ?

Despite the disappointing lack of papyri, a great number of inscriptions were recovered from the tomb – indeed, most of those objects offering a sufficiently large surface carry a text of some sort. These range from extracts from the funerary books, notably on the shrines (p. 100), to longer or shorter versions of the titulary (p. 24) and more spontaneous texts scribbled in hieratic on the young king's boxes, box-labels, wine jars, boxed provisions and storage vessels. But about Tutankhamun himself, they tell us disappointingly little.

(Left) Brightly painted scene of Tutankhamun before Ptah, the goddess Sakhmet behind: detail from a simple papyrus box (no. 271a) associated with the king's writing equipment.

(Below left) Two wooden labels (nos. 620:96, 620:109), with hieratic inscriptions recording the contents of the boxes to which they were once attached: 'gold rings' and 'clothes'.

(Bottom left) The 'papyri' of box no. 43, which, on unpacking, turned out to be nothing more than tightly folded items of royal underlinen.

(Below right) The lid of box no. 54 ddd, with black ink docket mentioning the gold rings it once held.

'Heirlooms'

(Below) Gilded and resin-coated wooden coffin (no. 320), containing a second coffin of gilded wood (no. 320a). This, in turn, held a third, miniature coffin of painted wood (no. 320b) and a tightly wrapped linen bundle (no. 320c).

'Among purely ritualistic paraphernalia belonging to a burial custom one finds simple family relics which must have carried many a human remembrance.'

Howard Carter

A good number of objects from the tomb bear th[e] names of earlier kings or members of the roy[al] family, objects which Carter rather loosely terme[d] 'heirlooms'. It is probable that relatively few objec[ts] may in the strictest sense be so described, the mo[st] apparent being the lock of Queen Tiye's ha[ir] contained, with the pendant figure of a squattin[g] king (probably Tutankhamun himself), within [a] nest of four coffins (no. 320) from the Treasury. Th[e] ivory palettes of his half-sisters, Meketaten an[d] Meritaten, may also be regarded as heirlooms. Mos[t] of the rest, at least so far as the inscribed material [is] concerned, would be better characterized as odd[s] and ends drawn together as required from variou[s] royal stores – though, if so, a deliberate sifting of th[e]

material might be detected. The almost total absence of certain names (Nefertiti and Kiya – if the latter was indeed the mother of Tutankhamun) is especially striking.

Many of these 'surplus' funerary objects – far more, one suspects, than can now be recognized – had originally been prepared for the burials of Amenophis IV–Akhenaten (at Thebes) and of Ankhkheprure Nefernefruaten. The majority of these pieces were fully reinscribed for their new owner, though in a few cases the original name can still be discerned beneath the palimpsest. Contrary to popular belief, there is nothing from the tomb inscribed with the nomen of Ankhkheprure Smenkhkare-djeserkhepru.

'Heirlooms'

Object number	Description	Name	Dimensions (centimetres)
1a	scarab	Tuthmosis III	l. 1.4
1k	box	Akhenaten, Nefernefruaten, Meritaten	l. 58
12n + 79 +574	box	Nefernefruaten, Meritaten; reinscribed	l. 26.5
44p	model adze	Amenophis III, Tiye	l. 9
46gg	sequins	'Ankhkheprure', Meritaten (?)	d. 1.7
48h	bow	'Ankhkheprure'; reinscribed	l. 134
54hh	box lid	Nefernefrure	l. 10
101s	linen shawl	'Ankhkheprure'	l. c. 200
256a	scarab chain	'Ankhkheprure'; reused	—
256b	mummy bands	'Ankhkheprure'; reused	—
261a	linen covering of Anubis	Akhenaten	—
261p(1)	pectoral	Akhenaten; reinscribed	w. 14.3
262	palette	Meritaten; Nefertiti	l. 21.9
266g	canopic coffinettes	Nefernefruaten; reinscribed	l. 39
281a	linen shawl on Mamu figure	Akhenaten	—
320d	miniature coffin with hair	Tiye	l. 13.2
333	whip stock	Tuthmosis (king's son)	l. 51
404	calcite vessel	Tuthmosis III	ht. 35
405	calcite vessel	Amenophis III(?), ?	ht. 30
410	calcite vessel	Tuthmosis III	ht. 41.5
448	calcite vessel	Amenophis III(?), ?	ht. c. 30
483	calcite vessel	Amenophis III	ht. 35.5
585u	glass mandragora fruit	Tuthmosis III	—
588	calcite vessel	Amenophis III, Tiye	ht. 41
596a	fan	Akhenaten	l. 104
620:13	clappers	Meritaten; Tiye	l. 15.7
620:40	faience bangle	Akhenaten	d. 7
620:41	faience bangle	Nefernefruaten	d. 7
620:42	faience bangle	Nefernefruaten	d. 7

Note
Two further ivory palettes from the tomb (not numbered in Carter's sequence) may be noted: one inscribed with the prenomen of Amenophis III, 'beloved of Re'; and another inscribed for Meketaten, noting her filiation to Nefertiti.

(Left) When unwrapped, the linen bundle (no. 320c) was found to contain (above) a solid gold image of a squatting king with bead collar and tasseled suspension cord.

(Left) The miniature third coffin (no. 320b) held a tiny, coffin-shaped box (no. 320d), inscribed with the name of Queen Tiye, wrapped in linen and smeared with unguents. Within this coffin was a plaited lock of hair (no. 320e) – the precious remembrance, perhaps, of a much-loved grandmother.

Chariots and Chariot Equipment

' On that day one [Akhenaten] was in Akhetaten, in the carpeted tent made for his majesty in Akhetaten ... The king appeared mounted on the great chariot of fine gold like Aten when he arises in the horizon and fills the two lands with his love. '

Boundary stela S at el-Amarna

Introduced into Egypt by the Hyksos in the sixteenth century BC, the chariot was throughout the New Kingdom closely associated with the king, who is constantly shown dominating the field of battle, the reins around his waist, firing his bow. Chariots begin to appear in Egyptian wall reliefs and paintings from the early 18th dynasty, and are mentioned as diplomatic gifts in the correspondence from el-Amarna. Until the discovery of Tutankhamun's tomb only two complete vehicles were known – one now in Florence, and another from the tomb of Yuya and Tjuyu (No. 46) – together with a miscellaneous array of chariot fittings and fragments from other tombs in the Valley of the Kings and elsewhere. The burial of Tutankhamun yielded six complete but dismantled chariots of unparalleled richness and sophistication, four found at the southeast end of the Antechamber and two along the north wall of the Treasury. Each had had its axle sawn through to enable it to be brought along the narrow corridor into the tomb, and each had been

Detail (left side) of the body of the first chariot (no. 122), with its relief decoration of gilded gesso and chevron and rishi inlays of carnelian and coloured glass. The medallion contains a wedjat-eye, with pendant uraeus, surmounting a neb-basket – conceivably a rebus of the royal prenomen.

The Egyptian chariot, as Tutankhamun's first 'state' vehicle (no. 122) shows, was broad, D-shaped in plan, widely tracked and open at the back. The use of bent wood and leather, together with elaborately constructed wheels (with rawhide tyres) made for great lightness with minimal sacrifice of strength.

broken down into its component parts for compactness when stored. Thrown about when the tomb was robbed, and roughly handled when the burial was tidied up, the confused and precarious heaps into which these parts had been thrown were a nightmare to untangle. But, after much delicate preservative work, five of the six chariots could be reassembled for display in the Cairo Museum. When reconstructed it was possible to see how markedly they differ in points of detail according to the various roles for which they had apparently been intended.

The first of the chariots (no. 122) is constructed with a bent wood body, 1.02m (3ft 4⅛in) wide and 0.44m (1ft 5⅜in) deep, partially filled with a thin wooden sheet. The frame is strengthened at the front with an additional top-rail, the space between it and the body decorated in openwork with a *sma-tawy* (union of the two lands) symbol flanked by captives.

The main outer and inner surfaces of the body are gessoed and overlaid with gold which is further embellished with bands of brightly coloured glass and stone inlay. The central inner and outer panels are decorated in raised relief with a winged solar falcon (identified in the inscriptions as Horus-of-Behdet), which hovers above the king's prenomen, nomen and the name of Ankhesenamun. On the lower part of these 'heraldic' panels, two *rekhyt*-birds (representing the people of Egypt) adore a *djed*-pillar (the Osiris Tutankhamun) flanked by *ankh*-signs, while, below, foreign captives are shown entangled in a *sma-tawy* motif. An inlaid *wedjat*-eye roundel is present on either side of the outer body.

The axle, 2.3m (7ft 6½in) long, the greater portion of which was still attached to the body when found, was decorated with inlaid gold bands; the wheels, removed from the axle when the chariot was placed in the tomb, are of the later, composite, six-spoked variety, like all the Tutankhamun specimens. The pole of the first chariot, heat-bent from a single length of straight-grained wood and embellished with gold, attaches to the main body in a socket beneath the rear floor bar, is held in position by lashing around the frontal floor bar, and is further supported by two strengthening rods connecting to the top rail. It connects with the two-horse yoke, of artificially bent hardwood overlaid with gold and with calcite terminals, at its distal end, where it was pegged and lashed into position.

The basic construction of the second chariot (no. 120), 2.89m (9ft 5¾in) overall, is similar to that of the

first. Here again, the entire surface is covered with gold and highlighted with coloured inlays. The running-spiral decoration of the outer body is interrupted by a vertical panel decorated with plant motifs, at the top of which is a 'heraldic' panel containing the cartouched prenomen and nomen of the king flanked on either side by his Horus name in a *serekh*. The entire inner surface of the chariot body is covered with relief decoration, consisting of a central *sma-tawy* emblem and bound captives, dominated at either edge by a standing royal sphinx.

These, the two finest vehicles recovered from the tomb, Carter identified as the king's 'state chariots',

(Above left) Arthur Mace and Alfred Lucas outside the laboratory in the tomb of Sethos II, stabilizing the surface of the second 'state chariot' body (no. 120).

(Above) Gilded Bes-mask with richly inlaid headdress; from the rear siding-frame of the second chariot (no. 120).

(Left) Bound Nubian and Asiatic captives modelled in relief on the gilded interior of the second 'state chariot' (no. 120). (Below) Detail of the relief.

171

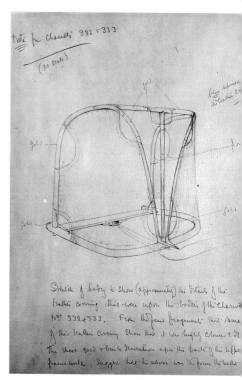

(Right) The reconstructed fourth chariot (no. 161), an undecorated and more practical hunting vehicle with open siding frame.

(Below right) Carter's sketch and comments on the leather body-covering of the fifth and sixth chariots (nos. 332, 333) from the Treasury.

(Below) Drawing of the fragmentary chariot wheel recovered during Carter's clearance of the tomb of Amenophis III in 1915. The complex construction of such wheels, using imported elm (strong and difficult to split) for the nave and native tamarisk for the cylindrical axle flange, may be clearly seen.

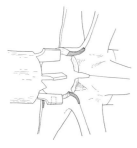

highly embellished and primarily intended for parade and ceremonial use. The equally lavish third chariot (no. 121), found with its pole still attached in the southeast corner of the Antechamber, perhaps falls into the same category, though the fenestrated side panels of this vehicle, which were evidently of leather, have now decayed. The original effect would have been similar to that of the first and second chariots – though as preserved the appearance is one of dragon-fly lightness not dissimilar to that of the fourth chariot (no. 161), an undecorated vehicle with hard-wearing wooden tyres characterized by Carter as a curricle, 'of … more open … lighter construction probably for hunting or exercising purposes'.

The tangle of parts making up Tutankhamun's fifth (no. 332) and sixth (no. 333) chariots was found in the Treasury. Only no. 333 has been reconstructed. Both were light in construction and again regarded by Carter as hunting vehicles. The first was essentially undecorated though with remains of leather panels to the body sides. The original presence of similar side panels was noted in the case of the rather more elaborate sixth chariot, here, according to Carter, 'highly coloured and decorated'.

Related equipment

With both groups of chariots was found a mass of related material. Twelve yoke saddles of gilded wood were present – one pair to each chariot. Artificially bent into an inverted U-shape, these saddles were surmounted by a reel-shaped knob of calcite by which the saddle was lashed to the yoke proper. A hole in the lower end of each terminal of the yoke saddle was intended to accommodate the harness straps. The leather of the harness had everywhere (due to the intermittent humidity) decayed beyond salvage into a black, glutinous

mass, but many of the gold foil appliqués which ha once decorated the bridlery were recovered, as w as several blinkers and bridle bosses. Ten 'che rowels' (nos. 152a–b, 162, c, d, etc) – wooden roc just over 0.65m (c. 2ft) long, with a central, copp spiked discus – also formed part of the char

(Above) A pair of gilded wooden blinkers (no. 122i) with glass-inlaid wedjat-eyes, from the bridle of the first 'state chariot' (no. 122).

(Left) Tutankhamun at hunt in his chariot: a detail of the king's ostrich-feather fan (no. 242). The charioteer stood on a leather-thonged floor covered with a rug of animal skin or tufted linen – an elastic footing made even more efficient by a flexible yoke-pole and by the placement of the axle at the rear of the body.

(Below left) Carter's reconstruction drawing showing the arrangement of the yoke and yoke saddles.

(Bottom left) A pair of 'check rowels' (nos. 152a–b) from the Antechamber. The lower specimen may be that seen on in situ shots resting upon the seat of one of the folding stools (no. 83).

(Below right) A fanciful reconstruction drawing by Carter showing the harness of one of the chariot-horses.

...rness, originally attached to the reins to distract a ...arrelsome male team. Four objects identified by ...e excavators as fly-whisks (nos. 148a–c, 168), ...35–0.43m (1ft 1¾in–1ft 4⅞in) long, perhaps orig- ...ally hung from the horses' sides. It may be noted ...at no bits were found; their metal content had ...idently proved too great a temptation to the ...mb's ancient plunderers.

...Three whip-stocks (nos. 50ss, 122u, 135cc) were ...und among the chariot debris in the Antechamber. ...e first of these, 0.503m (1ft 7¾in) long, of ivory ...ounted with gold, electrum and silver, is inscribed ...th the titulary of the king, 'who appears upon his ...am of horses as when Re ascends . . .' A fourth ...ip-stock, 0.51m (1ft 8⅛in) long of wood, gessoed ...d gilded, with a bronze tip and marbled glass knob,

formed part of group no. 333 from the Treasury. It is inscribed for 'The king's son, the troop commander, Tuthmosis, who repeats life'. The identity of this prince is uncertain; he may perhaps as easily be a son of Tuthmosis IV and younger brother of Amenophis III as the elder brother of Akhenaten. A further, fragmentary whip-stock said to come from the tomb, of painted ivory, takes the form of a galloping horse (not numbered in Carter's sequence).

One fragment of linen housing or trapper was recovered (group no. 332/333), its only possible royal parallel being a fragmentary example recovered by Carter from the tomb of Tuthmosis IV (Cairo CG 46526). A crescent-shaped piece of coarse, folded linen (group no. 333) has been identified as part of a neck strap.

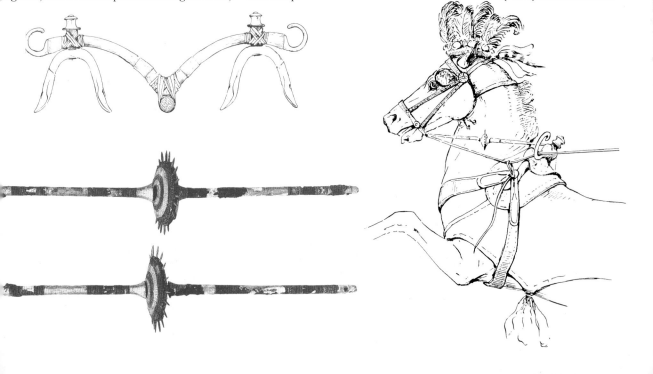

Weaponry

(Right) Bow case (no. 335) in the northwest corner of the Treasury. (Centre) A detail of the fine marquetry work on this bow case (obverse), showing an ibex and an oryx pierced by arrows.

(Below) From the Antechamber: a ceremonial self bow (no. 77a) with gilded grip and tips, and two elaborately decorated composite bows (nos. 48i(l), 48f).

Tutankhamun was buried both with items of defensive armour – a leather cuirass and eight shields – and with a good range of offensive weapons – including daggers, swords, bows, arrows, throwsticks, boomerangs and clubs; no battle-axes were found. The majority of these pieces were nonfunerary in origin and, to judge from their small size, a number may well have been used by the king during his lifetime.

Archery equipment

'The bows and arrows excited supreme interest. In design they are not unlike the conventional bow and arrow of modern times, but they display a remarkable ingenuity and thoroughness in construction. It was apparent that they had been placed in the tomb with Tutankhamen to assist his ancient Majesty in combating any enemies who might attempt to retard his progress from this world to the next.'

Daily Telegraph

The largest group of weaponry is the archery tack which was found scattered throughout the tom Clearance of the entrance corridor produced a sing bronze arrowhead (group no. 12n), one of tho broken by the robbers from arrows in the An chamber, which itself produced 13 composite bow 3 self bows, 2 quivers (both of linen, one reinforc with leather) and 112 arrows or arrowheads. In t Burial Chamber were a further 10 self bows and arrows, while the Treasury yielded an elabora inscribed wooden bow case (no. 335) 1.53m (c. 5

Tutankhamun's Bows

Object number	Descriptions	Length (metres)	Object number	Descriptions	Length (metres)
48f	double composite angular bow	1.2	228	self bow	1.94
			234	self bow	1.20
48g (1–2)	two composite angular bows	1.315 and 1.26	241	self bow	1.65
			244	self bow	1.91
48h	composite angular 'Bow of Honour'	1.34	246	self bow	1.77
			247	self bow	1.98
48i (1)	double composite angular bow	1.395	335a	three composite bows (?)	?
			370ff–ii	four composite angular bows	1.215 +; 1.12 +; 1.02 +; 1.11
48i (2)	composite angular bow	1.20			
48j (1–2)	two composite angular bows	1.105 and 1.13	370jj	composite bow	c. 1.11
48k (1–2)	two composite angular bows	1.12 and 1.125	370kk	short composite angular bow	0.72
48l	self bow	1.72	370 ll	miniature composite angular bow	0.34
70	unfinished self bowstave	1.78			
77a	self bow	1.59	596k–m	three short composite angular bows	1.02; 0.98; 0.885
77b	composite angular bow	1.25			
135z	composite angular bow	1.135	596n–o	two short composite bows	0.69; 0.74
153	composite angular bow	1.085			
222	self bow	1.21	596p–s	four short composite angular bows	0.635; 1.03; 0.905; 0.925
225a–b	two self bows	1.65 and 1.70			
226	self bow	1.25	596t	short self bow	0.67

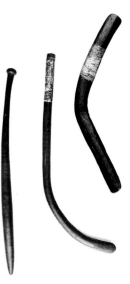

at least one bow of this type was among tribute sent by the Mitannian king Tushratta to the court of Amenophis III.

The longest of the 14 ordinary or 'self' bows from the tomb (one of which had been left unfinished) exceeded the length of the English long-bow – 1.9m (over 6ft). The shortest measured 0.67m (2ft 2⅜in) long. The material of these bows has never been scientifically examined.

Of the arrows from the tomb, all but 21 (which were constructed entirely of wood) had reed shafts (where examined, *Phragmites communis*, var. *isiacus*), made fletched (feathered) and with wooden nocks. The tips are of various specialized shapes, made from wood, ivory, bone, bronze, stone or glass. The wood employed in the construction of the arrows, which vary in length between 0.145 and 0.95m (5¾ and 37⅜in), has not been analyzed.

Slings, throwsticks, boomerangs and clubs

Among the miscellaneous weapons of sport and combat found by Carter in a large wooden box (no. 585) in the Annexe were two fragmentary slings of finely plaited linen-cord, each fitted with a pouch for the missile (a rounded pebble, several examples of which were recovered from the floor debris) and a loop at one end for attachment to the little finger. The type is one which has continued in use down to the present century – one correspondent was to draw Carter's attention to the similarity between the

(Above) Two clubs and a boomerang from the large white bow box (no. 370).

(Below) One of the two wooden 'snake batons' (nos. 620:11–12) found on the Annexe floor. A fowling scene (bottom), from the Theban tomb of Nebamun (No. 146), shows a similar weapon.

ong, covered with linen and leather, with marquetry, bark, faience and gold-leaf decoration, containing three composite bows. The Annexe, where so much of the king's weaponry had been stored, produced a white-painted bow box (no. 370), .67m (5ft 5¾in) long, 16 composite bows and ragmentary bowstrings, a self bow, 295 arrows and

bracers(?) to protect the inner arm from the released bowstring. Seven of the composite bows rom the Annexe had been stored in the bow box, together with some 254 arrows, and it is likely that the rest of the archery material found in this hamber had shared the same origin.

The powerful 'composite' or 'compound' bow – a laminated weapon consisting of a wooden core acked and/or faced with sinew or horn and wrapped in bark – was, like the chariot and the *hepesh*-sword, an Asiatic import of the Second intermediate Period and in frequent use during the New Kingdom. Before Carter's discovery of the omb, only 10 weapons of this type were known. Tutankhamun's impressive collection of at least 29, and perhaps 32, composite bows is thus the largest extant. The king's bows range in length from a child-sized 0.34 to 1.4m (1ft 1⅜in to 4ft 7in), and show considerable variation in their individual structure. Scientific examination has shown the wood employed to be ash (*Fraxinus* sp.), in one instance, manna ash (*F. ornus*); the bark, although it has not been positively identified, may be birch or cherry.

Like other composite bows, the Tutankhamun specimens are elaborately decorated and frequently inscribed. The best of them is the gold-sheathed and gold-granulated 'Bow of Honour' (no. 48h) – described by Carter as a 'work of almost inconceivable fineness', which was found with a number of other bows and staves laid on the bed no. 47 in the Antechamber. In the inscriptions of this bow, the name has been rather clumsily altered from 'Ankhkheprure'. As the Amarna correspondence reveals,

(Above) Three elaborate ivory boomerangs (nos. 620:6, 620:5, 620:4) from the Annexe floor.

(Right) Tutankhamun smites a lion: a ceremonial, openwork shield of gilded wood (no. 379b).

(Below) Pharaoh's leather scale armour, as found in Annexe box no. 587.

Tutankhamun slings and those employed 'in recent years' in the jungles of Malaya.

According to Carter, the boomerang (of curved or angled form, in type returnable and non-returnable) was primarily employed for fowling; the throwstick – of more or less fantastic form – probably for battle. Actual and model examples of both types (at least one fashioned from tamarisk wood) were recovered from the tomb in some numbers: in total, 34 from box nos. 367, 370, group no. 607, and among the Annexe floor debris (nos. 620: 4–12). With the exception of two specimens of gessoed and gilded wood capped with faience, found in a box (no. 54) in the Antechamber, all of these projectiles were recovered from the Annexe.

Of the Annexe specimens, the greater number had been thrown into a large white-painted bow box (no. 370), though others were recovered from boxes 367 and 607, and from the debris on the chamber floor. They included two 'snake-batons' (nos. 620:11–12) of a type well known from fowling scenes. One of the finest of Tutankhamun's boomerangs is a non-functional specimen of ivory, gold-capped at one end and inscribed for 'The good god, lord of the Two Lands, Nebkheprure, beloved of Ptah, south of his wall' (no. 620:6); two similar examples (nos. 620:4–5) were found with it on the Annexe floor. The majority of the projectiles were far more workmanlike affairs, of hardwood covered with strips of birch bark or painted in polychrome. Lengths varied from 26.5 to over 64cm (10⅜ to over 25in), weights from 50 to 260g (1⅘ to 9⅕oz).

The same box (no. 370) which furnished the bulk of the king's bows, boomerangs and throwsticks also contained a number of primitive hardwood

clubs, oddly curved or straight and cudgel-lik[e] some 70-85cm (27⅝–33½in) long, sometimes with [a] grip covered in birch bark. Other clubs of simil[ar] type were found among Carter's group no. 607, al[l] in the Annexe. In total, 13 such weapons were foun[d] one (no. 370h) was engraved with a standing bul[l]

Two decorated wooden maces (nos. 218, 23[7]) gessoed and gilded, had been placed between t[he] outermost and second shrines in the Buri[al] Chamber. They measure 81.8 and 82cm (32¼ an[d] 32¼in) long respectively.

Armour

The only item of true body armour recovered fro[m] the tomb was a close-fitting leather cuirass, found [in] a crumpled-up state in box 587 in the Annexe. It [is] described by Carter as 'made up of scales of thi[ck] tinted leather worked on to a linen basis, or lining, [in] the form of a . . . bodice without sleeves.' See also t[he] corslet from box no. 54 (p. 153).

Clearance of the Annexe produced, in additio[n] eight shields, of which four of the larger (ranging [in] height between 83.5 and 89cm (32⅞ and 35in) thoug[h] more delicate types, of gilded openwork, we[re] regarded by Carter as being 'of ceremonial purpos[e] only. The designs of these ceremonial shiel[ds] represent the king seated upon his throne (nos. 3[5,] 488b), as a sphinx trampling his enemies (no. 379[a,] or in human form smiting a lion with a curve[d] *khepesh*-sword (no. 379b). The four smaller (abo[ut] 74cm (29in) high) and more functional shields fro[m]

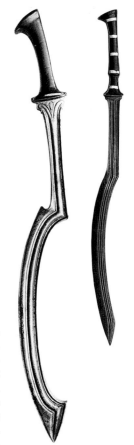

31.9cm (12½in) long, was found 'tucked ... obliquely' under one of the narrow, chased sheet 'girdles' that surrounded the waist, 'the haft to the right of the abdomen, the point of the sheath over the upper part of the left thigh'. The dagger sheath is of sheet gold, its outer surface delicately inlaid with a *rishi* pattern and fitted with a fennec- or desert-fox-head chape, the inner surface decorated in repoussé with an energetic chase-scene and incised with the king's name: 'The good god, lord of valour, Nebkheprure'. With its hardened gold blade, the ricasso elegantly chased with a palmette design, its elaborate grip richly granulated and inlaid with glass and semi-precious stones, the weapon is a masterpiece of the jeweller's art.

The second dagger (no. 256k) 34.2cm (13½in) long is even more startling, bearing a close resemblance to the weapons sent by the Mitannian king Tush-ratta to Amenophis III. Buried in the mummy wrappings along the right thigh, this dagger too was contained in a sheet-gold scabbard, decorated on its outer surface with a chased *rishi* pattern and again terminating in the head of a fennec, the back with a vertical palmette design contained within a rope border. Unlike that of the first dagger, it is uninscribed. The weapon proper is fitted with a grip closely similar to that of the first dagger, except that it is fitted with a pommel of sparkling rock crystal. But only when the dagger was drawn from the sheath was its true significance appreciated: 'the astonishing and unique feature of this beautiful weapon is that the blade is of iron, still bright and resembling steel!' This metal, of Hittite origin and of the greatest rarity and value, was destined to change the world.

e Annexe (nos. 488a, 492, 545, 566) are of solid nstruction, covered with either antelope or chee- skin. Each of them is decorated with a central nel of gilded gesso containing the prenomen and men of the king.

words and daggers

vo characteristic New-Kingdom *khepesh*-swords, type of Asiatic origin, were found in the Annexe. the first of these (no. 582a) made of bronze and asuring some 59.7cm (23½in) in length, was with a ass of sticks and staves in the southwest corner of e room. It is a heavy-backed, full-sized weapon, its rious, sickle-shaped blade cast as one with the ndle and the grip inlaid with panels of ebony or me other, dark-stained wood. Carter believed it to 'more fitted for a "crushing" than for a "cutting" ow, its convex edge being only partially deve- ped.' The second *khepesh* (no. 620:52), recovered om the debris on the Annexe floor, was in contrast very much smaller weapon, 40.6cm (16in) overall, ain cast in one piece from bronze and with dark- ood grips but lighter in weight and with a finely ged cutting blade. As Carter suggests, it was obably made for Tutankhamun as a child.

Two small (8.5 and 9cm (3⅜ and 3½in) long) gold nulets of *khepesh* form were also found in the bris of the Annexe floor (nos. 620:60–61).

The finest weapons buried with Tutankhamun ere the two daggers found wrapped in with the yal mummy (p. 177). The first of these (no. 256dd),

(Above left) A second ceremonial shield (no. 379a), again of gilded openwork, showing the king as a sphinx trampling his enemies.

(Above) The two bronze khepesh-*swords from the Annexe, that on the left (no. 582a) a full-sized weapon, that on the right (no. 620:52) evidently prepared for Tutankhamun as a child.*

Two daggers from the royal mummy, with blades of gold (no. 256dd) and iron (no. 256k): after watercolours by Winifred M. Brunton.

Sticks, Staves and Fans

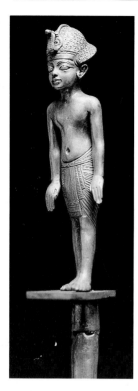

> ❛ The cloth the sticks were in was all falling away . . . and when the black from the cloth was brushed off they were perfect . . . Each stick was different; one was ebony and ivory, one was gold, a silver ferrule and a glass top, another gold bands with captives engraved on and beetle wings . . . another a reed with gold top. I cannot remember more but they were all different and of exquisite work. ❜
>
> Winifred Mace to her mother

Sticks and staves

The number of sticks and staves buried with Tutankhamun – some 130 complete and fragmentary examples, from the Antechamber, the Burial Chamber and the Annexe – led Carter to speculate that 'The young Tut.ankh.Amen must have been an amateur collector of walking sticks and staves'. Many of the forms were clearly ritual; others, however, showed signs of use.

The king's sticks and staves were of several different types: 'long staves with knobbed and forked tops and ferruled ends, crooked sticks, and curved sticks for killing snakes. Some beautifully mounted with gold and silver, others decorated with a marquetry of barks, or with the polished wood left plain'. One group from the Antechamber included four specimens ranging in length from 93.5 to 115c (36⅞ to 45¼in) with crooks carved and painted represent African and Asiatic captives (nos. 48a–c while with another group propped up inside t doors of the outermost shrine were two staffs, one gold (131.7cm (51⅞in)) and one of silver (130.5c (51⅜in)), surmounted by exquisite miniature effigi of the young king (nos. 235a–b). One stick stood o from the rest by its stark simplicity (no. 229, 181.3c (71¾in)) long. 'We wondered why such an ordina and plain reed should have been so richly mounte but the legend written upon it gave the touchi solution: "A reed which His Majesty cut with h own hand".'

(Above) Image of the child-king on golden staff no. 235a. With a matching silver staff, it is thought to have featured in the coronation.

(Below) Fighting sticks (bottom to top, nos. 582c–h), each fitted originally with a gold-mounted leather knuckle-guard. (Right) Fighting sticks in use: from the tomb of Amenmose (No. 19) at Thebes.

(Below) Detail from a Theban tomb painting of a king holding a stick like the gold-and marquetry-embellished one to the right (no. 227a). (Far right) The gold-mounted reed (no. 229).

'Such charming relics seem to elude time; many civilizations have risen and died away since that fan was deposited in this treasury. Such a rare, but in many ways familiar, object provides a link between us and that tremendous past. It helps us to visualize that the young king must have been very like ourselves.'

Howard Carter

Fans

In a land as hot and frequently airless as Egypt the fan was a necessary piece of equipment, intended to provide shade as well as a cooling breeze. Tutankhamun had been buried with eight – a single hand-held example and seven fans mounted on longer or shorter stocks for operation by a courtier. All are of the half-round, multi-feathered variety, and were distributed between the Burial Chamber (nos. 242 and 245), the Treasury (no. 272a), and the Annexe (nos. 389, 415, 596a, 599 and 600).

The most remarkable of Tutankhamun's fans was a small (18cm (*c.* 7in) long) but exquisite rotating hand-fan of ivory found in a white-painted wooden box (no. 272) in the Treasury. Its feathers, predominantly white with a shorter row of brown at the base, were preserved intact.

The first of the long fans was no. 242 (the 'Golden Fan'), deposited in the space between the third and fourth shrines, on the western side. Just over a metre in length (1.015m (*c.* 3ft 4in)), both the handle and the semi-circular 'palm' into which the feathers were originally inserted are covered with thick gold foil. Both sides of the palm are embossed and chased, the one with a scene of Tutankhamun hunting, the other with his triumphant return. The vertical inscription chased down the length of the handle records that the feathers of the fan (42 in all, before the depredations of insects, alternating white and brown) were obtained by the king 'while out hunting in the desert east of Heliopolis'.

The second stocked fan, no. 245 (the 'Ebony Fan'), was lying on the south side of the innermost shrine. Its palm is similarly covered with thick gold sheet, decorated in inlay work of coloured glass and calcite with the king's twin cartouches, while the ebony stock is decorated at intervals with inlaid bands.

The five fans from the Annexe varied in length between 60.96 and 121.9cm (24 and 48in) and their

materials from stained and gilded ivory, to wood with ornamented bark covering, and gold foil. Each had been fitted with 48 feathers. Where traces were preserved, it could be seen that the feathering had been stripped from the quills for part of the lower length, presenting a spoked effect. All except no. 596a, which carries the later form of the Aten cartouches and the prenomen and nomen of Akhenaten, were inscribed for Tutankhamun himself.

(Right) Tutankhamun returns from the chase in triumph: the reverse side of the Golden Fan (no. 242); and (far right) an ebony-stocked fan (no. 245), its gold-foil covered 'palm' inlaid with the prenomen and nomen of Tutankhamun.

(Below left) The king's small, rotating hand-fan as found in the bottom of box no. 272, its feathers preserved intact.

(Below right) Two of the fans from the Annexe (nos. 415, 600). The latter, when found, had the quills of its ostrich feathers still in place.

Beds and Headrests

Unlike the large, ritualistic couches which filled one wall of the tomb's Antechamber (p. 146), the smaller beds and bed-parts recovered from the Antechamber and Annexe were intended for use – or at least modelled upon the type of everyday bed found in the richer Egyptian households. In all, six such beds were found, two in the Antechamber and the remainder in the Annexe. All take the same general shape – feline-footed, dipping in the middle and fitted with a rectangular footboard.

The first of these (no. 47) Carter records as 'Resting upon [the] lion couch [no. 35] and probably in its original position', loaded up with a pile of sticks, bows and arrows from box no. 50. Constructed of wood (identified as ebony) and partially overlaid with gold leaf, this elegant bed measures some 1.85m by 0.9m (c. 7ft by 2ft 11⅜in), with maximum height at the foot end of 0.76m (2ft 5⅞in). The legs are strengthened with cross-stretchers, while two further stretchers, of curved, flattened form, clear the string-mesh mattress. The main feature of the bed is the footboard, which is divided into three panels, each containing an openwork figure of Bes. This bandy-legged dwarf-god, patron of the home and the hearth, is shown wearing a lotus crown, flanked on either side (in right and left profile) by a rampant lion resting upon a *sa* hieroglyph signifying 'protection'; night was a particularly vulnerable time. Each of the figures has a protruding tongue of ivory. The hieroglyphic inscriptions, incised and filled with yellow pigment, contain an elaborated version of the royal protocol.

A less elaborate, lime-washed bed (no. 80) was found on the central couch, 'obviously not in its

(Opposite top) An extra headrest: inscribed, of dark blue glass, and with gold foil edging to the 'pillow'. The superb quality and condition of the piece (now in Cairo) clearly identify it as a piece from the tomb, though it finds no mention in Carter's inventory.

(Right) The god Bes flanked by two rampant lions: a panel from the footboard of the 'ebony' bed (no. 47). The figures are painted blue and highlighted with gold leaf; the incised hieroglyphs, incorporating the prenomen and nomen of the king, are filled with yellow pigment.

(Opposite, left above) Two of the king's beds (nos. 466, 497) in position in the Annexe. (Left below) The gold-covered footboard of bed no. 466, with its string-mesh mattress. (Right) A detail of the footboard's central panel, decorated in relief with a sma-tawy ('binding of the Two Lands') motif.

riginal position', its painted, linen-weave mattress ierced by the cow-goddess's horns. It was unincribed. Bed no. 377, from the Annexe, had been imilarly roughly treated, being found 'on its side pon a heap of divers objects [at the] S. end of [the] hamber'. Its ebony frame is gessoed and covered ith gold leaf, the inner surface of the footboard ecorated with figures of the hippopotamus-headed 'hoeris and of Bes and its outer face with papyrus nd lotus motifs. The most notable feature of this oughly constructed piece, which Carter believed to e 'for sepulchral purpose', is the elaborate stringing f its mattress.

Two beds were recovered from the heap of debris t the north end of the Annexe. The first of these and t the same time the most spectacular of Tutankhmun's beds (no. 466) had its carved ebony frame ntirely covered in thick gold foil. Somewhat horter, at 1.75m (5ft 8⅜in), than the king's ebony edstead, scratches on the gold suggested to Carter hat this piece of furniture had seen use and was not rimarily a funerary piece. The footboard is again

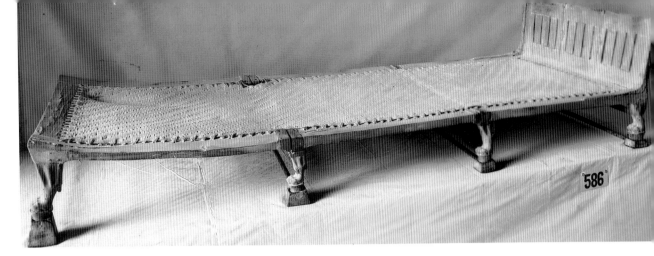

(Above) The king's folding bed (no. 586). (Right) Carter's unpublished record card, with notes and detailed drawings explaining the sophisticated hinging of the piece.

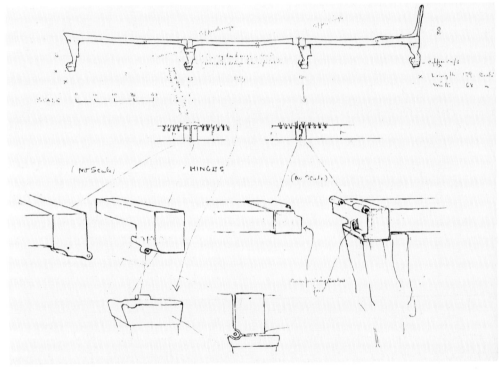

divided into three bordered panels, decorated with papyrus clumps and plant designs, the central panel carrying a large *sma-tawy* motif. The second bed from this heap (no. 497) was a great deal more modest – of simple wood construction, with its plain, panelled footboard broken away in antiquity and found leaning against the north wall.

The south end of the Annexe yielded the only intact, full-sized example of a travelling bed (no. 586) to have survived from ancient Egypt. Made of a light wood and measuring 1.79m (5ft 10½in) overall, its length is interrupted at two points by heavy, copper hinged-joints. The resultant lack of rigidity is compensated for by the provision of four extra legs, again of feline type, which are hinged to fold inwards when the bed is closed up in Z-form. At a mere 0.30m (c. 1ft) high this bed sits rather lower than the other beds from the tomb, but is generally similar in form. The footboard is panelled, like that of no. 497, and, like bed no. 80, it was originally painted over its entire surface (including its closely woven string mattress) in white, presumably limewash.

Headrests

Closely associated with the ritual couches (p. 146) and beds was a series of headrests which, suitably padded with linen, provided support during sleep. Eight were found in various parts of the tomb.

The characteristic New Kingdom headrest is of waisted form, produced in two or three parts, and 18cm or so (c. 7in) in height. Six examples of this type were recorded, the first (no. 21c), of gessoed and gilded wood, otherwise without decoration or

...scription, was recovered from the elaborate ...ainted Box positioned in front of the Burial ...hamber blocking; two similarly decorated head-...ests were found in the Annexe, in box nos. 547 and ...48. The three had perhaps been intended for the ...tual couches (p. 146). A rather better example (no. ...01o), of hard reddish-brown wood which Carter ...ntatively identified as cedar, was found in a black-...nd-white box with vaulted lid on top of the ...ippopotamus couch in the Antechamber. Blue-...ainted figures of Bes decorate either side of the ...ase, with a column of text, again in blue, on the ...ront and back containing the prenomen and nomen ...f Tutankhamun.

The majority of the tomb's headrests, like the ...eds themselves, came from the Annexe. The ...excavation' of a delightful 'table-shaped cabinet' ...no. 403) found lying on top of the jumble in the ...niddle of the chamber produced four headrests – ...hough Carter was of the opinion that 'These were ...ut there after the robbery and have, no doubt, ...nothing to do with the box itself.' The quality of all ...our headrests is superb. The first (no. 403a), made of ...urquoise-blue glass, now somewhat discoloured ...rom the damp of the tomb, is of the usual waisted ...orm, fashioned in two halves and joined at the ...entre of the column with a square wooden dowel. ...The join is covered by a narrow strip of gold foil, ...vidently attached to a central wooden 'washer', ...hased with alternating *ankh* ('life') and *was* ('domi-...ion') hieroglyphs. Both sides of the column carry a ...ertical inscription, one incorporating the preno-...men, the other the nomen. One corner of the base ...shows evidence of an ancient mend.

The second headrest (no. 403b) from this box is of ...leep blue faience, made in two pieces joined at the ...niddle, the joint concealed with a delicately inlaid ...gold band. Both front and rear facets of the column ...carry an elaborate cartouche in turquoise-blue glaze, ...one side containing the prenomen, 'Nebkheprure', ...he other the nomen, 'Tutankhamun, ruler-of-Upper-...Egyptian-Heliopolis'.

The two remaining headrests from this box (nos. ...403c and 403d), both of ivory, are each unique in ...design. In the first, which is made in two pieces, the ...central column is carved in the form of the kneeling ...air-god, Shu, supporting the curved top surface of ...the headrest (= the heavens) on his shoulders; the ...base is decorated with the two couchant lions of the ...eastern and western horizons, carved in the round to ...either side. The back of the pillar carries a vertical ...column of incised hieroglyphs (with blue-black fill) ...containing the king's prenomen. No. 403d takes the ...form of a miniature folding stool, with a flexible ...'rest' of threaded ivory beads, variously stained, like ...the headrest itself, in red, green and black. The outer ...surfaces of the pillow terminals are carved with Bes ...masks, while the gold-hinged, duck-headed legs (one ...of which is incised with Tutankhamun's prenomen) ...are steadied by horizontal, yellow-stained ivory feet.

Headrests inscribed with the names of Tutankhamun, from Annexe box no. 403. (Top) Headrest of turquoise-blue glass (no. 403a), of traditional, single-pillared form. (Centre) The folding headrest of tinted ivory (no. 403d), with beaded 'cushion', Bes masks and duck-headed legs. (Bottom) The ivory Shu headrest (no. 403c), with curved pillow and base decorated with the lions of the eastern and western horizons.

Chairs and Thrones

(Right) Inlaid 'Tutankhaten' cartouche from the right outer arm of the Golden Throne (no. 91).

(Below) The sumptuously inlaid back-panel of the Golden Throne (no. 91), showing a royal couple (identified by the altered inscriptions as Tutankhamun and Ankhesenamun) within a floral pavilion open to the life-giving rays of the sun.

The chair in ancient Egypt, as in many eastern countries, was a symbol of authority and prestige, and it came as no surprise to the excavators to find buried with Tutankhamun as with Tuthmosis IV and others before him a selection of chairs and stools scattered higgledy-piggledy throughout the Antechamber and the Annexe.

The most spectacular of Tutankhamun's six chairs – in Lord Carnarvon's words, 'one of the most marvellous pieces of furniture that has ever been discovered' – is the so-called 'Golden Throne' (no. 91). Found, curiously wrapped with a length of black linen, beneath the hippopotamus couch in the Antechamber, this 'throne', 1.04m (3ft 5in) high, is in reality an elaborated armchair of wood overlaid with sheet gold and silver ('dulled by age to an exquisite bloom') and inlaid with the usual blend of coloured glass, faience and semi-precious stones. The animal legs, originally linked by grilles (removed in antiquity by the tomb robbers) representing the 'binding of the Two Lands' (sma-tawy), are of a type which goes back to the beginnings of Egyptian furniture design. Here they adopt a leonine form, a theme continued in the apotropaic lion heads which protrude from the front. The openwork side-panels of the chair take the form of winged uraei adorned with the double crown of Upper and Lower Egypt which present the nomen of the king in its earlier -aten form. Four more uraei decorate the back of the throne, two on either side of the central stile.

The focus of this chair is the sloping back, with its inlaid scene (in the relaxed Amarna style) of the queen anointing her young husband with perfume within a floral pavilion open to the rays of the Aten which is here referred to in its later name-form. Certain details of this panel have been altered since it was first made – most noticeably the head-ornaments worn by the royal couple which in their final form cut through the life-giving rays of the disc. The queen's wig appears also to have been reduced in size, leaving the pleated ribbons of the fillet hanging unattached. The repoussé inscriptions to the left and right of the couple refer to them with the -amun forms of their names; these names too appear to have been altered. These alterations are perhaps to be construed as part of a refurbishment (not fully completed) to which the chair had been subjected before it was introduced into the tomb, and to which two hieratic notations on the rear right leg perhaps relate.

The throne's footrest (no. 90), 63.5cm (25in) long, had been placed sideways upon the inlaid chequerboard seat. Constructed of heavy wood, gessoed, gilded and inlaid with blue faience and yellow stone(?), the top surface carries a design consisting of three Nubians and three Asiatics, the chieftains of 'all foreign lands [who] are under his [the king's] feet'.

An uninscribed chair (no. 39), again from the Antechamber, is of similar design to the Golden

Throne. Made from African ebony with ivory inlay, its side panels overlaid with gold leaf, it had been prepared for Tutankhamun as a child, to judge from its small size (0.71m (2ft 4in) high). The mortise and tenon joints with which the chair is assembled are secured with bronze pins capped in gold. Unlike the flat seat of the more elaborate throne, that of the child's chair is made with a double curve, while the stretchers are more simplified.

One of the most elegant of the chairs buried with Tutankhamun was again found in the Antechamber (no. 87, 0.96m (3ft 1¾in) high, with its associated footrest, no. 88, 0.51m (2ft 8⅛in) long). The piece is constructed from an unidentified fine-grained wood, with tenon and mortise joints strengthened by gold-capped copper-alloy rivets. The deep-red colour of the base material is emphasized by a contrasting gold-foil overlay on the winged sun-disc, the wooden

(Above right) The so-called 'Ecclesiastical Throne' (no. 351), from the Annexe: a faldstool inscribed with both the 'Tutankhaten' and 'Tutankhamun' forms of the king's name. (Above) The top surface of the associated footrest no. 378.

(Below, left) Small ebony chair (no. 39), made for Tutankhamun as a child. (Below, centre) Sketch of chair no. 39, from Carter's unpublished notes.

(Below, right) Chair no. 82, bound with papyrus strips, and with back and seat in sheets of the same material: a sketch made by Carter.

back-bracers, and (before they were carried off by thieves) the openwork *sma-tawy* motifs between the animal legs. The seat of the chair is again double-curved, while the back carries an openwork representation of Heh, god of eternity, grasping notched palm ribs, an *ankh*-sign over one arm, kneeling upon the hieroglyph for gold – a complex interaction of symbols intended to convey the hope of long and prosperous life. The main inscription, cut in relief, comprises the names and titles of the king, here as 'Tutankhamun'.

Carter also recovered from the Antechamber, in a state of virtual collapse, a second chair of similar design (no. 82) though with an arrangement of vertical and diagonal bracings between the legs. The ebony framework of this chair, which stood 1.01m (3ft 3¾in) high, was held together merely by strips of papyrus, while sheets of papyrus had been employed to form the seat and back.

A third example of this type of chair (no. 349) comes from the Annexe. In its general shape closely similar to no. 87, though a mere 0.73m (2ft 4¾in) tall, the surface of this chair had been painted white. The sloping back again carries an openwork design, the main component of which is a falcon with crooked wings.

The most peculiar of the seats buried with Tutankhamun, 'thrown topsy-turvy in the S[outh] E[ast] corner of the [Annexe]' and 'tied up with strips of linen in similar manner to the throne' (no. 91), is a type of backed 'faldstool' (folding stool) commonly referred to as the 'Ecclesiastical Throne' (no. 351). Constructed from ebony covered in part with gold foil and richly inlaid with glass, faience and coloured stones, its double-curved seat (with panels of imitation animal skins, including cheetah and 'the blotchy markings of a hide like that of the Nubian goat') is suspended on a base fashioned as a duck-headed folding stool, here made permanently rigid. The geometric inlays of the sloping back, 1.02m (3ft 4½in) high, contain three vertical columns of text, in which the king is referred to in his earlier manifestation of Tutankhaten; the horizontal inscription above carries the king's name in its Tutankhamun form, while the main inlaid cartouches which flank the spread-winged Nekhbet vulture revert to the -aten form. At the top of the chair stands the Aten disc, with later-form cartouches. The -aten form of Tutankhamun's name is again found in the texts on the stiles at the rear of the throne. It is, as Carter observed, 'an important historical document with regard to the politico-religious vacillations of the reign.'

Associated with this throne was a simple, three-piece footrest (no. 378), 0.587m (1ft 11⅛in) long, similarly veneered and inlaid. Its top surface is divided into two, each stacked horizontally with alternating black and Asiatic bound captives – the 'Nine Bows', or traditional enemies of the Egyptian state.

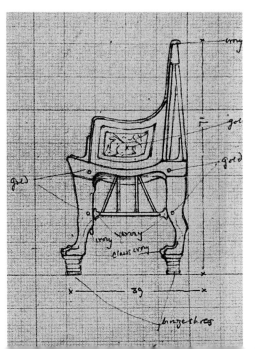

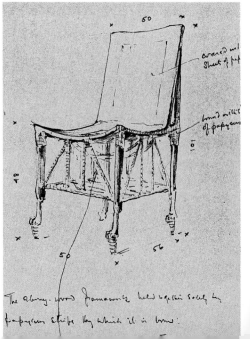

What may be a seventh chair (no. 33), albeit a very small one, low-backed and a mere 0.242m (c. 9½in) high, comes from the Antechamber; it was found balanced on top of the carrying chest no. 32 beneath the first of the ritual couches. The excavation records describe it, rather doubtfully, as a 'wooden stand' with 'slots cut out at each side, at top of back and front of seat', perhaps 'for side bars'. The information we have (which is very little) might indicate that the object was a low feeding chair used by Tutankhamun as an infant.

In addition to the footrests associated with the chairs and thrones enumerated above, eight further examples had been buried with Tutankhamun, both decorated (no. 30) and plain (nos. 67, 92, 414, 442b, 442e, 592, 613). Of those from the Annexe, Carter comments, 'Their dimensions seem appropriate only for a child'. With these footrests may be grouped a series of hassocks (nos. 34, 354, 361, 431b), evidently intended for the royal knee', 'of rush-work, lined with linen, and covered with elaborate polychrome beadwork. . . .' Dimensions for only two of these are recorded: nos. 34 and 354, with diameters of 26 and 29cm (10¼ and 11⅜in).

In all, 12 stools, of six distinct types, were found (nos. 66, 78, 81, 83–4, 139–40, 142b + 149, 412, 467, 511, 595). The first, represented by nos. 66, 81 and 84, ranging in height from 0.305 to 0.38m (c. 12 to 15in), is of simple, straight-legged form with double-curved seat and vertical and diagonal bracings; the second, somewhat similar, but with animal legs and *sma-tawy* grilles (nos. 78 and 467, at 0.345 (1ft 1⅝in) and 0.45m (1ft 5¾in) high respectively); the third, with 'turned' legs and horizontal stretchers (no. 142b + 149, 0.415m (1ft 4⅜in) high); the fourth, of folding type (nos. 83, 139–40), again under half a metre (c. 19½in) in height; and the fifth, of which only one example was recorded (no. 412), of tripod form, 0.29m (9⅞in) high, with animal legs and semi-circular seat. The type of no. 595, constructed from papyrus and palm-stalks and very badly preserved, is not clear.

Object no. 511, from the Annexe – rectangular in form, with bronze staples, a goose-feather filled cushion and leather carrying straps – Carter identified as a 'travelling stool'. This stool, 0.342m (1ft 1½in) long, and 0.205m (8in) high, was constructed from inferior wood improved by gilding and blue faience inlays; three of its four sides are decorated with a *sma-tawy* motif flanked by two bound captives on either side. The stool appears to be associated with the collapsible wooden canopy, no. 123, 'carried in the king's train wherever he went, and set up at a moment's notice to shield him from the sun'. The principal sections of this framework were found at the south end of the Antechamber with other elements recovered from the Annexe. Several parts of the canopy were missing, including the base. Its fabric covering, together with its metal fittings, had perhaps been carried off by the robbers.

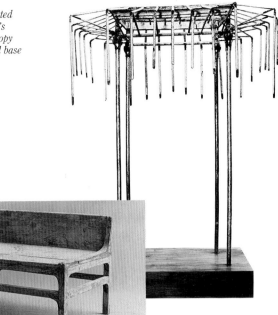

(Right) The reconstructed framework of the king's collapsible wooden canopy (no. 123). The original base was not found.

(Left, top to bottom) The royal 'feeding chair' (?) (no. 33); one of the tomb's three duck-headed folding stools (no. 140), lacking its seat; a white-painted, feline-legged stool (no. 467) with gilded sma-tawy grilles and double-curved seat designed to hold a cushion in position; and a white-painted tripod stool (no. 415), with feline legs, single sma-tawy grille and openwork seat in the form of two lions bound head to tail.

Boxes and Chests

Excluding the *shabti* boxes (p. 138), the variou ritual shrines (p. 130 *et seq*), the game-boxes (p. 160 the boxed provisions (p. 206) and the chest contain ing the two mummified foetuses (p. 123), the tom contained more than 50 boxes and chests. All of th boxes had been ransacked at the time of the theft and few contained even a fraction of the materia with which they had originally been packed. At leas two boxes (nos. 1k and 1l), found dismantled in th entrance debris, seem to have been employed by th robbers to carry off their loot: according to the dockets (p. 190), they had contained items of fin linen as well as silver vessels.

The boxes range in size from the smallest an most delicate, for cosmetics or trinkets, to large an functional carrying chests fitted with removabl pole-handles (no. 32) and elegant cabinets on lon slender legs (nos. 56, 403, 388 + 537). (See table Rectangular forms predominate, with sloping gabled or flat lids. Four boxes are cartouche-shaped and one, of veneered, barrel construction, is sem circular in shape. Several boxes (e.g. no. 56) hav secondary internal lids. The interiors of a grea many of the boxes (e.g. no. 315) are fitted wit wooden divisions, as if to receive specific objects o vessels. Materials and quality vary, from th beautifully finished calcite casket no. 40 found in th Antechamber to the irregularly made, yellow painted wood of its container-box no. 111 + 115 and the papyrus-pith construction of box no. 271a, wit its linen-lined interior. On the whole, however, eve with the most attractive of the boxes, the quality o the basic construction appeared to be poor, thoug the bad jointing we see today may be due at least i part to shrinkage.

The majority of Tutankhamun's boxes had bee closed by means of cord wrapped around the knobs

on the movable lid and end, to which a seal (p. 93) was then attached. Some containers, like no. 12n + 79 + 574, were fitted with gilded-copper side staples; such boxes 'were evidently intended to be used for travelling purposes, strapped either on the back of a beast of burden, or over the shoulders of a slave'. Copper hinges occur, for example on box no. 267 and on the 'toy chest' no. 585, both of which are fitted with an automatic catch: 'the fastening of the knob upon the lid is so notched on the inside that when the lid was closed and the knob turned, it locked the lid to the box'. In Carter's opinion, 'This

(Opposite, above) Bow-fronted travelling box (no. 12n + 79 + 574), perhaps in earlier days intended as a container for papyrus rolls.

(Opposite, below left) Calcite box (no. 40) of Tutankhamun and Ankhesenamun, with incised, colour-filled decoration and obsidian fastening knobs. When found, the box contained a mass of decayed hair and two hair balls wrapped in linen – remains of the royal marriage contract?

(Opposite, below right) Small panelled box (no. 56) on legs, with 'ebony' and ivory veneer and ivory fastening knobs. The interior is divided into six compartments, and fitted with a secondary hinged lid.

(Above) The portable chest (no. 32) in position in the Antechamber beneath the lioness couch (no. 35).

(Left) This type of large, portable chest (no. 32), with retractable handles, is well-known from tomb scenes going back to the Old Kingdom. Tutankhamun's, however, is the only example known to have survived.

(Left) The 'Painted Box' (no. 21), decorated over its entire outer surface with highly detailed scenes executed in tempera on a gesso base. The scene on the box side depicts Tutankhamun in battle against the Syrians; that visible on the lid shows the king hunting in the desert.

189

(Above) The lid of box no. 269, with hieroglyphs of ebony and tinted ivory spelling out the king's nomen: 'Tutankhamun, ruler-of-Upper-Egyptian-Heliopolis'.

(Above right) The cartouche-shaped box (no. 269) from the Treasury, found to contain jewellery, items of the royal regalia, linen, and a gilded mirror-case.

(Below) Box lid (no. 54hh) from the Antechamber, inlaid with the name and image of Nefernefrure, fifth daughter of Akhenaten. The box itself was not found.

contrivance . . . is the earliest automatic fastening hitherto known'.

As with other classes of object from the tomb, a number of pieces had originally been prepared during previous reigns. With box 1k, which carries the names of Akhenaten, Nefernefruaten and Meritaten, there had been no attempt to alter the earlier names, though on box 12n + 79 + 574 the cartouches of Nefernefruaten and Meritaten had been erased and written over with those of Tutankhamun and his consort. The inlaid wooden lid of a small box found in the Antechamber (54hh) carried the name of Nefernefrure, the fifth daughter of Akhenaten and Nefertiti; the box itself was not recovered.

The two finest boxes from the tomb are the Painted Box no. 21 from the Antechamber (des-

The Box Dockets

The majority of these dockets appear to have been written at the time the tomb was stocked; a very few, such as that inscribed upon box no. 575, may date from after the first robbery.

Object number	Translation
1k	The box of *kedet*-wood. Contents pertaining to the House-of-repelling-the-bowmen: byssus prepared as *mek*-material, different shawls of very good quality, 2; byssus prepared as *mek*-material, kerchiefs, 10; byssus prepared as *mek*-material, long *sedj*-loincloths, 20; byssus prepared as *mek*-material, long shirts, 7(?). Total of various choice linen, [3]9(?)
11	Contents: 1 silver *khenem*-vase; 3 silver jugs for milk
12n + 79 + 574	The *khetkhet*-objects of the king Nebkheprure life! prosperity! health! which belonged to the funeral
54	Contents: 17 blue faience *nemset*-ewers
54ddd	Gold seal rings belonging to the funeral
68	The equipment of His Majesty life! prosperity! health! when he was a child. Contents: copper handled-razors, knife-razors, and ewers; linen
101	Contents: 17 *djay*-lengths, for making up into 34 *daiu*-loincloths
267	Gold jewellery(?) for the funeral made [originally] for the bed-chamber of Nebkheprure
268	Gold *keb*-vase and *nemset*-vase which belonged to the funeral
272	The paraphernalia of the bed-chamber
283 (p. 130)	Gods
330 (p. 139)	Contents: *shawabtis* [*shabtis*] [made] of gold foil and cedar/cypress wood
386 + 388 + 537	Contents: kerchiefs and . . . shirt of fluffy(?) byssus
493 + 494	The equipment of His Majesty life! prosperity! health! when he was a child. Contents: frankincense [and] gum
547 + 615	Contents: fetish [and] *shabtis*
575 + 594	The equipment of Pharaoh life! prosperity! health! when he was a child. Gold: 1 *tekhbeset*-basket, 1 *qeb*-jar for carrying water(?), 1 *qeb*-jar for pure water(?), 2 sticks(?) for applying [black] eye-paint, 3 grasshoppers of gold, 2 *bensu*-vases [and] a basket of broken copper-bits(?)

ribed by Breasted as 'the work of a master artist of all time, compared with whom the greatest artists among the Greeks and of the Italian Renaissance and of the Louis XIV period are mere hacks'), and the ivory veneered box no. 540 + 551 from the Annexe. Breasted's rapturous comment on the Painted Box was characteristic of all who saw it. It is, indeed, one of the finest examples of miniature painting to have survived from ancient Egypt, considered by Carter to be 'one of the greatest artistic treasures' found. With its vaulted lid in position, it stands some 44.5cm (17½in) high; its length is 61cm (24in), its width 43cm (16⅞in). The tempera decoration covers each side (the king in battle against the Syrians, and against the Nubians), both ends (opposed images of the king as sphinx), and the lid (the king hunting

(Above) The royal 'toy chest' (no. 585), of solid construction, which when found contained a mix of objects: jewellery, a game-board, a pair of slings, and the king's fire-making equipment.

(Above left) The interior of box no. 585, showing the complicated arrangement of partitions and box-shaped drawers with sliding lids.

(Above) Scene of box-making from the tomb of Rekhmire (No. 100) at Thebes.

(Left) Hieratic docket from the white-painted wooden box (no. 1k) found in pieces at the tomb entrance.

Many of Tutankhamun's boxes were carefully veneered, using a variety of different woods or ivory. The decoration of the box shown here (no. 268), with its elaborate herringbone marquetry, had involved the gluing and attachment of more than 45,000 individual pieces.

(Below) The census: detail of a wall-painting from the tomb of Nebamun at Thebes. The two boxes with sloping lids are similar to examples found in the tomb of Tutankhamun.

(Above) Gilded wooden box (no. 44), with rich faience inlay and knobs of violet faience. The sides are decorated with the alternating prenomen and nomen of the king; the end of the box is decorated with opposed images of the kneeling Heh holding notched palm branches – a silent wish for eternal life.

desert game and lions). It had been employed originally to contain a range of children's clothing, some of which it still held when the tomb was first opened (p. 157). It took Mace and Lucas three weeks to empty.

The sloping lid no. 540 and the short-legged box from which it comes, no. 551, are constructed from a soft reddish-brown wood, overlaid with slabs of ivory carved in low relief and delicately stained, further embellished with inlays of faience, glass, calcite, ebony and ivory. On the front panel of the box we see 'the king seated upon a cushioned chair (decorated with garlands), shooting wild-fowl and fish with bow and arrow', while beside him squats the queen. The sides and back panels of the box are decorated with 'scampering animals – bulls, bull-calves, and ibexes – which, in some instances, are being attacked by a lion, a cheetah, a leopard, and hounds'. But, as Carter notes, the 'chief glory' of this

casket is the ivory panel upon the lid, 'carved in delicate low relief like a Greek coin'. Here, within a flower-bedecked pavilion, we see the slender Ankhesenamun presenting bouquets of flowers to her husband, who leans forward slightly upon his staff; below the couple, a boy and girl are shown kneeling, collecting mandrake fruits. Like the Painted Box, this casket too, though found empty, will perhaps originally have been employed to contain wearing apparel.

(Right) An indication of how much richer the tomb must once have been: a gold, openwork lid (no. 267c), found in the Annexe; the missing box was probably one of the many 'loose' pieces carried off by thieves in antiquity.

(Far right) Box no. 547 + 615, showing the mushroom-shaped interior fitting (reminiscent of the Abydos fetish) originally draped with a gold and faience beaded net.

Boxes and Chests

Object number	Material	Inscription	Details	Size (metres)
1k	wood, painted	Akhenaten, Nefernefruaten, Meritaten	vaulted lid; hieratic docket	l. 0.58
1l	wood, painted, veneered	Tutankhamun	flat lid; hieratic docket	—
12n(part) + 79 + 574	wood, veneered	Tutankhamun, Ankhesenamun; (orig. Nefernefruaten, Meritaten)	flat lid, round front; hieratic docket	w. 0.37
14a	wood, veneered		orig. flat lid? now missing	l. 0.11
14b	wood	Tutankhamun	cartouche-shaped	l. 0.122
21	wood, painted	Tutankhamun	vaulted lid; the Painted Box	l. 0.61
32	wood, veneered	Tutankhamun, Ankhesenamun	gabled lid	l. 0.83
40	calcite, painted	Tutankhamun, Ankhesenamun	vaulted lid	l. 0.33
42	reed, papyrus		flat lid	l. 0.305
43 + 522?			sloping lid; hieratic label	l. 0.33
44	wood, gilded and inlaid	Tutankhamun	sloping lid	l. 0.488
50	wood, painted	Tutankhamun	narrow, flat lid, legs	l. 1.36
54	wood, painted	Tutankhamun	flat lid; hieratic docket	l. 0.555
54hh	wood, inlaid	Nefernefrure	lid only	l. 0.10
54ddd	ivory	Tutankhamun	flat lid; hieratic docket	l. 0.156
56	wood, veneered		flat lid, legs	ht. 0.451
68	wood, painted		flat lid; razor box; hieratic docket	l. 0.30
101	wood, painted, veneered	Tutankhamun, Ankhesenamun	vaulted lid; hieratic docket	l. 0.90
111 + 115	wood, painted		vaulted lid; outer case of no. 40	l. 0.522
141	reed, papyrus		flat lid	l. 0.385
178	reed, papyrus		flat lid	l. 0.50
178a	reed, papyrus		flat lid	l. 0.50
179	ivory		fragment	—
267	wood, veneered		vaulted lid; hieratic docket	l. 0.454
267c	gold, open work		lid only	l. 0.064
268	wood, veneered	Tutankhamun	flat lid; hieratic docket	l. 0.262
269	wood, veneered	Tutankhamun	cartouche-shaped	l. 0.635
269a + 270b	wood		? lid; hieratic docket	—
270	wood		vaulted lid	l. 0.514
271	wood, veneered	Tutankhamun, Ankhesenamun	flat lid	l. 0.487
271a	papyrus, painted	Tutankhamun	flat lid	l. 0.235
272	wood		vaulted lid; hieratic docket	l. 0.664
279	wood, painted		gabled lid	l. 0.68
315	wood, painted		gabled lid	l. 0.603
316	wood, painted		gabled lid	l. 0.605
317	wood, painted		gabled lid	l. 0.61
367	wood			l. 0.585
367k	wood	Tutankhamun	cartouche-shaped	l. 0.112
370	wood, painted		bow-shaped	l. 1.62
376 + 548	wood, painted		flat lid	l. 0.67
386 + 388 + 537	wood	Tutankhamun	flat lid, legs; hieratic docket	ht. 0.68
403	wood	Tutankhamun	flat lid, legs	ht. 0.70
453	wood			l. 0.125
493 + 494	wood		sloping lid; hieratic docket	l. 0.283
522	wood		lid only	l. 0.274
540 + 551	wood, veneered	Tutankhamun, Ankhesenamun	sloping lid	l. 0.72
546 + 550	wood, veneered		flat lid	l. 0.65
547 + 615	wood		flat lid; hieratic docket	w. 0.40
575 + 594	wood, veneered		sloping lid; hieratic docket	l. 0.293
585	wood	Tutankhamun	flat lid	l. 0.652
587	wood			l. 0.53
618	reed, papyrus		flat lid	—
620:95	wood	Tutankhamun	cartouche-shaped	l. 0.12
620:121	wood(?), painted		lid only	l. 0.247

Inscribed strip from the lid of the dismantled box (no. 1k) found at the tomb entrance. The strip carries the cartouched names of Akhenaten and his co-regent Nefernefruaten, and that of the great royal wife Meritaten.

Tools and Lamps

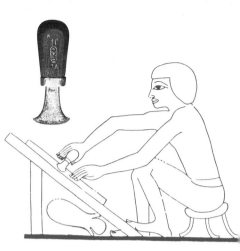

(Right) A leather-worker cutting sandal blanks with his curve-bladed knife: a scene from the tomb of Rekhmire (No. 100) at Thebes. Models of similar knives (shown is no. 620:59) were buried with Tutankhamun.

(Below) Two of the iron-bladed chisels from box no. 316 in the Treasury.

Tools and implements

Tutankhamun's tool-kit consisted of both ritual and practical items falling into four broad categories: mallets and chisels; knives; agricultural-type implements; and linear measures.

With the first group may be classed four small hones from the floor of the Annexe (no. 620:55), an ebony mallet(?), originally covered with gold(?), from box no. 46 in the Antechamber, a faience model pounder(?), 8.3cm (3¼in) long, from the Annexe floor debris (no. 620:27), and the electrum-bound wooden handle from a chisel or similar implement (no. 620:56). The blades of 16 further chisel-like implements had been fashioned not from the usual copper or bronze but from iron. All but one of them were found within box no. 316 in the Treasury; they are associated by some scholars with the 'opening of the mouth' ceremony depicted on the north wall of the Burial Chamber. The iron, of which no more than 4g was employed for all 16 blades, is probably of meteoric origin; when found, the metal was 'coated with oxide'.

Two finely polished flint knives (nos. 620:62 and 620:63), 11.5 and 10.5cm (4½ and 4⅛in) long, were recovered from the debris of the Annexe floor, while box no. 32 in the Antechamber contained seven model knives of limestone, ranging in length from 10.9 to 16.8cm (4¼ to 6⅝in); two model 'cutting knives' of painted wood, axe-shaped, were found in box no. 54 in the same chamber, and on the Annexe floor (no. 620:59). To judge from representations in the private

tomb of the vizier Rekhmire (No. 100) at Thebes they may well imitate a leather-worker's implements. A round-ended knife of sheet bronze, described by Carter as a spatula, was also recovered from the Annexe floor (no. 620:54).

The *shabti*-figures were well-equipped with model agricultural implements (p. 139). In addition to these may be noted a wooden model hoe of 'foundation deposit' type (no. 94b), an adze handle of white-painted wood (no. 100c), its blade evidently carried off by the robbers, and a second adze (no. 106a), larger in size and still retaining its bronze socketed blade. The bronze handle of a fine ritual adze (no. 402), 18.5cm (7⅜in) long, was found in the Annexe, inlaid in gold with the king's nomen and prenomen and still retaining its gold binding; it (gold?) blade was missing. Also from the Annexe come two 'ritualistic' sickles (nos. 561 and 620:64), both of wood. The more elaborate (no. 561), decorated with gold and electrum foil and inlays of calcite and glass, is inscribed with the king's prenomen and nomen and the epithet 'beloved of Hu' (personification of food). A model 'thrusting' hand mill for grinding corn, of sandstone and wood construction,

(Left) Wooden model hoe (no. 94b) from the Antechamber.

(Right) Ritual adze-handle (no. 402) of bronze with gold binding; the precious metal blade was evidently carried off at the time of the thefts.

(Far right) Ceremonial sickle (no. 561) sheathed in gold and electrum and inlaid with glass and calcite.

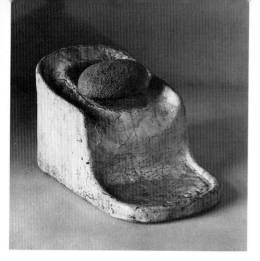

was found in the 'rough wooden box' no. 279 in the Treasury. For the wooden model granary (no. 277), see p. 145.

Six cubit measuring rods (1 cubit = 51cm), of 'dark red wood', come from box no. 50 in the Antechamber; but whether Carter was correct in believing the tall, shrine-shaped box no. 487 found in the Annexe to have 'once held a heavy metal standard cubit-measure' stolen by the robbers is debatable.

Lamps and torches

'It is I who hinder the sand from choking the secret chamber, and who repel that one who would repel him with the desert-flame. I have set aflame the desert(?), I have caused the path to be mistaken. I am for the protection of the Osiris [the deceased]'

Spell from the torch no. 263

Clearance of the Burial Chamber produced two calcite lamps (nos. 173, 174). The first, 51.4cm (20¼in) high, is really an elaborate stone vase, made in more than one piece and taking the form of a thin-walled

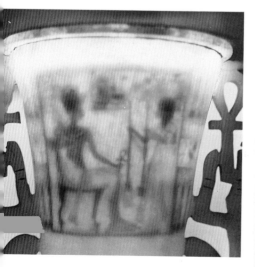

lotus chalice flanked by elaborately fretted 'handles'. The decoration of each handle contains a combination of symbols – the god Heh grasping a notched palm rib and *ankh* sign, the prenomen or nomen above – intended to convey the gift to Tutankhamun of millions of years. Both cup and handles are cemented onto a heavy, strutted pedestal carved from a single block of calcite. When employed as a lamp, the cup was part-filled with oil – perhaps sesame oil – traces of which still remained, and provided with a floating wick. When lit from within a scene becomes visible, painted upon the outer surface of a thin calcite liner cemented inside the cup. One side displays a scene of Queen Ankhesenamun presenting the seated king with the symbols of hundreds of thousands of years; the other side carries the king's prenomen and nomen between horizontal bands of petal ornament.

The second lamp is of triple form, 27cm (10⅝in) high, again of calcite though this time worked from a single block of stone. Like the first, it is of the floating-wick variety, its three oil reservoirs fashioned in the form of a large blue lotus flower flanked on either side by a white lotus, with a circular base from which the three stem. Each cup preserved traces of the original oil. The sepals of each cup are delicately incised, but there is no painted ornamentation like that of the larger lamp.

A smoke-blackened pottery dish (no. 86) some 19.3cm (7⅝in) in diameter was found beneath the ritual cow-couch. A lamp of a rather more practical sort, it had perhaps been employed by the tomb robbers or by one or other restoration party.

(Left) Model 'thrusting' hand mill (no. 279a) for grinding corn, with muller and saddle-stone of yellow quartzite. The saddle-stone is set into a gessoed wooden 'seat' fitted with a trough to catch the meal.

(Below left) Bowl of the first calcite lamp (no. 173), lit from the inside to show the scene (otherwise invisible) painted within the thickness of the translucent walls.

(Below) The second calcite lamp (no. 174), of triple-lotus form, carved from a single block of stone. When found, the three reservoirs still retained traces of the original oil.

(Above, left and right) One of four ritual torch and lamp supports (no. 41) taking the form of handled ankh-*signs set into bases of black-varnished wood. The torch shown here is of twisted linen.*

A third reed torch (no. 263), 8.3cm (3¼in) long, impregnated with pine resin and decorated with a gold-foil band, was found at the entrance to the Treasury. It had originally been slotted into a mud-brick base, incised with a spell for the protection of the dead king (see quotation p. 195).

Among the tools recovered from the tomb was an elaborate fire-drill which would have provided the flame to light torches and lamps of this sort. It was discovered in the king's 'toy chest' (no. 585) in the Annexe. Carter's description of its employment is as follows: 'The rotation was effected by means of a bow alternately thrust forwards and backwards, the thong of which having been first wound round the stock of the drill in which the fire-stick was fixed. In order to steady the drill the upper end was held in a socket (drill-head). . . . The round holes in which the fire-stick was rotated were made near the edges of the fire-stock, so that a vertical slot was created . . . which allowed the spark created to have free access to the tinder'. The drill stock measured 19.7cm (7¾in) in length.

It may be noted that the tomb also yielded a range of raw materials, including a small piece of lead, tin oxide, chalk, galena and malachite (see p. 158), red and yellow ochre, orpiment (arsenic trisulphide) and various other pigments (p. 166). Resin (in lumps, 'tears' and rods) and artificially shaped pieces of frankincense were also found.

Four ritualistic pieces found on the lion-couch in the Antechamber were, as Carter observed, 'absolutely new in type'. Each one is about 23cm (9in) tall and takes the form of an *ankh* sign of bronze fitted with enfolding arms, set into a black-varnished base. Two of the bases are fitted with tubular torch-holders of gilded bronze, one of which still retains its twisted linen torch. The remaining two bases appear to have been intended for use with a floating wick, though their bowls were now gone – 'Probably these were of gold and were stolen by the tomb-thieves'. Carter believed that, before the thefts, these 'candle-sticks' had been stored in box no. 316 in the Treasury: not only are they of an appropriate size for this box, but 'their wooden pedestals, coated with black resin, coincide with blotches of similar black material found on the bottom of the interior of the box'.

(Below, left and right) The Egyptians knew nothing of the flint striker, and the only method they employed for creating fire, from the beginning to the close of Pharaonic civilization, was by means of a fire-stick working on the same principle as the bow-drill. Tutankhamun's (no. 585aa) was evidently a far more efficient specimen than most, well designed and with the drill holes lined with resin to promote friction.

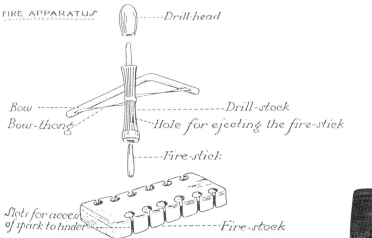

FIRE APPARATUS

Drill-head

Bow

Drill-stock

Bow-thong

Hole for ejecting the fire-stick

Fire-stick

Slots for access of spark to tinder

Fire-stock

(Left above) A pair of miniature vessels (nos. 394, 620:37), one of gold, the other of silver, perhaps part of the original contents of box no. 575 from the Annexe.

(Left and below) The finest of Tutankhamun's metal vessels: a pomegranate-shaped vase (no. 469), 13.4cm (5 $\frac{3}{10}$ in) tall, with serrated rim and bands of delicately chased floral decoration (as shown in Carter's sketches below). According to Carter, the metal contains a considerable proportion of gold 'and might be considered as either silver or electrum'. It had originally been fitted with a rush-work stopper, which was found inside together with the broken section of the rim; the remains of the 'dark brown material' the vessel contained could not be identified. The novelty value of the pomegranate, which was brought back to Egypt from Asia following the campaigns of Tuthmosis III, perhaps explains its popularity as a vessel form during the later years of the 18th dynasty.

Metal vessels

Only three metal vessels were found in the tomb, and all in the Annexe: no. 469, a silver pomegranate vase, beneath the oval basket no. 452; and nos. 394 and 620:37, a pair of small bag-shaped vessels, 3cm (1⅛in) or so in height, one of gold and one of silver, both rather battered. Carter believed that the latter were 'Possibly for writing or painting purposes'. They are perhaps two of the vessels mentioned in the docket to box no. 575 (p. 190).

The three vessels recovered by Carter clearly represent only a few of those originally buried with the king, if the box dockets (p. 190) are to be relied upon. The fate of the 'missing' pieces is fairly clear: they had been carried off for scrap at the time of the thefts.

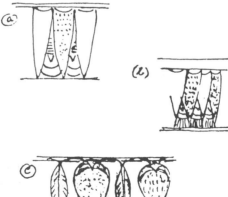

Stone Vessels

❝ His ornate vessels wrought of semi-translucent alabaster evoke surprise mingled with curiosity and admiration. Their strange forms seem almost to belong to wonderland. ❞

Howard Carter

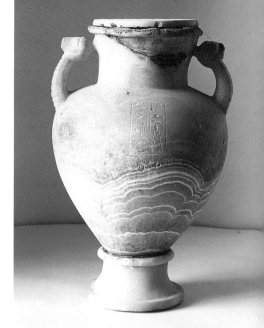

Stone vessels in ancient Egypt were commonly employed for the storage of precious oils and cosmetics, and this had been their principal function in Tutankhamun's tomb.

Several of the containers were of some considerable age (see table); Tuthmosis III, for example, for whom an oviform jar and amphora found in the Annexe were originally made, had himself been dead for a century when his vessels were buried in Tutankhamun's tomb. Other vessels from the Tutankhamun assemblage carried the cartouches of Amenophis III and Tiye, Tutankhamun's grandparents. A calcite jar stand carries on its under surface a hieratic docket recording the name of the scribe Djehutymose, son of Hatiay – a man already known from a graffito in the tomb of Tuthmosis IV (No. 43) as the assistant of the necropolis official Maya (p. 31). On the basis of the older royal names, Carter concluded that 'the majority of the commoner types appear to have been taken from a store and were not especially made for the funeral equipment'. A number of jars display old breaks and ancient repairs.

Over 80 vessels were represented in the tomb, of several different sorts, ranging from a *kohl* pot (p. 158), cups, simple bag-shaped jars, jugs, double vases, and a situla to large urns, amphorae, and elaborate vessels of fretwork and animal design – plus a sprinkling of bowls, lids, stoppers, stands and fragments. The vessels ranged in height from a few centimetres to almost a metre. The majority were

recovered from the Antechamber (some 36 pieces, including lids) and the Annexe (39), with further examples found elsewhere in and outside the tomb – including dummy vases, fragments and lids, from the stairway and the corridor (nos. 1g, 5a, 7); an elaborate vase (no. 210) more than 70cm (27⅝in) in height, cosmetic jar (no. 211, height 26.8cm (10½in)) and two lamps (for which see p. 195) from the Burial Chamber; and two calcite beakers (no. 261h, each 6.8cm tall (2⅝in)) from the Anubis shrine (p. 133) in the Treasury. The stone employed was predominantly calcite, frequently gilded, painted and sometimes inlaid with coloured glass and semi-precious stones. Serpentine and indurated limestone had also been employed for a small number of vessels.

(Above) The 'censored' text on pitcher no. 588 of Amenophis III and Tiye. The nomen was replaced during the Amarna period with a second example of the king's prenomen, 'Nebmaatre'.

(Right) An antique calcite amphora (no. 410) from the reign of Tuthmosis III, inscribed with its capacity – 14½ hin, or 6.67 litres.

(Far right) Jar (no. 420) with openwork 'envelope'.

(Left above) The discovery of decayed but still-viscid oils aroused much interest: the Daily Chronicle, *20 June 1929.*

(Left) The most elaborate stone vessel, containing aromatic gum-resin mixed with fat, was a perfume jar (no. 210) found within the doorway of the first outermost shrine. Its stopper had probably been carried off during the second robbery. The lion cosmetic jar (no. 211), pictured right, can be seen in the same photograph.

(Far right) Detail of the boat-shaped 'centre-piece' of calcite (no. 578) from the Annexe, with its superbly modelled dwarf steerswoman.

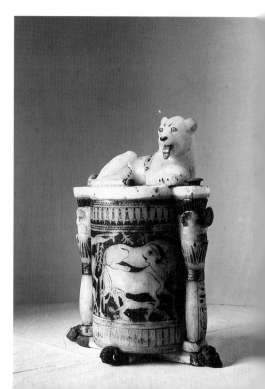

'With rare exception', the closed stone vessels had had their stoppers and lids removed and been ransacked by the tomb robbers. From the size and number of the vessels, the capacity of which ranged from 2.75 to 14 litres, Carter was able to estimate that 'at least 350 litres of oils, fats, and other unctuous materials' had originally been stored in the Annexe. A number of these jars still contained the remains of their original, fatty contents, Carter noting that the two 'craters' nos. 420 and 435, 25.8 and 47.6cm (10⅛ and 18¾in) high respectively, still showed 'Finger marks of thieves on [the] interior walls'. When the tomb was later tidied up, the empty vessels had been employed as containers for the smaller objects which had been scattered around by the robbers.

Inscribed Stone Vessels (all calcite)

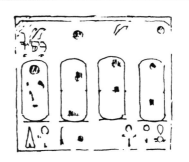

Evidence of co-regency? A drawing by Carter of the partially erased text panel of jar no. 405, where two sets of cartouches had originally been juxtaposed. Carter evidently believed the traces to conceal the names of Amenophis III and Akhenaten.

Object number	Name	Comments	Height (centimetres)
7		oil jar; hieratic docket	—
7a		oil jar; hieratic docket	—
7b		oil jar; hieratic docket	—
14	Tutankhamun	Wishing Cup	18
20		oil jar; hieratic docket	19
32b		oil jar; hieratic docket	c. 10
55		oil jar; hieratic docket	19.7
57	Tutankhamun	fret vase	52.9
60	Tutankhamun	fret vase	50.2
61	Tutankhamun	fret vase	61
127		oviform jar; semi-hieratic	35
173	Tutankhamun	fret lamp	51.4
210	Tutankhamun, Ankhesenamun	fret vase	70.2
211	Tutankhamun	cosmetic jar	26.8
360	Tutankhamun	cosmetic jar	68.3
385	Tutankhamun	amphora	66
404	Tuthmosis III	oviform jar	35
405	Amenophis III(?)	globular jar; two pairs of cartouches, erased	30
410	Tuthmosis III	amphora	41.5
420	Tutankhamun	jar	25.8
448	Amenophis III(?), ?	globular jar; two pairs of cartouches, erased	30.0
483	Amenophis III	handled jug; nomen erased and altered to prenomen	35.5
520	Tutankhamun, Ankhesenamun	jar	58.5
579	Tutankhamun, Ankhesenamun	lion vessel	60
584	Tutankhamun	ibex vessel	38.5
588	Amenophis III, Tiye	handled jug; nomen, erased and altered to prenomen	41
620:116/122	Djehutymose (scribe)	jar stand; hieratic docket	16

Oil jar (no. 584) modelled in the form of a bleating ibex.

Faience and Glass

Faience

Egyptian faience, a composite material consisting of a ground quartz body with alkaline glaze, is one of the most characteristic materials of ancient Egypt. It was used extensively from as early as the fourth millennium BC, and was employed in the tomb of Tutankhamun for inlays, terminals, jewellery, amulets, small sculpture (such as *shabti* figures – p. 136) and for small items of furniture, including headrests (p. 180). One of its principal uses, however, was for the production of vessels.

Several types of faience vessel were represented, including simple forms such as cups, jars and shallow dishes as well as peculiar ritual vessels of *hes-* and *nemset-*type, already well known from the tombs of Amenophis II (No. 35), Tuthmosis IV (No. 43) and elsewhere. In all, some 67 vessels were recovered, distributed between the Antechamber (with 34 vessels represented) and the Annexe (with 33). The bulk appear to have been contained within one box in each chamber: no. 54 in the Antechamber, and no. 461 in the Annexe. The former carried a docket specifying the contents as '17 blue faience *nemset-*ewers', of which 16 vessels (each about 10cm (*c.* 4in) high) and 17 stoppers were still present.

Glass

'There is absolutely no doubt that the tomb was robbed . . . I think, strangely enough, that glass was taken too, because . . . I did not see any glass, and in the passage leading down we found two bits . . . proving that glass had certainly been there and was either broken going in or coming out.'

Lord Carnarvon

Since the 18th dynasty was a period of large-scale glass production, it is curious that so few vessels and other objects of this material should have been recovered from the tomb. It seems probable, however, that there had originally been more: unlike faience, glass at this period was a costly and sought-after commodity; it could also be recycled, and much of the glass that had been buried with the king no doubt disappeared at the time his tomb was robbed.

A selection of faience vessels recovered from the tomb: (right) tea-pot-shaped nemset-*vessels (nos. 54zzz, 54z); (right below)* hes-*vases (nos. 461t, 461v); (below) miniature 'cups' (nos. 54u, 54t); and (bottom right) bag-shaped jars (nos. 620:30, 620:29), a further* hes-*vase (no. 620:31) and a drop-shaped jar (no. 399a).*

(Bottom left) The faience vessels of box no. 54, as found.

It is a view that Carter, who had a great interest in ancient glass, seems to have shared:

'A plain wooden box of oblong shape, which stood on the north side of the Canopic canopy, had its contents completely cleared by the tomb-plunderers. Its gable-shaped lid had been replaced the wrong way on, and only the packing material in its eight rectangular compartments was left. This material comprised pieces of papyrus reeds, shredded papyrus-pith and, at the bottom of each division, a small bundle of linen matting of long pile. There was not a trace of evidence as to what the original contents were, save that the careful arrangement of the packing suggested that the objects were of fragile nature – possibly glass.'

As Carter remarks on the object card for this box (no. 315): 'DAMN!!!'

The only glass vessels found in the tomb of Tutankhamun were three small specimens, one a small cup of translucent white (5.2cm (2in) high), the other two – a second cup and a small flask, each 5cm (1$\frac{9}{10}$in) high – of an indigo-blue colour. They came from the portable chest (no. 32) in the Antechamber. It is perhaps only by chance that these and a handful of other accessible glass objects – including large headrests (p. 182), a blue amulet of a squatting Amarna king (no. 54ff, 5.8cm (2$\frac{1}{4}$in) tall, the pair to no. 54ee, of calcite), and a model scribe's palette (p. 166) – should have survived at all.

(Far right) The tantalizing interior of box no. 315, with its carefully padded – but empty – compartments.

(Right) Found loose in the portable chest (no. 32): Tutankhamun's three remaining glass vessels: 32l, 32k, 32j.

(Below left) Two globular faience jars (nos. 31, 31a) in position in the Antechamber.

(Below right) Drop-shaped jars (nos. 54w, 54ccc) of blue-green and yellow faience.

315

Wine Jars and
Other Pottery

(Above) Blue-painted pottery jar (no. 203) from the Burial Chamber, of characteristic round-bottomed form for resting in the sand.

(Below) All 16 of the wine-jar sealings.

(Left) Ritual lidded vessel of blue-painted pottery (no. 23), from the Antechamber.

(Right) Two-handled wine-jars in the Annexe.

(Right centre) The two types of mud sealing on both the 'Syrian' and two-handled wine jars. A hole was left to allow the escape of carbon dioxide during secondary fermentation and was later sealed. One vessel in the tomb, sealed prematurely, exploded.

(Far right) 'Syrian' amphora no. 502, from the Annexe.

Given the number of artistic master-works buried with Tutankhamun, it is hardly surprising that Carter should have devoted little attention to the pottery from the tomb, which consists predominantly of plain, utilitarian vessels with a scattering of decorated specimens of blue-painted ware (e.g. nos. 9, 23–4, 203). The types fall into two main groups: open forms (dishes, bowls, saucers and cups), of which a dozen or so were found; and closed forms (jars), of which more than 50 were recovered, at least 30 of them wine-amphorae. No open-form vessels appear to have been found beyond the Annexe and Burial Chamber blockings; while the bulk of the closed forms came from the Annexe. No pottery of any sort appears to have been recovered from the Treasury.

Many of the smaller dishes and bowls had been employed as lids, plastered in position to close the mouths of the smaller round-bottomed storage jars. These jars for the most part contained food provisions (p. 205). Several of them (nos. 614a–i, ranging in height from 7.2–16.4cm ($2\frac{7}{8}$–$6\frac{1}{2}$in), and no. 406, at 44cm ($17\frac{3}{8}$in)) carry hieratic dockets specifying their original contents (which were somewhat mixed when discovered). Two further vessels from group no. 614 are a small amphora (no. 614j), 18cm (c. 7in) high, with rush-bound handles and a clay seal, and a single-handled jar (no. 614k), 13cm ($5\frac{1}{8}$in) tall, with rush-bound handle and plastered top; both of these vessels, according to their dockets, contained honey.

The largest group of ceramic vessels is that of the wine jars, of which more than 30 complete examples were found in the Burial Chamber and Annexe, together with fragments of others in the debris of the entrance staircase and corridor – the residue of the material reburied in Pit 54 following the first robbery (see p. 38). Tutankhamun's wine jars are of two main types: two-handled, measuring up to 80cm ($31\frac{1}{2}$in) tall, of which more than 24 specimens were recovered (nos. 362, 392, 411, etc.); and single-handled, slightly smaller at 50cm ($19\frac{5}{8}$in) or more in height, of which Carter records at least five examples. Although it has been claimed that the latter class of amphora with long neck and single strap handle is of Syrian origin, it is now thought likely that these marl-ware vessels, as indeed all of the pottery buried with Tutankhamun, were of local Egyptian manufacture.

Twenty-six of the wine vessels carry ink-written hieratic dockets which usually specify the date of the vintage, beverage type, vineyard, and the name of the vintner (see table). From these dockets Carter deduced that 68 per cent of the king's wines came from the 'domain of the Aten', a mere 5 per cent from the Amun temples, and some 27 per cent from his own vineyards. Among other information indirectly furnished by the dockets is the length of the king's reign: no wine produced later than Year 9 of Tutankhamun can with certainty be identified among the burial furnishings.

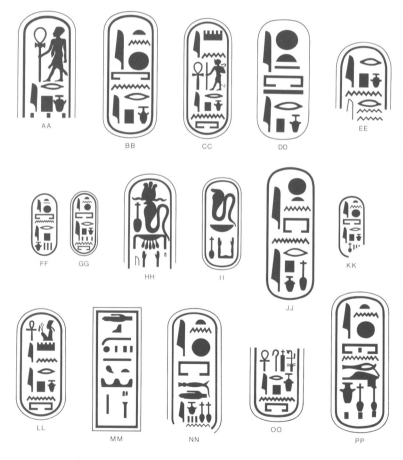

AA BB CC DD EE
FF GG HH II KK
JJ
LL MM NN OO PP

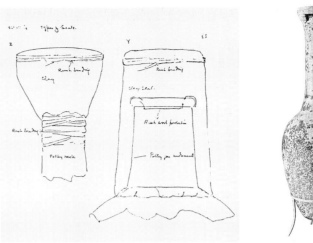

Tutankhamun's Wine List

Object number	Year	Type	Vineyard	Chief vintner	Seal
413	4	sweet wine	House of Aten life! prosperity! health! of the Western River	Aperreshep	FF?
486	4	wine	(ditto)	Nen	DD
362	4	pomegranate wine(?) of very good quality	(ditto)	Nen	—
568	4	wine	House of Tutankhamun life! prosperity! health! in the Western River	Kha	LL
392	4	pomegranate wine(?) of very good quality	House of Aten of the Western River	Khay	NN?
434	5	wine	(ditto)	Any	JJ?
523	5	wine	(ditto)	Pawah	—
411	5	sweet wine	House of Aten from Tjaru	Penamun	—
549	5	wine	House of Aten of the Western River	Nania	—
509	5	sweet wine	(ditto)	Nakht	—
489	5	wine	(ditto)	Nakhtsobk	BB
571	5	sweet wine	House of Aten from Qaret	Ramose	JJ
206	5	pomegranate wine(?) of very good quality	House of Aten of the Western River	Rer	—
180	5	wine	House of Tutankhamun-ruler-of-Upper-Egyptian-Heliopolis in the Western River	Kha	—; handle: House of the Ruler
560	5	wine	House of Tutankhamun life! prosperity! health! in the Western River	Kha	CC; handle: House of the Ruler ...
508	5	wine	House of Tutankhamun-ruler-of-Upper-Egyptian-Heliopolis life! prosperity! health! in the Western river	Kha	CC
570	5	wine	House of Tutankhamun-ruler-of-Upper-Egyptian-Heliopolis in the Western River	Kha	—; handle: House of the Ruler
—	9	wine	House of Aten on the Western River	Pay?/Khay?	—
516	9	wine	House of Tutankhamun-ruler-of-Upper-Egyptian-Heliopolis life! prosperity! health! in the Western River	May	—
539	9	wine	House of Aten on the Western River	Nebnefer	—
11	9	wine	House of Aten in the Western River	Nakhtsobk	—
195	9	wine	House of Aten of the Western River	Sennefer	—; handle: House of Aten
541	9	wine	House of Tutankhamun-ruler-of-Upper-Egyptian-Heliopolis life! prosperity! health!	Sennefer	AA?; handle: House of the Ruler
500	10	wine of good quality	from Iaty	—	MM
563	31	wine	House ... of the Western River[?]	...	—
490	—	—	[?Gift of] the vizier Pentu	—	—

Baskets

' They [the baskets] show by their symmetry the natural aptitude of the expert workman. The "strokes" employed in their construction appear to be precisely the same as those used today by the native basket-makers. Some of the smaller and finer weaved examples are adorned with patterns formed by interweaving stained with natural grasses. The coarser specimens are made of fibre "skeins" from the fruit-bearing stalks of the date palm, bound with fronds of the *dom*-palm, or, as in some cases, the date-palm, which were in all probability first soaked in water to render them both leathery and pliable. '

Howard Carter

(Right and below) The three main types of basket buried with Tutankhamun: oval (no. 440a), round (no. 357) and bottle-shaped (no. 589a).

(Far right, above) Partitioned reed tray (no. 119), recovered from beneath the pile of chariots at the south end of the Antechamber. The tray had been designed to hold a different fruit or berry in each compartment; as found, it contained chariot elements, a sealed linen bag, two dom-palm fruits, a fragment of bread(?) and a few seeds. The lid to this tray (no. 26) had been employed by Carnarvon and Carter to conceal their entry-hole into the Burial Chamber.

(Far right, below) A selection of the baskets as found at the north end of the Annexe.

So far as containers are concerned, the large number of boxes the tomb produced (p. 188) was exceeded only by the quantity of baskets: the Annexe, where most of them had been stored, produced an astonishing 116, with others scattered throughout the tomb. The majority of these baskets had been employed to hold food provisions (p. 206); of those that still did 60 per cent contained fruits, 26 per cent seeds of various sorts, with 1 per cent containing bread for beer-making. Other baskets, such as no. 119, contained a jumble of objects thrown in at the time the tomb was cleared up by the necropolis inspectors.

The baskets themselves, almost all coil-made from date and *dom*-palm leaves, ranged in size from 10.16 to 45.72cm (4 to 18in). They were of a variety of shapes – round (two large and 30 small, two of the latter variety with suspension strings), oval (10 large, 69 medium-sized, and two small) and 'bottle-shaped' (a mere three examples), with flattened or raised lids. Several had simple patterns worked in a contrasting colour. In type and general appearance, Tutankhamun's baskets are ageless: Carter noted that 'On certain festivals the modern Egyptians still take similar baskets of fruits to the tomb of their deceased relatives', and indeed similar examples of basketry work are still sold in Aswan today.

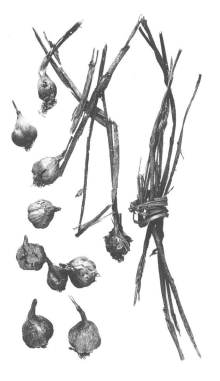

Tutankhamun's funerary provisions scattered throughout the tomb. Other foodstuffs had been recovered from Pit 54 (p. 39) in 1907.

A basic staple of the Egyptian diet was and still is bread, eaten alone or with onions (or garlic, of which box no. 32 yielded a small bunch – *Allium sativum*), and beer. It is not surprising, therefore, that the king should have been provided with a range of different types of bread and quantities of raw grain contained in baskets (for example, nos. 401, 439, 473, 531), a model grinder (no. 279a) (p. 195) and a model granary (no. 277) (p. 145). The baskets and granary included among their contents barley (*Hordeum vulgare*) and emmer wheat (*Triticum dicoccum*), with some, presumably accidental, admixture of leguminous and other plant seed. Actual examples of bread or cakes were recovered from the Antechamber (no. 99, 119e?) and Annexe (nos. 620:112, 620:117) floors, where they had been thrown by the tomb robbers. Those from the Annexe were the best preserved: Carter describes them as semi-circular in shape, varying in size from 9.5 to 13cm (3¾ to 5⅛in) in length, and enclosed 'in a mesh of rush-work'; a dozen or more were found. The bread's original taste can only be guessed at: according to Lucas, it 'is very cellular and has the appearance of petrified sponge'. The composition of one trefoil-shaped loaf or cake (no. 620:117) is described as 'a mixture of meal and fruits'. Other specimens of bread were recovered from at least one of the Annexe baskets (p. 204); Carter believed that they were intended for beermaking, and it has been further suggested that the two wood and copper strainers from the Treasury (no. 274) were perhaps associated with this process.

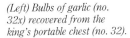

(Left) Bulbs of garlic (no. 32x) recovered from the king's portable chest (no. 32).

' The finding of canned beef 3,350 years old in Tutankhamen's tomb is admitted by cold storage experts to be a record. Mr. Raymond, hon. secretary of the British Cold Storage Association, says the record, so far as cold storage is concerned in this country, stands at eighteen years. '

Daily Mail

Although there was, of course, no 'canned' beef buried in the tomb, Tutankhamun had been sent to the grave accompanied by a range of foods in order that his *ka* might not go hungry in the next world. Most of this sustenance had originally been stored in separate baskets (p. 204) and pottery vessels (p. 202) in the Annexe; but, thanks to the activities of the tomb robbers, Carter and his team found remains of

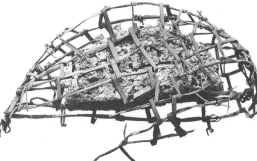

Three small loaves of bread (group no. 620:112), the specimen on the right encased in a rush-work mesh.

Meat was supplied in the form of 48 egg-shaped, two-piece boxes (no. 62), 27 to 56cm (10⅝ to 22in) long, whitened on the outside and varnished with resin on the inside, and containing a variety of joints (see table). The particular cut had been noted on the outside of several boxes, but the degree of carelessness was such that only rarely do the contents match the written description. Further meat provisions originally buried in the tomb were recovered from Pit 54. They included the shoulder blade of a cow and the ribs of a sheep or goat. The bulk of the protein from Pit 54, however, is made up of the wings and breasts of nine ducks (four small teal, *Anas crecca*; two shovellers, *Spatula clypeata*; one gadwall, *Chaulelasmus streperus*; with two unidentified) and four geese (a brent – *Branta bernicla*; a white-fronted – *Anser albifrons*; and two large bean geese – *Anser fabalis*).

The legumes and pulses from the tomb included chick-peas (*Cicer arietinum*), lentils (*Lens culinaris = Lens esculenta*) with an incidental scattering of peas (*Pisum* sp.). Of these provisions, many were found mixed with grain in the model granary and elsewhere. A small pottery vessel from the Annexe (no. 614f) contained a mixture of lentils and fenugreek (*Trigonella foenum-graecum*); while a wine jar (no. 509), again from the Annexe, Carter noted had 'Dried *lens* in interior'.

Among the spices and flavourings buried with the king, the bulk of them again contained in baskets stored in the Annexe, were juniper berries (*Juniperus oxycedrus*) (four baskets), coriander (*Coriandrum sativum*) (two baskets), fenugreek, sesame (*Sesamum indicum*) and black cumin (*Nigella sativa*). Also noted was a branch of *Thymbra spicata* (from box no. 367). The *Chaerophyllum* sp.? from the pottery jar no. 614a is almost certainly misidentified.

For sweetening, Tutankhamun had taken with him two jars of honey (nos. 614j–k) which were stored in the Annexe. A good selection of fruits was also found, including stoned dates (*Phoenix dactylifera*), contained in a large pottery dish (no. 154) from the Antechamber and six small round baskets (nos. 348, 356, etc.) in the Annexe. Examples of the ubiquitous *dom*-palm fruit were recovered from 12 of the larger Annexe baskets (nos. 346, 363, 366, etc.), as well as from a large basket (no. 97) in the Antechamber; other, stray examples were found in the corridor debris (no. 12r), and in the Antechamber in box no. 115 and in the reed tray no. 119. Dried

Tutankhamun's 'canned beef': egg-shaped boxes of white-painted wood (no. 62), coated with black resin on the interior and packed with various joints of meat, as found stacked beneath the cow-couch (no. 73) in the Antechamber.

Boxes of Prepared Food

Group number 62	Docket	Contents
b,d,q,s	head	scapula (shoulder blade) an ox
h,p,v,qq	heart	humerus of an ox
u,aa	back	radius of an ox
a,dd	spine	lumbar vertebrae of an o
e,l,n	tibia	femur
t,kk,oo,rr	(part of a leg)	tibia
f,m,ff,hh	rib	ribs of an ox
ee,jj	breast(?)	sternum
i,o	spleen	tongue of an ox
nn	goose	goose

and 20 unmarked boxes

'. . . out of ten items only three, or at most four, sh an agreement between the outside marking and the contents – an amazing example of carelessness. It ... not less astonishing to see the consistency in carelessness: boxes marked in the same way conta the same wrong part of an animal. It is clear that t boxes had been marked in advance and that some were expected to contain parts of the body which were not included at all; such boxes therefore were systematically used for other joints.'

Jaroslav Če

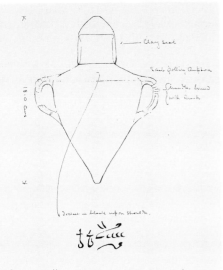

grapes (*Vitis vinifera*) were found in the Annexe baskets 471 and 518b, as well as in the 'bottle-shaped baskets' nos. 364 and 451. Jujubes (*Zizyphus spina christi*) were particularly well represented in the tomb, mostly in the Annexe where 36 medium-sized baskets were filled with them. Seeds of safflower (*Carthamus tinctorius*), often used as a red or yellow dye, were also found, here perhaps for making oil. The range of basket-stored commodities included persea fruit (*Mimusops laurifolia*, formerly *M. schimperi*) (three baskets), grewia fruit (*Grewia tenax*) (four baskets), cocculus fruit (*Cocculus* sp.), sycamore figs (*Ficus sycomorus*), and watermelon seeds (*Citrullus lanatus*) (11 baskets) for planting or chewing. Other 'nibbles' included almonds (*Prunus dulcis* = *P. amygdalus*).

Although Tutankhamun was supplied with the raw materials for its manufacture in the afterlife, no actual beer seems to have been buried with him. The boy may well have preferred fruit juice, perhaps grape, the sugary remnants of which Lucas identified in one of the tomb's calcite jars.

For Tutankhamun's wines, see pp. 202–03.

Insect life

It is hardly surprising that the quantity of food and edible matter buried with the young king should have attracted a range of insect life. Several calcite jars (nos. 16, 58, 60, 61) and the painted wooden box no. 111 + 115 contained the remains of several small, farinaceous beetles: the so-called cigarette or tobacco beetle (*Lasioderma serricorne*), the bread beetle (*Stegobium paniceum*, formerly *Sitodrepa panicea*), and *Gibbium psylloides* of the Spider Beetle group. Such domestic pests are commonly found in stored food, and have been known to feed off stored animal matter – hence their presence in the king's perfume jars.

Lucas notes the remains of small spiders and their webs, while 'various wooden objects', including the sticks found within the first shrine, 'contain holes manifestly made by insects . . . in the tomb'. No further information is available; for spiders, at least, this is regrettable, since they are otherwise peculiarly absent from the Egyptian record.

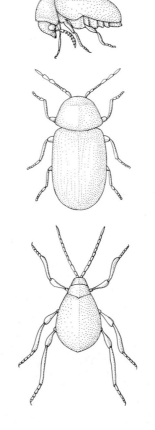

(Above left) Small pottery amphora (no. 614j) found in the Annexe. The hieratic inscription on the side of the vessel reads: 'Honey of good quality'.

(Above right) Oval basket (no. 97) filled with fruits of the dom-palm.

Tutankhamun's companions in death: Lasioderma serricorne, *the so-called cigarette or tobacco beetle; and the bread and spider beetles* Stegobium paniceum *and* Gibbium psylloides.

207

Epilogue: Tutankhamun Life, Death and Rebirth

‘ Live thy *Ka*, and mayst thou spend millions of years, thou lover of Thebes, sitting with thy face to the north wind, and thy eyes beholding felicity. ’

Inscription on the 'Wishing Cup' (obj. no. 14)

Like all Egyptians of wealth, Tutankhamun took with him to the grave everything that ritual or personal preference dictated he would require for a happy and contented existence in the next life; and, by a miracle, most of the objects buried in the tomb over those March days in 1323 BC remained for Lord Carnarvon and Howard Carter to disinter more than 3,000 years later.

Because of its relatively intact state, the tomb of Tutankhamun spans the millennia with peculiar ease; it excites all of the senses in a way in which no other archaeological find before or since has done. We see the king's youthful image standing before us in the portrait figures which once guarded the Burial Chamber entrance; we know the raucous blast of his trumpets, which have sounded again on more than one occasion; the privileged few are able to grasp the same reed stick which Tutankhamun cut with his own hand while walking one day down by the river; the resins and unguents lavished upon the king in death continue, even now, to give off their heavy, aromatic scent; while the taste of the foods, wines and juices of which the boy was fond are as familiar in Egypt today as they ever were.

Pharaoh's god-like mask begins to slip, to reveal a creature as frail and human as ourselves: a boy like any other, packed off to the next world as if to boarding school, accompanied by ample supplies of clean linen, hampers of his favourite foods, his prized possessions, and a lock of his beloved grandmother's hair. Yet in this, his final manifestation, Tutankhamun was no longer the malleable child: he had grown into a wilful adolescent, his father's son, eager to assert himself. And he was probably murdered for it.

The burial of Pharaoh was fast and careless, within a hastily adapted private sepulchre, the corpse equipped with a rag-bag mix of whatever new, old and adaptable funerary equipment was readily to hand. The funerary cortège, followed by the highest officials of the land and by crowds of ululating women, wound its way up the Valley. The ritual 'opening of the mouth' was performed by Ay, Tutankhamun's heir and successor, and the coffined corpse lifted into the sarcophagus in the partially decorated Burial Chamber. As the mis-matched lid of the sarcophagus was lowered into position, it cracked across: the toes of the outer coffin foot, sitting proud, were summarily adzed off, splashed with resin, and the lid again set in place, its break concealed beneath a covering of tinted plaster.

The troublesome young king had been laid to rest, but his burial preparations continued for several days. The task of erecting the shrines began, an operation again carried through in a hasty and careless manner, the panels wrongly orientated and ritually useless, roughly banged into place with mallets, damaging the decorated surfaces. With the shrines in position, a partition wall was erected between the Antechamber and the Burial Chamber, and the south wall of the latter painted to complement the walls already decorated. A rectangular doorway within this partition allowed access to the workmen and to those priests involved in the final stocking of the Treasury and in arranging the sticks, bows, oars and other objects found scattered in and around the shrines. In due course, this wall was closed with a dry-stone blocking, plastered on its outer surface and sealed by the officials present. The Annexe and Antechamber were stocked in a ramshackle way with more of the royal funerary equipment, and their doorways closed; the entrance corridor was filled with the embalming refuse and more food provisions, the outer corridor-blocking erected, and the tomb entrance buried from sight.

Tutankhamun had gone – but he was not yet forgotten. Within a short time of the burial, perhaps during the uncertain period following the four recorded years of Ay's reign, the tomb was entered by robbers. The robbers, familiar with the tomb and perhaps drawn from among the very men who had first filled it, ransacked the burial for metals, linen, glass and precious oils – anything inconspicuous or recyclable. The robbery was detected by the necropolis guards before the intruders had been able to break through into the Burial Chamber, and the entrance corridor was filled with rubble as a deterrent to further theft. But robbers returned a short time later, burrowing through the corridor fill, this time penetrating as far as the outermost gilded shrine surrounding the sarcophagus. They were again detected, and this time caught. The gruesome fate that awaited them ensured that the tomb would not be robbed again. Within a matter of years, it had been completely forgotten.

Tutankhamun still lies within his outermost coffin in the tomb he has occupied for more than 3,300 years – a span of time which has seen the rise and fall of Athens and Rome, the birth and crucifixion of Christ, the coming of Islam, the Renaissance and the Industrial Revolution. After so many centuries, Pharaoh's sad presence still pervades the sepulchre and the objects from it; and the fascination of this presence, as much as the lure of old, continues to draw to him and his treasures illions of visitors every year. These visitors, by peaking Tutankhamun's name, cause him to live, he so fervently wished, every minute of every day, round the vastness of a modern world he could ever have imagined.

Tutankhamun was a king unwanted by his subjects, ignored by his successors and forgotten for more than 30 centuries; thanks to the discovery of his tomb by Lord Carnarvon and Howard Carter, he has been reborn as Egypt's most famous son, to achieve true immortality at last.

Tutankhamun emerging from the shadows: detail of a gilded wooden shabti *figure (no. 330e) from the Treasury.*

The Story
of the
Tomb

The Burial

1323 BC
January–March
Tutankhamun dies
Empty private sepulchre enlarged and adapted for
the king's use
North, east and west walls of the Burial Chamber
decorated
Sarcophagus introduced
Canopic equipment and other items installed in
Treasury
Coffins and royal mummy installed in sarcophagus
Shrines erected around sarcophagus
Antechamber–Burial Chamber partition wall
erected
South wall of Burial Chamber decorated
Final stocking of Treasury and Burial Chamber
Burial Chamber blocked off
Annexe and Antechamber stocked with funerary
goods
Annexe blocked off
Final stocking of Antechamber
Antechamber doorway blocked off
Entrance corridor stocked with burial goods
Corridor blocked off
Entrance stairway buried

c. 1319 BC
First robbery, with access to Antechamber and
Annexe
Burial put back in order by necropolis officials
Closure of robbers' breach in Antechamber
blocking
Material stored in corridor removed for reburial in
Pit 54
Corridor filled with rubble
Closure of robbers' breach in outer doorway
Burial of entrance
Second robbery, perhaps over several days, with
access to all chambers
Robbers apprehended
Burial put back in order by necropolis officials
Closure of robbers' breach in Burial Chamber
blocking
Closure of robbers' breach in Antechamber
blocking
Refilling of robbers' tunnel through corridor fill
Closure of robbers' breach in outer doorway
Burial of entrance

c. 1151–43 BC
Huts for workmen engaged on quarrying tomb of
Ramesses VI erected immediately over entrance
to Tutankhamun's tomb

c. 1000 BC
Tomb of Tutankhamun missed when work began
on dismantling royal necropolis

The Discovery

1922
1 November
Start of season
4 November
Discovery of first step
5 November
Outer blocking revealed
25 November
Corridor fill revealed
26 November
Access to Antechamber and view of Annexe
28 November
Access to Burial Chamber and Treasury
29 November
Official opening of Antechamber and Annexe
30 November
First press reports
27 December
First object removed from Antechamber: Painted
Box no. 21

1923
9 January
Carnarvon signs contract with the *Times*
16 February
Opening of Burial Chamber
5 April
Death of Lord Carnarvon (buried 28 April)
14 May
First objects leave for Cairo Museum (arrive
22 May)

1924
12 February
Lifting of sarcophagus lid
13 February
Strike
15 February
Lock-out
12 April
Carter leaves England for U.S. lecture tour (until 2
July)

1925
13 January
New concession to continue work
13 October
Lid of outer coffin removed
23 October
Lid of second coffin removed
28 October
Lid of inner coffin removed and royal mummy
revealed
11 November
Start of autopsy on mummy

1926
24 October
Start of work in Treasury

927
0 October
tart of work in Annexe (completed 15 December)

930
0 November
inal objects removed from tomb: shrine elements

1932
Spring
Final objects conserved for shipment to Cairo

1939
2 March
Death of Howard Carter

Object class	A	B	C	D	E	F
archery equipment		●	●	●	●	●
baskets			●			●
beds			●			●
bier				●		
boat models					●	●
boomerangs and throwsticks			●			●
botanical specimens		●	●	●	●	●
boxes and chests	●		●		●	●
canopic equipment					●	
chairs and stools			●			●
chariot equipment			●		●	●
clothing			●	●	●	●
coffins (king)				●		
coffins (other)					●	
cosmetic objects		●	●		●	●
cuirass						●
divine figures			●	●	●	
fans				●	●	●
foodstuffs			●			●
gaming equipment		●	●			●
gold mask				●		
granary model					●	
hassocks			●			●
jewellery, beads, amulets	●	●	●	●	●	●
labels		●	●	●		●
lamps and torches			●	●	●	
mummies				●	●	
musical instruments			●	●		●
pall and framework				●		
portable pavilion			●			●
regalia			●	●	●	●
ritual couches			●			
ritual objects			●	●	●	●
royal figures		?	●	●	●	
sarcophagus				●		
sealings	●	●	●	●	●	●
shabtis and related objects		●	●		●	●
shields						●
shrines			●	●	●	●
sticks and staves			●	●	●	
swords and daggers				●		●
tools			●		●	●
vessels	●	●	●	●	●	●
wine jars	●	●		●		●
writing equipment			●		●	●

The Objects: Where They Were Found

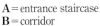

A = entrance staircase
B = corridor
C = Antechamber
D = Burial Chamber
E = Treasury
F = Annexe

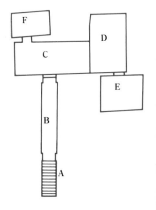

Exhibitions and Displays

The Exhibitions

1961–1962
United States of America

Washington DC
November–December 1961

1962–1963
United States of America

Philadelphia
January–February 1962
New Haven
February–March/April 1962
Houston
April–May 1962
Omaha
May–June/July 1962
Chicago
July–August 1962
Seattle
August–September/October 1962
San Francisco
October–November/December 1962
Cleveland
December 1962–January 1963

1963–1964
United States of America

Boston
February–April 1963
Saint Louis
April–May 1963
Baltimore
June–July 1963
Dayton
from July 1963
Detroit
August–September 1963
Toledo
September–October 1963
Richmond
December 1963–January 1964
New York
from January 1964

1964–1965
Canada

Montreal
Toronto
November–December 1964
Winnipeg
December 1964–January 1965
Vancouver
January–February 1965
Quebec
March–April 1965

1965–1966
Japan

Tokyo
August–October 1965
Kyoto
October–November 1965
Fukuoka
December 1965–January 1966

1967
France

Paris
February–August 1967

1972
England

London
March–December 1972

1973–1974
USSR

Moscow
December 1973–May 1974
Leningrad
July–November 1974

1975
USSR

Kiev
January–March 1975

1976–1977
United States of America

Washington DC
from September 1976

1977–1978
United States of America

Chicago
to July 1977
New Orleans
September 1977–January 1978

1978–1979
United States of America

Los Angeles
February–May 1978
Seattle
July–November 1978
New York
December 1978–April 1979
San Francisco
May–October 1979

1979–1980
Canada

Toronto
November 1979–January 1980

1980–1981
West Germany

West Berlin
February–May 1980
Cologne
June–October 1980
Munich
November 1980–February 1981
Hanover
February–April 1981
Hamburg
May–July 1981

Note: dates given in some cases include storage, travelling and mounting times.

Museums and Collections

Egypt

The great travelling exhibitions of Tutankhamun's funerary treasures have now ceased because of concerns for the welfare of the objects, which, inevitably, were beginning to suffer from constant packing, travelling, unpacking and handling. Fortunately, visiting Egypt itself has never been easier or cheaper; and there is much to be said for seeing the young king in the context of his native land. The following is a brief check-list of Tutankhamun-related material in Egyptian collections; for the larger monuments, see pp. 26–9.

Cairo

The greater part of the king's funerary equipment is on display on the upper floor of the Egyptian Museum, Cairo, some of it as first set out by Carter himself; a few of the Cairo pieces are in storage. The second and third (innermost) coffins and the gold mask are shown with the jewellery in room 4; the shrines, canopic assemblage and animal couches in galleries 8, 9 and 10. The remainder of the material is displayed in the run of galleries 15, 20, 25, 30, 35, 40, and 45, at the end of which Tutankhamun's two guardian figures stand sentinel.

Much of the botanical material recovered from the tomb is now in the Agricultural Museum, Dokki;

while one of the foetuses is in the Department of Anatomy of the University of Cairo.

Luxor

The gilded cow head from the tomb, two pairs of sandals, 63 gilded bronze pall-rosettes, six arrows and two boat models are on display in the Luxor Museum of Ancient Egyptian Art.

Other objects from Tutankhamun's tomb, including many of the black-varnished shrines and baskets, lie in storage in a tomb on the Theban west bank. These pieces are not accessible to the general public.

The tomb of Tutankhamun is No. 62 in the Valley of the Kings. The remains of the young king lie in a box within the outermost gilded coffin, which still sits within the quartzite sarcophagus in the painted Burial Chamber. The lid of the sarcophagus has been replaced with a panel of plate glass, so that the coffin within can be seen by the tomb's many visitors.

The plaster from the tomb's sealed doorways lay for many years in the tomb of Ramesses XI, Carter's original storeroom; it has now been transferred back to the tomb of Tutankhamun itself. Other, minor objects from Carter's clearance of the Tutankhamun entrance corridor are among materials brought to light between 1977 and 1979 by John Romer during his clearance of the Ramesses XI tomb, where they are now stored.

Outside Egypt

Those unable to visit Egypt need not despair. Objects dating from the period in which Tutankhamun lived and reigned may be seen in any of the larger European and American museums, including the British Museum in London, the Louvre in Paris, and the collections of Brussels, Munich, West Berlin, Leiden, Turin, Chicago and Philadelphia (cf. pp. 26–9.).

The best objects discovered by Theodore Davis in Pit 54 in the Valley of the Kings are in the Metropolitan Museum of Art in New York; other pieces from the Pit 54 assemblage were de-accessioned in the 1950s, and are now in the American Museum of Natural History in New York, and elsewhere. A representative selection of botanical specimens from the tomb of Tutankhamun was presented in 1933 to the Royal Botanic Gardens, Kew, on long-term loan. A group of textile fragments is in the Victoria and Albert Museum.

The magnificent collection of Egyptian art assembled by Lord Carnarvon and Howard Carter is now one of the treasures of New York's Metropolitan Museum of Art; further antiquities and personal memorabilia from the fifth Earl's pre-Tutankhamun days are on display at Highclere Castle in Hampshire, the Carnarvon family home. Other Carter-related objects are to be found in Brooklyn, Detroit, St Louis, Kansas City and elsewhere.

Further Reading

Much, of greater and lesser importance, has been written on Tutankhamun and his time, and the following selection makes no claims to be exhaustive; readers wishing for a more comprehensive listing are referred to G.T. Martin's *A Bibliography of the Amarna Period* (forthcoming). For sources of quotations, including contemporary press reports, see p. 218.

Abbreviations

AcOr	Acta Orientalia
AJA	American Journal of Archaeology
ANM	Annals of the Náprstek Museum
ASAE	Annales du Service des Antiquités de l'Égypte
AW	Aramco World
BMB	The Brooklyn Museum Bulletin
BH	Buried History
BIFAO	Bulletin de l'Institut français d'archéologie orientale
BMMA	Bulletin of the Metropolitan Museum of Art
BSEG	Bulletin de la Société d'Égyptologie, Genève
CdE	Chronique d'Égypte
CH	Current History
GM	Göttinger Miszellen
HM	Historical Metallurgy
JARCE	Journal of the American Research Center in Egypt
JCS	Journal of Cuneiform Studies
JEA	Journal of Egyptian Archaeology
JNES	Journal of Near Eastern Studies
JPK	Jahrbuch Preussischer Kulturbesitz
JRAI	Journal of the Royal Anthropological Institute
JSSEA	Journal of the Society for the Study of Egyptian Antiquities
Karnak	Cahiers de Karnak
MDAIK	Mitteilungen des Deutschen Archäologischen Instituts Abteilung Kairo
MDOG	Mitteilungen der Deutsche Orient-Gesellschaft zu Berlin
NGM	National Geographic Magazine
OLZ	Orientalistische Literaturzeitung
OS	Orientalia Suecana
PCR	Photo-ciné-revue
RAA	Revue des arts asiatiques
RdE	Revue d'Égyptologie
RdT	Recueil de Travaux relatifs à la philologie et à l'archéologie égyptiennes et assyriennes
SAK	Studien zur altägyptischen Kultur
VA	Varia Aegyptiaca
ZÄS	Zeitschrift für Ägyptische Sprache und Altertumskunde

I. Published works

General

Baines, J., and J. Málek *Atlas of Ancient Egypt* (Oxford and New York, 1980)

Brovarski, E., S.K. Doll and R.E. Freed *Egypt's Golden Age. The Art of Living in the New Kingdom, 1558–1085 BC* (Boston, 1982)

D'Auria, S., P. Lacovara, and C.H. Roehrig *Mummies and Magic. The Funerary Arts of Ancient Egypt* (Boston, 1988)

Faulkner, Raymond O. *The Ancient Egyptian Book of the Dead* (ed. Carol Andrews, London, 1985)

Hayes, W.C. *The Scepter of Egypt*, II (New York, 1959)

Helck, W., and E. Otto (eds.) *Lexikon der Ägyptologie* (Wiesbaden, 1975–)

Hornung, E. *Conceptions of God in Ancient Egypt* (London, 1983)

—— *Tal der Könige* (2nd ed., Munich, 1983)

Lichtheim, M. *Ancient Egyptian Literature*, II. *The New Kingdom* (Berkeley, 1976)

Lucas, A., and J.R. Harris *Ancient Egyptian Materials and Industries* (London, 1962; repr. 1989)

Porter, B., and R.L.B. Moss *Topographical Bibliography of Ancient Egyptian Hieroglyphic Texts, Reliefs, and Paintings* I–VII (various eds., Oxford, 1927–)

Tutankhamun and his time

Aldred, C. *Akhenaten and Nefertiti* (London and New York, 1973)

—— *Akhenaten, King of Egypt* (London and New York, 1988)

—— 'The beginning of the el-'Amārna period', *JEA* 45 (1959), pp. 19–33

—— 'Egypt: the Amarna period and the end of the Eighteenth Dynasty', *Cambridge Ancient History*, II/2 (Cambridge, 1975), chap. 19

—— 'The end of the el-'Amārna period', *JEA* 43 (1957), pp. 30–41

—— *Tutankhamun's Egypt* (London, 1972)

Allen, J.P. 'The natural philosophy of Akhenaten', in W.K. Simpson (ed.), *Religion and Philosophy in Ancient Egypt* (Yale, 1989), pp. 89–101

—— 'Two altered inscriptions of the late Amarna period', *JARCE* 25 (1988), pp. 117–26

Amer, A.A.M.A. 'A further note on Maya', *Orientalia* ns 55 (1986), pp. 171–3

—— 'Tutankhamun's decree for the chief treasurer Maya', *RdE* 36 (1985), pp. 17–20

(Anon.) *The Tombs of the Kings: a handbook to the objects directly relating to Akhenaten and Tutankhamen in the British Museum* (London, 1923)

Anthes, R. *Die Büste der Königin Nofret Ete* (Berlin, 1954)

Baikie, J. *The Amarna Age: a Study of the Crisis of the Ancient World* (London, 1926)

Bell, L. 'Aspects of the cult of the deified Tutankhamon', *Mélanges Gamal Eddin Mokhtar*, I (Cairo, 1985), pp. 31–59

Bennet, J. 'The Restoration Inscription of Tut'ankhamun', *JEA* 25 (1939), pp. 8–15

Berlandini, J. 'Un dromos de Toutânkhamon du Xe pylône de Karnak', *Karnak* VI, 1973–7 (Cairo, 1980), pp. 247–60

—— 'Le protocole de Toutânkhamon sur les socles du dromos du Xème pylône à Karnak', *GM* 22 (1976), pp. 13–20

Bourriau, J. 'A private stela of the reign of Tutankhamun in the Fitzwilliam Museum', in J. Baines and others (ed.), *Pyramid Studies and Other Essays presented to I.E.S. Edwards*
(London, 1988), pp. 110–13

Budge, E.A.W. *Tutankhamen, Amenism, Atenism and Egyptian Monotheism* (London, 1923)

Capart, J., and others *Tout-Ankh-Amon* (2nd ed., Brussels, 1950)

Cooney, J.D. *Amarna Reliefs from Hermopolis in American collections* (Brooklyn, 1965)

Danilova, I.E., and I.S. Katznelson (eds.) *Tutankhamon i ego vrema* (Moscow, 1976)

Davies, Nina M., and A.H. Gardiner *The Tomb of Ḥuy, Viceroy of Nubia in the Reign of Tut'ankhamūn* (London, 1926)

Davies, N. de G. *The Rock Tombs of El Amarna*, I–VI (London, 1903–08)

Desroches-Noblecourt, C. *Tutankhamen. Life and Death of a Pharaoh* (London, 1963)

Dijk, J. van, and M. Eaton-Krauss 'Tutankhamun at Memphis', *MDAIK* 42 (1986), pp. 35–41

Eaton-Krauss, M. 'Tutankhamun at Karnak', *MDAIK* 44 (1988), pp. 1–11

Engelbach, R. 'Material for a revision of the history of the Heresy Period of the XVIIIth Dynasty', *ASAE* 40 (1940), pp. 133–65

Fairman, H.W. 'Tutankhamun and the end of the 18th dynasty', *Antiquity* 46 (1972), pp. 15–18

Fazzini, R. *Tutankhamun and the African Heritage: a View of Society in the Time of the Boy King* (New York, 1978)

Gabolde, M. 'Ay, Toutankhamon et les martelages de la stèle de la restauration de Karnak (CG 34183)', *BSEG* 11 (1987), pp. 37–61

Giles, F.J. *Ikhnaton, Legend and History* (London, 1970)

Gohary, J. *Akhenaten's Sed-Festival at Karnak* (London, 1990)

—— 'Nefertiti at Karnak', in J. Ruffle and others (ed.), *Glimpses of Ancient Egypt* (Studies Fairman) (Warminster, 1979), pp. 30–31

Gunn, B. 'Notes on the Aten and his names', *JEA* 9 (1923), pp. 168–76

—— 'Notes on two Egyptian kings', *JEA* 12 (1926), pp. 252–3

Güterbock, H.G. 'The deeds of Suppiluliuma as told by his son, Mursili II', *JCS* 10 (1956), pp. 41–68, 75–98, 107–30

Habachi, L. 'Unknown or little-known monuments of Tut 'ankhamun and of his viziers', in J. Ruffle and others (ed.), *Glimpses of Ancient Egypt* (Warminster, 1979), pp. 32–41

Hall, H.R.H. 'Objects of Tut'ankhamūn in the British Museum', *JEA* 14 (1928), pp. 74–7

Hanke, R. *Amarna-Reliefs aus Hermopolis* (Hildesheim, 1978)

Hari, R. *Horemheb et la reine Moutnedjemet, ou la fin d'une dynastie* (Geneva, 1964)

Harris, J.E., and others 'Mummy of the "Elder Lady" in the tomb of Amenhotep II', *Science* 200/4346 (9 June 1978), pp. 1149–51

Harris, J.R. 'Contributions to the history of the Eighteenth Dynasty, 2. Amenhotpe III: a terminus for the co-regency with Akhenaten', *SAK* 2 (1975), pp. 98–101

—— 'Akhenaten or Nefertiti?' *AcOr* 38 (1977), pp. 5–10

—— 'The date of the "Restoration" stela of Tutankhamun', *GM* 5 (1973), pp. 9–11

—— 'A fine piece of Egyptian faience', *Burlington Magazine* 119/890 (May, 1977), pp. 340–43

—— 'Kiya', *CdE* 49 (1974), pp. 25–30

—— 'Nefernefruaten', *GM* 4 (1973), pp. 15–17

—— 'Nefernefruaten regnans', *AcOr* 36 (1974), pp. 11–21

—— 'Nefertiti rediviva', *AcOr* 35 (1973), pp. 5–13

Ielck, W. 'Kijê', *MDAIK* 40 (1984), pp. 159–67

Kemp, B.J., and others *Amarna Reports*, I– (London, 1984–)

Khouly, A. el-, and G.T. Martin *Excavations in the Royal Necropolis at El-'Amarna* (Cairo, 1987)

Krauss, R. 'Der Bildhauer Thutmose in Amarna', *JPK* 20 (1983), pp. 119–32

—— *Das Ende der Amarnazeit* (Hildesheim, 1978)

—— 'Kija – ursprüngliche Besitzerin der Kanopen aus KV 55', *MDAIK* 42 (1986), pp. 67–80

Krauss, R., and D. Ullrich 'Ein gläserner Doppelring aus Altägypten', *JPK* 19 (1982), pp. 199–212

Legrain, G. 'La grand stèle de Toutankhamanou à Karnak', *RdT* 29 (1907), pp. 162–73

—— 'Notes d'inspection, XXVII. Le protocole de Toutankhamon', *ASAE* 6 (1905), p. 192

—— 'Notes d'inspection, LII. Un duplicatá de la grande stèle de Toutankamanou à Karnak', *ASAE* 8 (1907), pp. 256–8

Loeben, C. 'Eine Bestattung der *grossen königlichen Gemahlin Nofretete* in Amarna? Die Totenfigur der Nofretete', *MDAIK* 42 (1986), pp. 99–107

Manniche, L. 'The wife of Bata', *GM* 18 (1975), pp. 33–5

Martin, G.T. *The Hidden Tombs of Memphis* (London and New York, 1990)

—— *The Memphite Tomb of Ḥoremḥeb, Commander-in-Chief of Tut'ankhamūn*, I– (London, 1990–)

—— *The Royal Tomb at El-'Amarna*, I–II (London, 1974–89)

Meltzer, E.S. 'The parentage of Tut'ankhamūn and Smenkhkarē', *JEA* 64 (1978), pp. 134–5

Morkot, R. 'Nakhtmin, the supposed viceroy of Ay', *Wepwawet* 1 (1985), p. 4

Murnane, W.J. *Ancient Egyptian Coregencies* (Chicago, 1977)

—— 'Tutankhamun on the Eighth Pylon at Karnak', *VA* 1 (1985), pp. 59–68

Peet, T.E., L. Woolley, and others *The City of Akhenaten*, I– (London, 1923–)

Pendlebury, J.D.S. *Tell el-Amarna* (London, 1935)

Perepelkin, G. (= I.I.) *The Secret of the Gold Coffin* (Moscow, 1978)

Perepelkin, I.I. *Keīe i Semnekh-ke-re* (Moscow, 1979)

—— *Perevorot Amen-khotpa IV*, I–II (Moscow, 1967–84)

Ratié, S. 'Quelques problèmes soulevés par la persécution de Toutankhamon', *Hommages à François Daumas*, II (Montpellier, 1986), pp. 545–8

Ray, J.D. 'The parentage of Tutankhamūn', *Antiquity* 49/113 (March, 1975), pp. 45–7

—— Review-article, D.B. Redford, *Akhenaten, the Heretic King*, *GM* 86 (1985), pp. 81–93

Redford, D.B. *Akhenaten, the Heretic King* (Princeton, 1984)

—— *History and Chronology of the Eighteenth Dynasty of Egypt: Seven Studies* (Toronto, 1967)

—— 'Once again the filiation of Tutankhamun', *JSSEA* 9/3 (June, 1979), pp. 111–15

Reeves, C.N. 'A further occurrence of Nefertiti as *ḥmt nsw '3t*', *GM* 30 (1978), pp. 61–9

—— 'New light on Kiya from texts in the British Museum', *JEA* 74 (1988), pp. 91–101

—— 'The tomb of Tuthmosis IV: two questionable attributions', *GM* 44 (1981), pp. 49–55

—— *Tutankhamun Pocket Guide* (Reading/London, 1987)

—— 'Tuthmosis IV as "great-grandfather" of Tut'ankhamūn', *GM* 56 (1982), pp. 65–9

Roeder, G. *Amarna-Reliefs aus Hermopolis* (Hildesheim, 1969)

Sa'ad, R. 'Fragments d'un monument de Toutânkhamon retrouvés dans le IXe pylône de Karnak', *Karnak* V 1970–72 (Cairo, 1975), pp. 93–109

Samson, J. *Amarna, City of Akhenaten: Nefertiti as Pharaoh* (London, 1978)

Schaden, O.J. *The God's Father Ay* (University Microfilms, 1978)

—— 'The granite colossi of Amun and Amonet at Karnak', *GM* 38 (1980), pp. 69–73

Schlögl, H.A. *Echnaton-Tutanchamun Fakten und Texte* (Wiesbaden, 1983)

Schulman, A.R. "Ankhesenamūn, Nofretity, and the Amka affair', *JARCE* 15 (1978), pp. 43–8

—— 'The Berlin "Truauerrelief" (no. 12411) and some officials of Tut'ankhamūn and Ay', *JARCE* 4 (1965), pp. 55–68

—— 'Excursus on the "military officer" Nakhtmin', *JARCE* 3 (1964), pp. 124–6

—— 'Some observations on the military background of the Amarna period', *JARCE* 3 (1964), pp. 51–69

Seele, K.C. 'King Ay and the Close of the Amarna Age', *JNES*, 14 (1955) pp. 168–80

Simpson, W.K. 'The head of a statuette of Tut'ankhamūn in the Metropolitan Museum', *JEA* 41 (1955), pp. 112–14

—— *Heka-Nefer and the Dynastic Material from Toshka and Arminna* (New Haven/Philadelphia, 1963)

Smith, R.W., D.B. Redford, and others *The Akhenaten Temple Project*, I– (Warminster/Toronto, 1976–)

Tawfik, S.'Aton studies, 3. Back again to Nefer-nefru-Aton', *MDAIK* 31 (1975), pp. 159–68

Vergote, J. *Toutankhamon dans les archives hittites* (Istanbul, 1961)

Weigall, A.E.P.B. *The Life and Times of Akhnaton, Pharaoh of Egypt* (London, 1922)

Wijngaarden, W.D. van 'Objects of Tut'ankhamūn in the Rijksmuseum of Antiquities at Leiden', *JEA* 22 (1936), pp. 1–2

Search and discovery

Allen, T.G. 'Discoveries at the tomb of Tutenkhamon', *CH* 20 (1924), pp. 363–73

Brackman, A.C. *The Search for the Gold of Tutankhamen* (New York, 1976)

Breasted, C. *Pioneer to the Past. The Story of James H. Breasted* (London, 1948)

—— 'Over the threshold of Tut-ankh-Amen's tomb', *Asia* 23 (1923), pp. 437–41, 465, 468

Breasted, J.H. *Some Experiences in the Tomb of Tutenkhamon* (Chicago, 1923)

Capart, J. *The Tomb of Tutankhamen* (London, 1923)

Carnarvon, The Earl of, and H. Carter *Five Years' Explorations at Thebes, a record of work done, 1907–1911* (Oxford, 1912)

Carter, H. 'Report on the tomb of Zeser-ka-ra Amenhetep I, discovered by the Earl of Carnarvon in 1914', *JEA* 3 (1916), pp. 147–54

—— *Six Portraits of the Thothmes Family* (n.p., n.d.)

—— 'A tomb prepared for Queen Hatshepsuit and other recent discoveries at Thebes', *JEA* 4 (1917), pp. 107–18

—— 'A tomb prepared for Queen Hatshepsuit discovered by the Earl of Carnarvon (October, 1916)', *ASAE* 16 (1916), pp. 175–82

—— *The Tomb of Tut.ankh.amen: statement with documents, as to the events which occurred in Egypt in the winter of 1923–24, leading to the ultimate break with the Egyptian Government* (London, 1924)

Carter, H. (and A.C. Mace) *The Tomb of Tut.ankh.Amen*, I–III (London, 1923–33)

Cone, P. (ed.) *The Discovery of Tutankhamun's Tomb* (New York, 1976)

Cottrell, L. *The Secrets of Tutankhamen* (London and New York, 1978)

Davis, T.M., and others *The Tombs of Harmhabi and Touatânkhamanou* (London, 1912)

—— *The Tomb of Hâtshopsîtû* (London, 1906)

—— *The Tomb of Iouiya and Touiyou* (London, 1907)

—— *The Tomb of Queen Tîyi* (London, 1910)

—— *The Tomb of Thoutmôsis IV* (London, 1904)

Drower, Margaret S. *Flinders Petrie. A Life in Archaeology* (London, 1985)

Gardiner, Sir Alan H. *My Early Years* (n.p., n.d.)

—— *My Working Years* (n.p., n.d.)

Hoving, T. *Tutankhamun: the Untold Story* (New York and Harmondsworth, 1978)

Lawton, J. 'The last survivor', *AW* 32/6 (Nov.–Dec., 1981), pp. 10–21

Mace, A.C. 'Work at the tomb of Tutenkhamon', *BMMA* Dec. 1923, Part II (Egyptian Expedition 1922–23), pp. 5–11

Naville, E., and others *The Temple of Deir el Bahari*, I–VI (London, 1895–1908)

Newberry, P.E., and others *Beni Hasan*, I–IV (London, 1893–1900)

—— *El Bersheh*, I–II (London, 1893–4)

New York, Metropolitan Museum of Art *Wonderful Things: the Discovery of Tutankhamun's Tomb* (New York, 1976)

Peck, W.H. 'The discoverer of the tomb of Tutankhamun and the Detroit Institute of the Arts', *JSSEA* 11 (1981), pp. 65–7

Petrie, W.M.F. *Tell el Amarna* (London, 1894)

Reeves, Nicholas *Ancient Egypt at Highclere Castle* (Highclere, 1989)

Romer, J. *Valley of the Kings* (London, 1981)

Silverman, D. 'The curse of the curse of the Pharaohs', *Expedition* 29/2 (1987), pp. 56–63

Smith, G. Elliot *Tutankhamen and the Discovery of his Tomb by the late Earl of Carnarvon and Mr Howard Carter* (London, 1923)

Smith, Joseph Lindon *Tombs, Temples and Ancient Art* (ed. Corinna Lindon Smith, Norman, 1956)

Weigall, A. *Tutankhamen and Other Essays* (New York, 1924)

Williams, M.O. 'At the tomb of Tutankhamen', *NGM* 43/5 (May, 1923), pp. 461–508

Winlock, H.E. *Materials Used at the Embalming of King Tūt-'ankh-Amūn* (New York, 1941)

—— *The Treasure of Three Egyptian Princesses* (New York, 1948)

Wynne, B. *Behind the Mask of Tutankhamen* (London, 1972)

The Tomb and its Treasures

(See also the works by Carter (and Mace), Cone, Cottrell and New York, Metropolitan Museum of Art, and others listed in the previous section.)

Aldred, C. *Jewels of the Pharaohs* (London, 1971)

—— *Tutankhamun: Craftsmanship in Gold in the Reign of the King* (New York, 1979)

Anthes, R. *Tutankhamun Treasures* (exhibition catalogue, Washington 1961)

—— Tutankhamun Treasures/Trésors de Toutankhamon (exhibition catalogue, Montreal, 1964)

Assaad, H., and D. Kolos *The Name of the Dead: Hieroglyphic Inscriptions of the Treasures of Tutankhamun Translated* (Mississauga, 1979)

Bacon, E. (ed.) *The Great Archaeologists* (London, 1976)

Baker, Hollis S. *Furniture in the Ancient World. Origins and Evolution 3100–475 B.C.* (London, 1966)

Beinlich, H. 'Das Totenbuch bei Tutanchamun', *GM* 102 (1988), pp. 7–18

Beinlich, Horst and Mohamed Saleh *Corpus der hieroglyphischen Inschriften aus dem Grab des Tutanchamun* (Oxford, 1989)

Bimson, M. 'Glass in the Tutankhamun treasure', *6e Congrès de l'Association Internationale pour l'Histoire de Verre*, Cologne, 1–7 juillet 1973, *Annales* (Liege, 1974), pp. 291–4)

Bosse-Griffiths, K. 'Further remarks on *Wrt ḤḲꜣw*', *JEA* 62 (1976), pp. 181–2

—— 'The Great Enchantress in the little golden shrine of Tut'ankhamūn', *JEA* 59 (1973), pp. 100–108

Černý, J. *Hieratic Inscriptions from the tomb of Tūt'ankhamun* (Oxford, 1965)

—— 'Three regnal dates of the Eighteenth Dynasty', *JEA* 50 (1964), pp. 37–9

Cherf, W.J. 'Some forked staves in the Tut'ankhamūn collection', *ZÄS* 115, (1988), pp. 107–10

Coghlan, H.H. 'Copper artefacts from Tutankhamun's tomb', *HM* 9/2 (1975), pp. 64–7

Connolly, R.C., R.G. Harrison and S. Ahmed 'Serological evidence for the parentage of Tut'ankhamūn and Smenkhkarē' *JEA* 62 (1976), pp. 184–6

Cooney, J.D. 'Three ivories of the late XVIII Dynasty' *BMB* 10/1 (1948), pp. 1–16

Crowfoot, G.M., and N. de G. Davies 'The tunic of Tut'ankhamūn', *JEA* 27 (1941), pp. 113–30

Davies, Nina M., and A.H. Gardiner *Tutankhamun's Painted Box* (Oxford, 1962)

Davies, W.V. 'Tut'ankhamūn's razor-box: a problem in lexicography', *JEA* 63 (1977), pp. 107–11

Desroches-Noblecourt, C. 'La cueillette du raisin à la fin de l'époque amarnienne: Tutankhamon fut-il portraituré sous l'aspect d'un petit prince?' *JEA* 54 (1968), pp. 82–8

—— *Toutankhamon et son temps* (exhibition catalogue, Paris, 1967)

Drenkhahn, R. 'Eine Umbettung Tutanchamuns?' *MDAIK* 39 (1983), pp. 29–37

Drioton, E. 'La cryptographie de la chapelle de Toutânkhamon', *JEA* 35 (1949), pp. 117–22

Eaton-Krauss, M. 'Die Throne Tutanchamuns: vorläufige Bemerkungen', *GM* 76 (1984), pp. 7–10

—— 'The titulary of Tutankhamun', in J. Osing and G. Dreyer (ed.), *Form und Mass: Beiträge zur Literatur, Sprache und Kunst des alten Ägypten* (Fs. Fecht) (Wiesbaden, 1987), pp. 110–23

Eaton-Krauss, M., and E. Graefe *The Small Golden Shrine from the Tomb of Tutankhamun* (Oxford, 1985)

Edwards, I.E.S. *Treasures of Tutankhamun* (exhibition catalogue, London, 1972)

—— *Treasures of Tutankhamun* (exhibition catalogue, New York, 1976)

—— *Tutankhamun: his Tomb and its Treasures* (New York, 1976)

—— *Tutankhamun's Jewelry* (New York, 1976)

—— 'Zoomorphic anomalies in Tutankhamun's treasures', *AJA* 83 (1979), pp. 205–6

Fox, P. *Tutankhamun's Treasure* (London, 1951)

Gardiner, A.H. 'Tut'ankhamūn's gold dagger', *JEA* 27 (1941), p. 1

—— 'Tut'ankhamūn's iron dagger', *JEA* 28 (1942), p. 1

Germer, Renate *Die Pflanzenmaterialien aus dem Grab des Tutanchamun* (Hildesheim, 1989)

Gruen, S.W. 'A note on the separation of *di 'nḫ* from its complement *mi R'* on inscribed objects', *GM* 18 (1975), pp. 21–2

Harrison, R.G. 'An anatomical examination of the pharaonic remains purported to be Akhenaten', *JEA* 52 (1966), pp. 95–119

—— 'Post mortem on two pharaohs. Was Tutankhamun's skull fractured?' *BH* (1972), pp. 18–24

—— 'Tutankhamun's postmortem', *The Lancet* (1973), 259

Harrison, R.G. and A.G. Abdalla 'The remains of Tutankhamun', *Antiquity* 46 (1972), pp. 8–14

Harrison, R.G., R.C. Connolly and A. Abdalla 'Kinship of Smenkhkare and Tutankhamen demonstrated serologically', *Nature* 224 (25 Oct. 1969), pp. 325–6

Harrison, R.G., and others 'A mummified foetus from the tomb of Tutankhamun', *Antiquity* 53 (1979), pp. 19–21

Hepper, F. Nigel *Pharaoh's Flowers: Plants of Tutankhamun's Tomb* (London, 1990)

Hoolihan, P.F., and S.M. Goodman 'Comments on the identification of birds depicted on Tutankhamun's embossed gold fan', *JSSEA* 9/4 (August, 1978), pp. 219–25

Hornung, E. 'Ein aenigmatisches Unterweltsbuch', *JSSEA* 13 (1983), pp. 29–34

Hummel, S. 'Tut-ench-Amun auf dem Leoparden', *OS* 23–24 (1974–5), pp. 65–7

Jéquier, G. 'À propos de grands lits de Toutânkhamon', *RdT* 40 (1923), pp. 205–10

Jones, D. *Model Boats from the Tomb of Tut'ankhamūn* (Oxford, 1990)

Keating, R. 'Blowing Tutankhamun's trumpet', *The Listener* 87/2246 (13 April 1972), pp. 479–80

Kessler, D. 'Zu den Jagdszenen auf dem kleinen goldenen Tutanchamunschrein', *GM* 90 (1986), pp. 35–43

Kirby, P.R. 'The trumpets of Tut-ankh-Amen and their successors', *JRAI* 77 (1947), pp. 33–45

Krauss, R. 'Zum archäologischen Befund im thebanischen Königsgrab Nr. 62', *MDOG* 118 (1986), pp. 165–81

Larson, J. 'The Heb-sed robe and the "ceremonial robe" of Tut'ankhamūn', *JEA* 67 (1981), pp. 180–81

Leek, F.F. 'How old was Tut'ankhamūn?', *JEA* 63 (1977), pp. 112–15

—— *The Human Remains from the Tomb of Tut'ankhamūn* (Oxford, 1972)

Leibovitch, J. *A Guide to the Treasures of Tut-ankh-Amun* (Cairo, 1945)

Lesko, L.H. *King Tut's Wine Cellar* (Berkeley, 1977)

Littauer, M.A., and J.H. Crouwel *Chariots and Related Equipment from the Tomb of Tut'ankhamūn* (Oxford, 1985)

—— 'Unrecognized linch pins from the tombs of Tut'ankhamūn and Amenophis II: a reply', *GM* 100 (1987), pp. 57–61

Loeben, C. 'Abbildungskonkordanz zwischen der englischen und deutschen Ausgabe von Carters Tutanchamun-Publikation (mit Verweis auf der Handlist)', *GM* 40 (1980), pp. 69–80

Lucas, A. 'Notes on some objects from the tomb of Tut-ankhamun', *ASAE* 41 (1942), pp. 135–47

—— 'Notes on some of the objects from the tomb of Tut-Ankhamun', *ASAE* 45 (1947), pp. 133–4

Luxor Museum *The Luxor Museum of Ancient Egyptian Art. Catalogue* (Cairo, 1979)

McLeod, W. *Composite Bows from the Tomb of Tut'ankhamūn* (Oxford, 1970)

—— *Self Bows and Other Archery Tackle from the Tomb of Tut'ankhamūn* (Oxford, 1982)

Mallakh, K. El, and A.C. Brackman *The Gold of Tutankhamen* (New York, 1978)

Manniche, L. 'The body colours of gods and men in inlaid jewellery and related objects from the tomb of Tutankhamun', *AcOr* 43 (1982), pp. 5–12

—— *Musical Instruments from the Tomb of Tut'ankhamūn* (Oxford, 1976)

Montagu, J. 'One of Tut'ankhamūn's trumpets', *JEA* 64 (1978), pp. 133–4

Murray, H., and M. Nuttall *A Handlist to Howard Carter's Catalogue of Objects in Tut'ankhamūn's Tomb* (Oxford, 1963)

Musgrove, P. 'Prehistoric aeronautics', *Hemisphere* 19/9 (September, 1975), pp. 10–14

New York, Metropolitan Museum of Art *Treasures of Tutankhamun at the Metropolitan Museum of Art* (New York, 1978)

Osborn, D.J. 'Corrections and identifications of the alabaster ibexes in Tutankhamun's treasures', *JEA* 73 (1987), pp. 243–4

Pfister, R. 'Les textiles du tombeau de Toutankhamon', *RAA* 11 (1937), pp. 207–18

Piankoff, A. *Les chapelles de Tout-Ankh-Amon* (Cairo, 1951–2)

—— *The Shrines of Tut-Ankh-Amon* (ed. N. Rambova, New York, 1955)

Piotrovsky, B.B., and others *Sokrovishcha grobnitsy Tutankhamona* (exhibition catalogue, Moscow, 1973–4)

Podgorski, T. 'The position of Tutankhamun's feathered corselet against iconographic sources', Cairo, 5th International Congress of Egyptologists, *Abstracts of Papers* (Cairo, 1988), p. 220

Reed, C.A., and D.J. Osborn 'Taxonomic transgressions in Tutankhamun's treasures', *AJA* 82 (1978), pp. 273–83

Reeves, C.N. 'On the miniature mask from the Tut'ankhamūn embalming cache', *BSEG* 8 (1983), pp. 81–3

—— 'Tut'ankhamūn and his papyri', *GM* 88 (1985), pp. 39–45

—— *Valley of the Kings. The Decline of a Royal Necropolis* (London, 1990)

Riesterer, P. *Das Ägyptische Museum Kairo*, II. *Grabschatz des Tut-ench-Amun* (3. Auflage, Bern/Cairo, 1972)

Ritner, R.K. 'Unrecognized decorated linch pins from the tombs of Tutankhamon and Amenhotep II', *GM* 94 (1986), pp. 53–6

Robins, G. 'Isis, Nephthys, Selket and Neith represented on the sarcophagus of Tutankhamun and in four free-standing statues found in KV 62', *GM* 72 (1984), pp. 21–5

—— 'The proportions of figures in the decoration of the tombs of Tutankhamun (KV 62) and Ay (KV 23)', *GM* 72 (1984), pp. 27–32

—— 'Two statues from the tomb of Tutankhamun', *GM* 71 (1984), pp. 47–50

Ross, E. Denison *The Art of Egypt through the Ages* (London, 1931)

Rowe, A. 'Inscriptions on the model coffin containing the lock of hair of Queen Tyi', *ASAE* 40 (1940–41), pp. 623–7

Saleh, M., and H. Sourouzian *The Egyptian Museum Cairo* (Mainz, 1987)

Seton-Williams, M.V. *Tutanchamun: der Pharao, das Grab, der Goldschatz* (Frankfurt am Main, 1980)

Settgast, J., and others *Tutanchamun* (Berlin exhibition catalogue, Mainz, 1980; similar catalogues were prepared for the *Tutanchamun* exhibitions in Cologne, Hamburg, Hanover and Munich)

Silverman, D.P. 'Cryptographic writing in the tomb of Tutankhamun', *SAK* 8 (1980), pp. 233–6

—— *Fifty Wonders of Tutankhamun* (New York, 1978)

—— *Masterpieces of Tutankhamun* (New York, 1978)

Spiegelberg, W. 'Zu dem Grabfunde des Tutenchamun', *OLZ* 28 (1925), cols. 140–44

—— 'Zu den Jagdbildern des Tutenchamun', *OLZ* 38 (1938), cols. 569–71

Steindorff, G. 'Die Grabkammer des Tutanchamun', *ASAE* 38 (1938), pp. 641–67

Tait, W.J. *Game-boxes and Accessories from the Tomb of Tut'ankhamūn* (Oxford, 1982)

Tawfik, S. 'Tutanchamuns Grab: Provisorium oder kunstvolles Novum?', in *Studien zu Sprache und Religion Ägyptens. Zu Ehren von Wolfhart Westendorf*, II (Göttingen, 1984), pp. 1131–9

Teeter, E. 'Enameling in Ancient Egypt?', *AJA* 85 (1981), p. 319

Thibault, J. 'La masque d'or de Toutankhamon radiographié', *PCR* (May, 1968), pp. 216–17

Thomas, J. *Les boomerangs d'un Pharaon* (n.p., 1989)

Vandersleyen, C. 'L'iconographie de Toutankhamon et les effigies provenant de sa tombe', *BSEG* 9–10 (1984–5), pp. 309–21

—— 'Pour qui a été creusée la tombe de Toutankhamon?', in *Studia Paulo Naster Oblata* (ed. J. Quaegebeur), II (Louvain, 1982), pp. 263–7

—— 'Quelques énigmes eclaircies, à propos de la tombe de Toutankhamon', *BSEG* 8 (1983), pp. 97–9

Vilimkova, M. 'Pectoralien in Form von Tutanchamuns ersten Namen *Nb-ḥprw-Rʿ* und ihre Varienten', *ANM* 9 (1980), pp. 163–9

Wilkinson, A. *Ancient Egyptian Jewellery* (London, 1971)

—— 'Evidence for Osirian rituals in the tomb of Tutankhamun', in *Pharaonic Egypt: the Bible and Christianity* (ed. S. I. Groll, Jerusalem, 1985), pp. 328–40

—— 'Jewellery for a procession in the bed-chamber in the tomb of Tut'ankhamūn', *BIFAO* 84 (1984), pp. 335–45

Wood, R.W. 'The purple gold of Tut'ankhamūn', *JEA* 20 (1934), pp. 62–5

Zabkar, L.V. 'Correlation of the transformation spells of the Book of the Dead and the amulets of Tutankhamun's mummy', in *Mélanges offerts à Jean Vercoutter* (Paris, 1985), pp. 375–88

II Archival and miscellaneous sources

The bulk of Howard Carter's papers relating to the discovery and clearance of the tomb are in the Griffith Institute, Oxford, together with a set of Harry Burton's photographic negatives; a further set of negatives is in the Metropolitan Museum of Art in New York.

The voice of Carter himself may be heard on the BBC double LP *BBC 1922–1972. Fifty Years of the BBC*, issued in 1972, together with a brief snatch of the Tutankhamun trumpets broadcast. The original recordings may be consulted in the BBC Sound Archives in London. Contemporary newsreel footage of the clearance is held by the National Film Institute in London, and by Visnews, London. The film footage taken by Harry Burton is in the Metropolitan Museum of Art, New York.

Sources of Quotations

p. 1 'A story . . . and women' H. Carter and A.C. Mace, *The Tomb of Tut.ankh.Amen* I, p. 1. **p. 10** 'when I . . . as this' Lord Carnarvon, *Daily Telegraph*, 12 January 1923; 'Mr Carter, . . . is wonderful"' *Daily Telegraph*, 12 January 1923; 'There is . . . ever made' Griffith Institute (GI), Gardiner archive, press cuttings. **p. 16** 'So let . . . as dust' J.H. Breasted, *A History of Egypt* (2nd ed., New York, 1910), p. 334; 'blast of god' Manetho, *Aegyptiaca*, fr. 42: W.G. Waddell, *Manetho* (Cambridge, Ma./London, 1948). **p. 17** ' . . . a monument . . . fine gold' mortuary temple stela of Amenophis III (Cairo CG 34025), M. Lichtheim, *Ancient Egyptian Literature* II (Berkeley, 1976), p. 44. **p. 18** 'The good . . . his maker . . .' Lichtheim, *Literature* II, p. 49; 'There is . . . Neferkheprure-waenre [Amenophis IV] . . .' Great Hymn to the Aten, Lichtheim, *Literature* II, p. 99. **p. 19** 'one whom . . . himself instructed' statue-stela of Bek (West Berlin 1/63), B. Fay, *Egyptian Museum Berlin* (Berlin, 1985), p. 78; 'How many . . . of Egypt' Lichtheim, *Literature* II, p. 98; 'O lord . . . thy creatures' Breasted, *History*, pp. 373–74; 'The resemblances . . . literary interdependence' Lichtheim, *Literature* II, p. 100, n. 3. **p. 20** 'owing to . . . upon him' A. Weigall, *JEA* 8 (1922), p. 194. **p. 22** 'The study . . . in need' Carter, *Tut.ankh.Amen* III, p. viii. **p. 23** 'My husband . . . am afraid!' and 'such a . . . whole life' Güterbock, *JCS* 10 (1956), pp. 96 ff. **p. 24** 'The mystery . . . quite dispersed' Carter, *Tut.ankh.Amen* II, p. 20. **p. 33** 'Woe unto . . . cast down' A. Erman, *ZÄS* 42 (1905), p. 106; C. Aldred, *Akhenaten, King of Egypt* (London, 1988), p. 306. **p. 36** '. . . if Mr. Theodore Davis . . . cease work' H. Burton, quoted in *Manchester Guardian*, 27 January 1923. **p. 37** 'under a . . . rock' Th. M. Davis, *The Tombs of Harmhabi and Touatânkhamanou* (London, 1912), p. 135. **p. 38** 'I fear . . . now exhausted' Davis, *Harmhabi*, p. 3. **p. 40** 'Mr. Carter . . . an excavator' M.S. Drower, *Flinders Petrie. A Life in Archaeology* (London, 1985), p. 194; 'It is . . . miserably incomplete' GI, Carter archive, VI, autobiographical sketch. **p. 42** 'I have . . . can't help!' GI, Carter archive, VI, autobiographical sketch; 'very much . . . for liquor' P.E. Newberry, *JEA* 25 (1939), p. 68; 'cut and knocked about' GI, Carter archive, V, telegram to Lord Cromer, 8 Jan. 1905; 'and wrote . . . to return' Newberry, *JEA* 25 (1939), p. 68. **p. 43** 'There is . . . the beautiful' W.H. Peck, *JSSEA* 11 (1981), p. 66. **p. 44** 'We once . . . the Kings' P. Cone (ed.), *The Discovery of Tutankhamun's Tomb* (New York, 1976), p. v; 'like "a flash"' *The Autocar*, 9 June 1900, p. 556; 'I only . . . go up' British Museum (Egyptian Antiquities), letter from Carnarvon to E.A.W. Budge, 10 Dec. 1909; 'dressed for . . . the sunlight' Joseph Lindon Smith, *Tombs, Temples and Ancient Art* (ed. Corinna Lindon Smith, Norman, 1956), pp. 79–80. **p. 45** 'The finds . . . historical interest' *Egypt Exploration Fund (EEF) Archaeological Report 1911–12*, p. 23; 'I thought . . . at Luxor' Weigall archive, letter from Carnarvon to Weigall, 14 April 1907; 'If I . . . requisite data' Weigall archive, letter from Carnarvon to Weigall, undated; 'small excavation at Gurneh' Weigall, *EEF Archaeological Report 1907–08*, p. 7. **p. 46** 'on account . . . whole area', GI, Gardiner archive, letter from Newberry to Gardiner, 25 December 1947; 'late Ptolemaic' GI, Carter archive, IV. **p. 47** 'To amass . . . of study' J. Capart, *The Tomb of Tutankhamen* (London, 1923), p. 92; 'Carter suggested . . . this fashion' Highclere Castle (Egyptian archive), draft of an article by the sixth Earl of Carnarvon, undated; 'You have . . . for 80,000£' and 'I personally . . . scarcely credit' British Museum (Egyptian Antiquities), letter from Carnarvon to Budge, 4 Feb. 1912; 'I saw . . . asked 1500 . . .' British Museum (Egyptian Antiquities), letter from Carnarvon to Budge, 4 March 1913; 'Should she . . . its value' and 'I would . . . the price' *The Times*, 18 May 1923. **p. 48** 'I believe . . . Amenhotep I' British Museum (Egyptian Antiquities), letter from Carnarvon to Budge, 11 March 1914; 'I told . . . man again' Weigall archive, letter from Carnarvon to Weigall, 14 April 1907. **p. 50** 'At last . . . arrival; congratulations' Carter and Mace, *Tut.ankh.Amen* I, p. 90. **p. 51** 'some thirteen . . . The Valley' Carter and Mace, *Tut.ankh.Amen* I, p. 87; 'The design . . . in search?' Carter and Mace, *Tut.ankh.Amen* I, pp. 89–90; 'it seems . . . should take' General Sir John Maxwell, Egypt Exploration Society, *Report of the 35th Ordinary General Meeting, 1921*, p. 7. **p. 53** 'On the . . . of Tut.ankh.Amen' Carter and Mace, *Tut.ankh.Amen* I, p. 92. **p. 54** 'At first . . . of gold' Carter and Mace, *Tut.ankh.Amen* I, pp. 95–96; 'the day . . . see again' Carter and Mace, *Tut.ankh.Amen* I, p. 94. **p. 55** 'I have . . . intact' GI, Gardiner archive, press cuttings, letter from Carnarvon to Gardiner, 1 December 1922. **p. 56** 'While in . . . this assistance' Carter and Mace, *Tut.ankh.Amen* I, p. 107; 'Carter has . . . of him', GI, Gardiner archive, press cuttings, letter from Carnarvon to Gardiner, 28 Nov. 1922; 'Thanks message . . . Continental, Cairo' Cone, *Discovery*, p. xiv; 'Only too . . . effect. Lythgoe' Cone, *Discovery*, p. xv; 'by nature . . . high-strung' C. Breasted, *Pioneer to the Past. The Story of James H. Breasted* (London, 1948), p. 325. **p. 57** 'the more . . . be trusted . . .' GI, Newberry archive, letter from Carter to Newberry, 27 Oct. 1911; 'to do . . . eventual publication' and 'this was . . . staggering assignment' Breasted, *Pioneer*, p. 324; 'The scratchy . . . any robbers' J. Lawton, *Aramco World* 32/6 (Nov.–Dec. 1981), p. 21. **p. 58** 'Excitement had . . . could accomplish' Carter and Mace, *Tut.ankh.Amen* I, p. 105; 'no matter . . . valuable information' GI, Carter archive, VI, autobiographical sketch. **p. 60** 'These were . . . the Museum' A. Lucas, *ASAE* 41 (1942), p. 135; 'road by . . . years before' Carter and Mace, *Tut.ankh.Amen* I, pp. 176–77. **p. 61** 'It had . . . the trust' Carter and Mace, *Tut.ankh.Amen* I, p. 125. **p. 62** 'Our great . . . of it' letter, 20 March 1923, quoted Sir Alan H. Gardiner, *My Early Years* (n.p., n.d.) p. 68; '. . . all sane . . . with contempt' Carter, *Tut.ankh.Amen* II, p. xxv; 'the most . . . sealed tomb' quoted *Daily Express*, 24 March 1923. **p. 63** 'Poor Ld. C. . . . the morning' GI, Carter archive, Tutankhamun, diary; 'Death shall . . . of Pharaoh' G. Barker, *The Epic Discovery of Tutankhamen's Tomb* (London, 1972), p. 32; 'elementals . . . guard the tomb' GI, Gardiner archive, press cuttings, unattributed; 'if he . . . to live' Weigall, *Tutankhamen and Other Essays* (New York, 1924), p. 89. **p. 64** '. . . the atmosphere . . . too much . . .' Mace archive, letter, 26 Jan. 1923; 'The whole . . . from him' Mace archive, letter, 21 Feb. 1924. **p. 65** '. . . there are . . . will happen . . .' Mace archive, letter from Winifred Mace to her mother, 23 Dec. 1923; 'spoiling the . . . every Egyptologist' and 'looking desperately . . . a fury' Mace archive, letter from Winifred Mace to her mother, 13 Feb. 1924; 'a full . . . Egyptian government' Carter, *The Tomb of Tut.ankh.amen. Statement*, prefatory note. **p. 66** 'Owing to . . . the tomb' *The Times* 14 Feb. 1924; 'there is . . . been entrusted' T. Hoving, *Tutankhamun: the Untold Story* (New York, 1978), p. 359; 'The question . . . about it . . .' Mace archive, letter, 16 April 1923; 'Little imagination . . . surprising results' GI, Gardiner archive, unattributed press cutting. **p. 67** 'What a . . . of Tutankhamun' Hoving, *Tutankhamun*, p. 338; 'the preliminary narrative' Carter, *Tut.ankh.Amen* III, p. vi. **p. 70** 'The masons' . . . the walls' and 'a few . . . the floors' and 'bonded with . . . of timber' and 'When this . . . burial chamber' and 'traces of . . . or torch' GI, Carter archive, Tutankhamun, notes on tomb and tomb plan; 'minute particles . . . limestone surface' Carter, *Tut.ankh.Amen* III, p. 160; 'With the . . . that moisture' GI, Carter archive, Tutankhamun, notes on tomb and tomb plan. **p. 72** 'rough, conventional . . . severely simple' Carter, *Tut.ankh.Amen* II, p. 29; 'small brown . . . sealed up' Carter, *Tut.ankh.Amen* II, p. 26. **p. 75** '. . . in the rubbish . . . beyond recovery' GI, Carter archive, Tutankhamun, card 'General – outside entrances of tomb'; 'bearing [a] . . . and animals' GI, Carter archive, I.J.387, no. 434; '(?)Mortar trough' GI, Carter archive, I.J.387, no. 435; 'In the lower . . . [Amenophis] III' Carter and Mace, *Tut.ankh.Amen* I, p. 93; 'Why this . . . for safety' Carter and Mace, *Tut.ankh.Amen* I, p. 93. **p. 76** 'As we . . . them askance' Carter and Mace, Tut.ankh.Amen I, p. 94; 'probably the . . . own excavation' and 'like the . . . dark flint' Carter and Mace, *Tut.ankh.Amen* I, p. 94; 'seemed to . . . a cache' and 'Darkness and . . . anxious expectation . . .' GI, Carter archive, Tutankhamun, diary, 26 Nov. 1922. **p. 77** all quotes: GI, Carter archive, Tutankhamun, cards. **p. 78** 'Gradually the . . . before us . . .' Carter and Mace, *Tut.ankh.Amen* I, pp. 98–99. **p. 79** 'The impression . . . in antiquity' *The Times*, 19 Dec. 1922. **p. 81** 'Clearing the . . . of spillikins' and 'So crowded . . . a nightmare' Carter and Mace, *Tut.ankh.Amen* I, p. 123; 'Wonderful things' Carter and Mace, *Tut.ankh.Amen* I, p. 96. **p. 82** 'Rows of . . . the discovery' Cairo Museum, diary of the Hon. Mervyn Herbert; '. . . when, after . . . the ceiling . . .' Carter and Mace, *Tut.ankh.Amen* I, pp. 179–82. **p. 83** 'full of . . . the body' Carter, *Tut.ankh.Amen* III, p. 41. **p. 84** 'Brown with . . . its fabric' Carter, *Tut.ankh.Amen* II, p. 33. **p. 86** '. . . a low . . . innermost chamber' Carter and Mace, *Tut.ankh.Amen* I, pp. 183–85; 'in order . . . the objects . . .' Carter, *Tut.ankh.Amen* III, p. 32. **p. 88** 'purely funerary . . . religious character' Carter, *Tut.ankh.Amen* III, p. 32; 'with rare . . . been disturbed' Carter, *Tut.ankh.Amen* III, p. 34. **p. 89** 'Peering beneath . . . left it' Carter and Mace, *Tut.ankh.Amen* I, pp. 103–04; '. . . firstly, nearly . . . of them' Carter, *Tut.ankh.Amen* III, p. 104. **p. 90** 'showed [a] . . . contained it' GI, Carter archive, Tutankhamun, card no. 106d. **p. 92** 'The seals . . . Pyramid Texts . . .' GI, Carter archive, Tutankhamun, report on the large seal impressions; 'The grouping . . . last employed' GI, Carter archive, Tutankhamun, notes on the large sealings. **p. 95** 'Now that . . . than once . . .' Carter and Mace, *Tut.ankh.Amen* I, pp. 92–93; 'One [robber] . . . an earthquake', Carter and Mace, *Tut.ankh.Amen* I, p. 10; 'reminded Carter . . . *his* tomb?' Breasted, *Pioneer*, p. 321. **p. 97** 'a handful . . . gold rings' Carter and Mace, *Tut.ankh.Amen* I, p. 138; 'We are . . . upon them' Carter and Mace, *Tut.ankh.Amen* I, pp. 138–39; 'seem to . . . sadly scamped' Carter and Mace, *Tut.ankh.Amen* I, p. 139. **p. 98** 'I shall . . . the lid' *The Times*, 18 Dec. 1922. **p. 100** 'The [second] . . . ancient Pharaoh' Carter, *Tut.ankh.Amen* II, pp. 33–34; 'We bumped . . . embarassing positions' and 'eighty-four . . . manual labour' Carter, *Tut.ankh.Amen* II, p. 41. **p. 101** 'owing to . . . the structure' GI, Carter archive, Tutankhamun, notes on sepulchral shrines; 'like a . . . with stars' Breasted, *Pioneer*, p. 334; 'Mr. Carter's . . . the world"' *Egyptian Gazette*, 27 Jan. 1925. **p. 105** 'The decisive . . . left it' Carter, *Tut.ankh.Amen* II, p. 45; 'When Carter . . . actual presence' Breasted, *Pioneer*, p. 336; 'the crack . . . sarcophagus] lid' and 'it to . . . one piece' Carter, *Tut.ankh.Amen* II, p. 50. **p. 106** 'The sarcophagus . . . indistinct form . . .' Breasted, *Pioneer*, p. 341; 'an impression . . . of death' Carter, *Tut.ankh.Amen* II, p. 52. **p. 107** 'It was . . . as exciting' Carter, *Tut.ankh.Amen* II, p. 72; 'of no little difficulty' Carter, *Tut.ankh.Amen* II, p. 73; 'stout copper wire' and 'Strong metal eyelets' Carter, *Tut.ankh.Amen* II, p. 76. **p. 108** 'Mr. Burton . . . could lift' Carter, *Tut.ankh.Amen* II, p. 78; 'with a thick . . . the ankles' GI, Carter archive, Tutankhamun, card no. 255. **p. 109** 'This pitch . . . completely removed' GI, Carter archive, Tutankhamun, card no. 255. **p. 110** 'The lid . . . king disclosed' Carter, *Tut.ankh.Amen* II, p. 82. **p. 111** 'We opened . . . upon him . . .' Papyrus eopold-Amherst, Capart, Gardiner and B. van de Walle, *JEA* 22 (1936), p. 171; 'Before us, . . . the nguents' Carter, *Tut.ankh.Amen* II, pp. 82–83. **p. 16** 'The youthful . . . many years' Carter, *'ut.ankh.Amen* II, p. xxiii; 'some kind . . . a part' arter, *Tut.ankh.Amen* II, p. 186; 'the mode . . . New mpire' Carter, quoted in F.F. Leek, *The Human emains from the Tomb of Tut'ankhamūn* (Oxford, 972), p. 6. **p. 117** 'parallel to . . . above it' D.E. Derry nd Saleh Bey Hamdi, quoted in Leek, *Human emains*, p. 12; 'so firmly . . . free it' and 'Eventually ve . . . with success' and 'beautiful and . . . finally evealed' Carter, quoted in Leek, *Human Remains*, p. ; 'within the . . . 18–22 years' R.G. Harrison and A.B. bdalla, *Antiquity* 46/181 (March 1972), p. 11. **p. 118** . . as much . . . is put . . .' *Herodotus. The Histories*, anslated by A. de Selincourt (Harmondsworth, 1972), . 160. **p. 119** 'One thing . . . out dazed' Mace archive, etter, 17 Feb. 1923; 'a monument not easily forgotten' Carter, *Tut.ankh.Amen* III, p. 50. **p. 121** 'There was . . was left' Carter, *Tut.ankh.Amen* III, p. 50. **p. 123** . . had one . . . a Rameses' Carter, *Tut.ankh.Amen* III, . 28. **p. 128** 'Strange and . . . other objects . . .' Carter nd Mace, *Tut.ankh.Amen* II, p. 112. **p. 130** 'We will . . the room . . .' Carter, *Tut.ankh.Amen* III, p. 51. **p. 132** 'The statuettes . . . one another' Carter, *Tut.ankh.Amen* III, p. 54. **p. 133** 'These comparatively . . . to us' GI, Carter archive, Tutankhamun, notes on figures; 'while fastened . . . he neck' Carter, *Tut.ankh.Amen* III, p. 41; 'seem to . . . f mummification' Carter, *Tut.ankh.Amen* III, p. 42. **p. 134** 'possibly comprise . . . the tomb' Carter, *Tut.ankh.Amen* III, p. 42. **p. 135** '. . . a system . . . uman imaginations' Carter, *Tut.ankh.Amen* III, p. 36. **p. 136** 'O *shabti* . . . shall say' R.O. Faulkner, *The Ancient Egyptian Book of the Dead* (London, 1985), p. 36. **p. 137** 'In the . . . of death' Carter, *Tut.ankh.Amen* III, p. 83. **p. 140** 'These are . . . consider modern' Carter, *Tut.ankh.Amen* II, p. 15. **p. 142** 'Among these . . . to traverse' Carter, *Tut.ankh.Amen* III, p. 57. **p. 145** 'showing a . . . centuries ago' Carter, *Tut.ankh.Amen* III, pp. 63–64. **p. 146** 'The immense . . . centuries' sleep"' *Yorkshire Post*, 25 January 1923. **p. 149** '. . . after three . . . a lever' Carter and Mace, *Tut.ankh.Amen* I, pp. 131–32; 'acclamations and . . . camera clicks' Mace archive, letter from Mace to his wife Winifred, 1 Feb. 1923. **p. 150** '. . . in many . . . symbolical device' Carter, *Tut.ankh.Amen* III, p. 71; 'hanging on . . . the stones' Carter, *Tut.ankh.Amen* III, p. 76. **p. 153** 'is of . . . Amen creeds' Carter, *Tut.ankh.Amen* III, p. 134. **p. 154** 'a fine cambric-like linen' Carter, *Tut.ankh.Amen* II, p. 112. **p. 155** 'The most . . . his garments . . .' *Manchester Guardian*, 27 Jan, 1923; 'We have . . . at them' Mace archive, letter, 6 Jan, 1923; 'Cloth in . . . of soot' Carter and Mace, *Tut.ankh.Amen* I, p. 159; 'probably used . . . or robes' Carter, *Tut.ankh.Amen* I, p. XXV. **p. 156** 'I made . . . his own . . .' Mace archive, letter, 21 Jan. 1923. **p. 157** 'neatly folded' and 'were possibly . . . go with' Carter, *Tut.ankh.Amen* III, p. 126. 'When these . . . wonderful things' *The Times*, 1 Feb. 1923; 'a design . . . Lower Egypt' GI, Carter archive, Tutankhamun, card no.

620:119. **p. 160** 'a pathway . . . some way' T. Kendall, in E. Brovarski, S. K. Doll and R.E. Freed, *Egypt's Golden Age* (Boston, 1982), p. 264; 'The contest . . . Near East . . .' Carter, *Tut.ankh.Amen* III, p. 131. **p. 161** 'were probably . . . ancient times' Carter, *Tut.ankh.Amen* III, p. 132. **p. 162** 'had suffered . . . the thieves' GI, Carter archive, Tutankhamun, card no. 593. **p. 165** 'raucous and powerful' and 'rather the . . . or cornet' H. Hickmann, *La trompette dans l'Égypte ancienne* (Cairo, 1946), p. 33; 'the Egyptian . . . single pitch' J. Montagu, *JEA* 64 (1978), p. 134. **p. 166** 'actually the . . . the king' Carter, *Tut.ankh.Amen* III, p. 80; 'The colours, . . . been used' Carter, *Tut.ankh.Amen* III, p. 80. **p. 167** '. . . one hoped, . . . of document' Carter, *Tut.ankh.Amen* III, p. 81; 'among the . . . towards him . . .' *The Times*, 2 Jan. 1923; 'box of papyri' Capart, *Tutankhamen*, p. 39; 'discoloured rolls of linen' Gardiner, *The Times*, 14 Feb. 1923; 'at least . . . be discovered' Gardiner, *The Times*, 14 Feb. 1923; 'ritual . . . linear hieroglyphs' and 'too decayed . . . difficulty decipherable' Carter, *Tut.ankh.Amen* II, p. 119. **p. 168** 'Among purely . . . human remembrance' Carter, *Tut.ankh.Amen* III, p. vii. **p. 170** 'On that . . . his love' Lichtheim, *Literature* II p. 49. **p. 172** 'of . . . more . . . exercising purposes' Carter, *Tut.ankh.Amen* II, p. 60; 'highly coloured and decorated' M.A. Littauer and J.H. Crouwel, *Chariots and Related Equipment from the Tomb of Tut'ankhamūn* (Oxford, 1985), pp. 56, 74. **p. 174** 'The bows . . . the next' *Daily Telegraph*, 17 Jan. 1923. **p. 175** 'work of almost inconceivable fineness' Carter and Mace, *Tut.ankh.Amen* I, p. 113. **p. 176** 'made up . . . without sleeves' Carter, *Tut.ankh.Amen* II, p. 143; 'of ceremonial purpose' Carter, *Tut.ankh.Amen* III, p. 142. **p. 177** 'more fitted . . . partially developed' Carter, *Tut.ankh.Amen* II, p. 137; 'tucked . . . obliquely' and 'the haft . . . left thigh' Carter, *Tut.ankh.Amen* II, p. 131; 'the astonishing . . . resembling steel!' Carter, *Tut.ankh.Amen* II, p. 135. **p. 178** 'The cloth . . . exquisite work' Mace archive, letter, 31 Jan. 1924; 'The young . . . and staves' Carter, *Tut.ankh.Amen* III, p. 135; 'long staves . . . left plain' Carter, *Tut.ankh.Amen* III, p. 135; 'We wondered . . . own hand"' Carter, *Tut.ankh.Amen* II, p. 36. **p. 179** 'Such charming . . . like ourselves' Carter, *Tut.ankh.Amen* II, p. 69, re: fan no. 272a. **p. 180** 'Resting upon . . . original position' GI, Carter archive, Tutankhamun, card no. 47; 'obviously not . . . original position' GI, Carter archive, Tutankhamun, card no. 80. **p. 181** 'on its . . . [the] chamber' GI, Carter archive, Tutankhamun, card no. 377; 'for sepulchral purpose' GI, Carter archive, Tutankhamun, card no. 377. **p. 183** 'These were . . . box itself' GI, Carter archive, Tutankhamun, card no. 403. **p. 184** 'one of . . . been discovered' *The Times*, 6 Feb. 1923; 'dulled by . . . exquisite bloom' Carter and Mace, *Tut.ankh.Amen* I, p. 118. **p. 186** 'thrown topsy-turvy . . . the [Annexe]' and 'tied up . . . the throne' and 'the blotchy . . . Nubian goat' GI, Carter archive, Tutankhamun, card no. 351; 'an important . . . the reign' Carter, *Tut.ankh.Amen* III, p. 113. **p. 187** 'wooden stand . . . side bars' GI, Carter archive, Tutankhamun, card no. 33; 'Their dimensions . . . a

child' Carter, *Tut.ankh.Amen* III, p. 115; 'intended for the royal knee' Carter, *Tut.ankh.Amen* III, p. 115; 'of rush-work . . . polychrome beadwork . . .' Carter, *Tut.ankh.Amen* III, p. 220; 'travelling stool' GI, Carter archive, Tutankhamun, card no. 511; 'carried in . . . the sun' Carter and Mace, *Tut.ankh.Amen* I, p. 120. **p. 189** 'were evidently . . . a slave' Carter, *Tut.ankh.Amen* III, p. 119; 'toy-chest' Carter, *Tut.ankh.Amen* III, p. 122; 'the fastening . . . the box' Carter, *Tut.ankh.Amen* III, p. 121; 'This contrivance . . . hitherto known' Carter, *Tut.ankh.Amen* III, p. 121. **p. 191** 'the work . . . mere hacks' Breasted, quoted in *The Morning Post*, 22 Dec. 1922; 'one of . . . artistic treasures' Carter and Mace, *Tut.ankh.Amen* I, p. 110. **p. 192** 'The king . . . and arrow' and 'scampering animals . . . and hounds' and 'chief glory' and 'carved in . . . Greek coin' GI, Carter archive, Tutankhamun, card no. 540 + 551. **p. 194** 'coated with oxide' Lucas, in Carter, *Tut.ankh.Amen* III, p. 90; 'foundation deposit' GI, Carter archive, Tutankhamun, card no. 94b. **p. 195** 'rough wooden box' Carter, *Tut.ankh.Amen* III, p. 62; 'dark red wood' GI, Carter archive, Tutankhamun, card nos. 50dd-ff; 'once held . . . cubit-measure' Carter, *Tut.ankh.Amen* III, p. 127; 'It is . . . [the deceased]' Carter, *Tut.ankh.Amen* III, pp. 40–41. **p. 196** 'absolutely new in type' Carter and Mace, *Tut.ankh.Amen* I, p. 113; 'Probably these . . . tomb-thieves' Carter and Mace, *Tut.ankh.Amen* I, p. 219; 'their wooden . . . the box' Carter, *Tut.ankh.Amen* III, p. 93; 'The rotation . . . the tinder' GI, Carter archive, Tutankhamun, notes on objects. **p. 197** 'Possibly for . . . painting purposes' GI, Carter archive, Tutankhamun, card no. 620:37; 'and might . . . or electrum' and 'dark brown material' GI, Carter archive, Tutankhamun, card no. 469. **p. 198** 'His ornate . . . to wonderland' Carter in E. Denison Ross, *The Art of Egypt through the Ages* (London, 1931), p. 45; 'the majority . . . funeral equipment' GI, Carter archive, Tutankhamun, notes on objects. **p. 199** 'With rare exception' GI, Carter archive, Tutankhamun, notes on objects; 'at least . . . unctuous materials' Carter, *Tut.ankh.Amen* III, p. 145; 'Finger marks . . . interior walls' GI, Carter archive, Tutankhamun, notes on objects. **p. 200** 'There is . . . coming out' Carnarvon, quoted in the *Daily Telegraph*, 1 Dec. 1923. **p. 201** 'A plain . . . possibly glass' Carter, *Tut.ankh.Amen* III, p. 86; 'Damn!!!' GI, Carter archive, Tutankhamun, card no. 315. **p. 204** 'They [the baskets] . . . a pliable' Carter, *Tut.ankh.Amen* III, pp. 149–50; 'On certain . . . deceased relatives' Carter, *Tut.ankh.Amen* III, p. 150. **p. 205** 'The finding . . . eighteen years' *Daily Mail*, 20 Jan. 1923; 'in a mesh of rush-work' GI, Carter archive, Tutankhamun, notes on objects; 'is very . . . petrified sponge' Lucas, *ASAE* 45 (1947), p. 134; 'a mixture . . . and fruits' GI, Carter archive, Tutankhamun, card no. 620:117. **p. 206** 'Dried *lens* in interior' GI, Carter archive, Tutankhamun, card no. 519; '. . . out of . . . other joints' J. Černý, *Hieratic Inscriptions from the Tomb of Tut'ankhamūn* (Oxford, 1965), p. 18. **p. 207** 'various wooden . . . the tomb' Carter, *Tut.ankh.Amen* II, p. 166. **p. 208** 'Live thy . . . beholding felicity' Carter and Mace, *Tut.ankh.Amen* I, p. 190.

Acknowledgments and Illustration Credits

Acknowledgments

For information, comments, advice and practical assistance, the author would like to thank the following individuals and institutions: Cyril Aldred; Birmingham City Library; Janine Bourriau; the British Museum, London; the Brooklyn Museum; the Cairo Museum; the Earl of Carnarvon; John Carter; Peter Clayton; the Detroit Institute of Arts; Dr Marianne Eaton-Krauss; Dr I.E.S. Edwards; the Egypt Exploration Society, London; Dr Irving Finkel; Prof. J.R. Harris; Peter Hayman; F. Nigel Hepper; Highclere Castle; T.G.H. James; Dr Dilwyn Jones; Kodansha Ltd, Tokyo; Dr Rolf Krauss; Peter Lacovara; John Lawton; Dr Christopher Lee; Dr Diana Magee, Dr Jaromír Málek, Elizabeth Miles and Fiona Strachan (Griffith Institute, Oxford); Dr Lise Manniche; Prof. G.T. Martin; the Metropolitan Museum of Art, New York; Philippa Moore and Vronwy Hankey (Arthur Weigall archive); the Museum of Fine Arts, Boston; the Natural History Museum, London; Margaret Orr (Arthur Mace archive); W.H. Peck; A.R. Reeves; Dr Gay Robins; Dr Catharine Roehrig; John Ross; Dr John Tait; Dr John Taylor; Times Newspapers Ltd; Sheila Watson; and Toyo Yoshizaki.

Illustration Credits

Abbreviations: a-above; b-below; c-centre; l-left; r-right

Author's archives 44b, 67b, 131r, 134b
Birmingham City Library (Benjamin Stone archive) 37b
Borchardt, *Statuen und Statuetten von Königen und Privatleuten*, III 31ar (Cairo CG 779a)
Bourriau, in J. Baines and others (ed), *Pyramid Studies and Other Essays in Honour of I.E.S. Edwards* 32a (Fitzwilliam E SS 54)
British Museum 16a (EA 43467), 19ar (EA 89), 29a (EA 2), 53a, 59b, 149a, 149c, 152c (EA 920), 175bl (EA 37977), 192ar (EA 37978)
The Brooklyn Museum 23b (71.89)
Cairo Museum 17ar (JE 38257), 19ac (JE 55938), 128l, 148, 163r, 164l, 170b, 172a
Carter, *Six Portraits of the Thothmes Family* 42a
Carter, Blackman, Brown and Buckman, *Beni Hasan*, IV 40bl
Carter and Mace, *The Tomb of Tut.ankh.Amen*, I 157b; III 196bl

Crowfoot and Davies, *JEA* 27 (1941) 156bl
Daressy, *Statues de divinités* 26r (Cairo CG 38488)
Davies, *The Rock Tombs of El Amarna*, VI 19br, 157al
Davies, *The Tomb of Rekh-mi-rē' at Thebes* 194ar
Davies and Gardiner, *Ancient Egyptian Paintings*, II 144b
Davies and Gardiner, *The Tomb of Antefoker* 163l
Davies and Gardiner, *The Tomb of Ḥuy* 32b, 93br
Davis, *The Tomb of Iouiya and Touiyou* 43al, 43ar
Davis, *The Tomb of Queen Tÿyi* 20cr, 21a, 21bl, 21br
Davis, *The Tomb of Thoutmôsis IV* 41b (Cairo CG 46097), 97bc
Davis, *The Tombs of Harmhabi and Touatânkhamanou* 30a (Cairo JE 57438), 33bl, 38al (Cairo JE 57438)
Desroches-Noblecourt, *Ramsès le Grand* 171br
Detroit Institute of Arts 43b (30.371)
Egypt Exploration Society 20cl, 31b, 66b, 166br
Fischer, in Helck and Otto (ed) *Lexikon der Ägyptologie* VI ('Stöcke und Stäbe') 178c, 178bc
Gardiner, *JEA* 27 (1941) 177bl
Gardiner, *JEA* 28 (1942) 177br
Griffith Institute (Howard Carter archive) 12a, 33a, 42c, 49al, 49bl, 50a, 51, 52, 53b, 54, 55a, 58a, 59a, 60, 61al, 61ar, 62, 64, 65, 66a, 67al, 70, 71, 72, 73, 74b, 75, 76, 77, 79, 80, 81, 83, 84, 85, 87, 88, 90, 91, 93bl, 94, 95, 96b, 97al, 97ar, 97bl, 97br, 100a, 101a, 104l, 105, 108, 109al, 109ar, 109bl, 112r, 112a, 113, 113br, 116, 117l, 118l, 119l, 121a, 124r, 125, 128r, 130, 131l, 131c, 134a, 135, 136r 137al, 137b, 138, 139, 140, 142, 143, 145, 146–147b, 149b, 150l, 152al, 152ar, 152bl, 152br, 153al, 153b, 155br, 156a, 156c, 156bc, 156br, 157ar, 158, 159ar, 159b, 160a, 160b, 161, 162, 164r, 165bl, 165br, 166a, 166bl, 167c, 167b, 168, 169, 170a, 171a, 171bl, 172b, 173, 174, 175a, 175br, 176, 177ar, 178al, 178ar, 178bl, 178br, 179, 181cl, 181bl, 182, 183, 185a, 186, 187, 188b, 189a, 189c, 190, 191, 192b, 193, 194al, 194c, 194b, 195a, 195br, 196a, 196br, 197, 198, 199, 200, 201, 202a, 203, 204, 205, 206, 207al
Harrison and Abdalla, *Antiquity* 46/181 (March, 1972) 118r
Harrison and others, *Antiquity* 53/207 (March 1979) 124l
Highclere Castle (Carnarvon archive) 40a, 44l, 44r, 45a, 45bl, 45br, 46al, 46ar, 46bl (H 267), 46br (H 290), 48a, 48b (H 118 etc.), 49ar (H 294), 49br (H 272), 63a
Illustrated London News 61b, 165a
Jéquier, *L'Architecture et la décoration dans l'ancienne Égypte*, I 16b, 28
Kodansha Ltd 1, 6, 10r, 14–15, 102, 103, 110l, 115, 122a, 126–127, 129b, 133, 141b, 144a, 147r, 150a, 155a, 159al, 177al, 180, 184b, 185b, 188a, 189b, 192al (photographs originally reproduced in Mallakh and Brackman, *The Gold of Tutankhamen*, first published by Kodansha Ltd, Tokyo)
Lacau, *Stèles du Nouvel Empire* 24br (Cairo CG 34183)
Leek, *Human Remains from the Tomb of Tut'ankhamûn* 117r
Lehnert and Landrock 34–35, 41ar, 68–69, 153ar, 207ar

Macadam, *The Temples of Kawa*, II 29bl
Martin, *The Royal Tomb at El-'Amarna*, II 25b
Metropolitan Museum of Art, New York 21cr (30.8.54), 25a (50.6), 31al (23.10.1), 38b, 39ac, 39cl, 39cr, 39bl, 40br (26.7.1395), 47l (26.7.1412), 47r (26.7.1400)
Philippa Moore and Vronwy Hankey (Arthur Weigall archive) 42b, 58bl
Museum of Fine Arts, Boston 18l (Cairo Temp. 29/5/49/1), 33br (50.3789)
Naville, *The Temple of Deir el Bahari*, I 41al
Margaret Orr (Arthur Mace archive) 57a
Piankoff, *The Shrines of Tut-Ankh-Amon*, 18a (Cairo Temp. 30/10/26/12), 100c
Pusch, *Das Senet-Brettspiel* I 160c (Louvre)
Nicholas Reeves 2, 10l, 11, 37a (Cairo JE 38330), 67ar, 104r, 106, 107, 110r, 111, 114, 119ar, 119br, 122b, 123, 129a, 132, 136l, 137ar, 141a, 146a, 150b, 154a, 155bl, 167a, 181a, 181br, 184a, 195bl, 209
Reeves, *JEA* 74 (1988) 23a (British Museum EA 58179)
Roeder, *Amarna-Reliefs aus Hermopolis* 24a
John Ross 27, 98–99
Albert Shoucair 151, 154c, 154b
Spink and Son Ltd 19bl (Berlin/West 1/63)
Staatliche Museen, Berlin/West 22l (21300), 24bl (21239)
Staatliche Museen, Berlin/DDR 17l (14442), 22r (17813)
Tait, *JEA* 49 (1963) 29br (Eton College ECM 1887)
Thibault, *PCR* (May, 1968) 114ar
Times Newspapers Ltd 58–59b; 92b
Weigall, *The Glory of the Pharaohs* 63b
Western, *JEA* 59 (1973) 172l
Winlock, *Materials used at the Embalming of King Tūt-'ankh-Amūn* 38ar, 39al, 39br

The publishers would also like to acknowledge the work of the following illustrators:

Ian Bott 50b, 78, 82, 86, 89, 109br
Christine Barratt and Nicholas Reeves 9
Sue Cawood 4–5 (after Piankoff, *The Shrines of Tut-Ankh-Amon*) 96a, 100–101b (after *Treasures of Tutankhamun at the Metropolitan Museum of Art*), 120–121b (after *Treasures of Tutankhamun at the Metropolitan Museum of Art*)
Tracy Wellman 13, 17b, 19al (after Davies, *The Rock Tombs of El Amarna*, II, IV), 20a, 20b (after *The Berkeley Map of the Theban Necropolis*, flyer), 25r (after Eaton-Krauss, in Osing and Dreyer, *Form und Mass*), 26l, 30b (based upon Trigger, Kemp, O'Connor and Lloyd, *Ancient Egypt: a Social History* (Cambridge, 1983), fig. 3.4), 36, 55b (after *The Berkeley Theban Mapping Project*, flyer), 71 (after Griffith Institute, Carter archive, Tutankhamun), 74a (after Robins, *GM* 72 (1984), 92–93a (after GI, Carter archive, Tutankhamun), 94c (after GI, Carter archive, Tutankhamun), 112–113 (after GI, Carter archive, Tutankhamun), 120a (after GI, Carter archive, Tutankhamun), 202a (after GI, Carter archive, Tutankhamun), 207b